Further Education Re-formed

After more than a century of being undervalued, further education has been thrust into the limelight. How have the colleges fared? How have they been shaped by the new arrangements for funding, governance, inspection and the new qualifications framework? What do those running the colleges and working in them make of the changes? What difference will the re-definition to lifelong learning make and what are the colleges' prospects for the new millennium?

Further Education Re-formed is the definitive account of where further education has got to and where it might be heading. Containing specially commissioned papers by the leading figures in the field of further education, this book sets out the situation as it is now and looks forward to the developments of the coming years. It will be vital reading for anyone concerned with further education in particular, and education in general, whether as a policy-maker, governor, manager, teacher, employer or student.

Contributors: John Pratt; David Melville and Deirdre Macleod; Roger McClure; Richard Dimbleby and Clive Cooke; Dan Taubman; Michael Shattock; George Edwards; Julian Gravatt and Ruth Silver; Annette Zera and Tom Jupp; Patrick Coldstream; Guardino Rospigliosi; Jim Donaldson; Geoff Stanton.

Alan Smithers and **Pamela Robinson** are co-directors of the Centre for Education and Employment Research at the University of Liverpool and have published a number of influential books and reports. In 1993, their *Changing Colleges: Further Education in the Market Place* was the first quantitative study of the emerging sector. Professor Smithers was special adviser to the House of Commons Select Committee in its recent inquiry into further education.

New Millennium Series

How Shall We School Our Children?
Edited by Colin Richards and Philip H. Taylor

Early Education Transformed
Edited by Lesley Abbott and Helen Moylett

Special Education Re-formed
Beyond Rhetoric
Edited by Harry Daniels

Higher Education Re-formed
Edited by Peter Scott

Further Education Re-formed
Edited by Alan Smithers and Pamela Robinson

Further Education Re-formed

**Edited by Alan Smithers and
Pamela Robinson**

London and New York

First published 2000 by Falmer Press
11 New Fetter Lane, London EC4P 4EE

Simultaneously published in the USA and Canada
by Falmer Press
Garland Inc., 19 Union Square West, New York, NY 10003

Falmer Press is an imprint of the Taylor & Francis Group

© 2000 Alan Smithers and Pamela Robinson;
Chapter 15 © Geoff Stanton

Typeset in Garamond by Taylor & Francis Group
Printed and bound in Great Britain by
Biddles Ltd, Guildford and King's Lynn

British Library Cataloguing in Publication Data
A catalogue record for this book is available from the British Library

Library of Congress Cataloging in Publication Data
A catalog record for this book has been requested

ISBN 0–750–70907–3 (hbk)
ISBN 0–750–70906–5 (pbk)

Contents

Contents

Figures and Tables

Figures

Tables

Acronyms

AC	Audit Commission
ACM	Association for College Management
ACVIC	Association of Catholic Sixth-Form Colleges
AfC	Association for Colleges
AFE	Advanced Further Education
ALF	Average Level of Funding
AoC	Association of Colleges
APC	Association of Principals of Colleges
APVIC	Association of Principals of Sixth-Form Colleges
BERA (SIG)	British Educational Research Association (Special Interest Group)
BTEC	Business and Technology Education Council
CAT	College of Advanced Technology
CEER	Centre for Education and Employment Research
CEF	Colleges' Employers' Forum
CIHE	Council for Industry and Higher Education
CNAA	Council for National Academic Awards
CSE	Certificate of Secondary Education
CSR	Comprehensive Spending Review
DES	Department of Education and Science
DETR	Department of the Environment, Transport and the Regions
DfEE	Department for Education and Employment
DLE	Demand-Led Element
DTI	Department of Trade and Industry
ED	Department of Employment
EHE	Enterprise in Higher Education
ERDF	European Regional Development Fund
ESRC	Economic and Social Research Council
FE	Further Education
FEDA	Further Education Development Agency
FEFC	Further Education Funding Council
FENTO	Further Education National Training Organization
FERA	Further Education Research Association

FERN	Further Education Research Network
FEU	Further Education Unit
FTE	Full-Time Equivalent
GCE	General Certificate of Education
GCSE	General Certificate of Secondary Education
GNVQ	General National Vocational Qualification
HE	Higher Education
HEFC	Higher Education Funding Council
HMI	Her Majesty's Inspectors
HND	Higher National Diploma
IES	Institute for Employment Studies
ISR	Individualized Student Record
ITO	Industry Training Organization
LEA	Local Education Authority
LMC	Local Management of Colleges
LMS	Local Management of Schools
LSC	Learning and Skills Council
MSC	Manpower Services Commission
NACETT	National Advisory Council for Education and Training Targets
NAO	National Audit Office
NATFHE	National Association of Teachers in Further and Higher Education
NCC	National Curriculum Council
NCVQ	National Council for Vocational Qualifications
NGfL	National Grid for Learning
NFER	National Foundation for Educational Research
NOCN	National Open College Network
NTO	National Training Organization
NVQ	National Vocational Qualification
ONC	Ordinary National Certificate
OND	Ordinary National Diploma
PAC	Public Accounts Committee
PCFC	Polytechnics and Colleges Funding Council
PES	Public Expenditure Survey
PFI	Public Finance Initiative
PPP	Public/Private Partnership
QCA	Qualifications and Curriculum Authority
RAE	Research Assessment Exercise
RDA	Regional Development Agency
SFCEF	Sixth-Form Colleges' Employers' Forum Ltd
SHA	Secondary Heads Association
SRB	Single Regeneration Budget
SVQ	Scottish Vocational Qualification
TAC	Tariff Advisory Committee
TEC	Training and Enterprise Council

Acronyms

TSC	Training Standards Council
TVEI	Technical and Vocational Education Initiative
UCAS	Universities and Colleges Admissions Service
UDACE	Unit for the Development of Adult and Continuing Education
UfI	University for Industry
ULEAC	University of London Examinations and Assessment Council
WRNAFE	Work-Related Non-Advanced Further Education

1   Introduction

The Making of a New Sector

Alan Smithers and Pamela Robinson

On 1 April 1993, a new sector of education was born. Under the provisions of the Further and Higher Education Act 1992, 465 colleges were taken out of local authority control in England (there were parallel arrangements in Wales, but Scotland and Northern Ireland continued to handle things differently) and given a Funding Council of their own. In future, this would be their main channel of public financial support. The reasons for the profound change are not wholly clear. On an optimistic interpretation, it was to bring the colleges out of the shadows to take their rightful place, along with schools and universities, as one of the three great pillars of the educational system. But there were hints too of darker motives. The then Conservative government's great embarrassment over the poll tax and its urgent need to reduce local authority spending come to mind. Removing the colleges was, in any case, part of the gradual stripping away of local authority functions which had also seen the polytechnics transferred and the attempt made to encourage schools to opt out. Behind this attrition, one suspects, was the unrequited hope that the LEAs (often thought troublesome by central government) might just wither away.

One great advantage of the creation of the sector was to enable us to see just how many colleges there were (Smithers and Robinson, 1993). But the very diversity of the sector does lend support to the suspicion that it had been to some extent thrown together. As well as the further education colleges themselves, the sector was made to include sixth-form colleges which were essentially schools and a variety of specialist colleges. It is true that the backbone of the sector consisted of 224 general colleges and 63 tertiary colleges. The general colleges are those whose histories are discussed in Chapter 2. Many were once the local 'tech' and geared to training apprentices for local industry. But others saw themselves as mainly offering second-chance education, with particular concern for example for ethnic minorities. The tertiary colleges like the general colleges had substantial involvement in the education of the over 18s, but were also the main or sole providers of education for the sixteen- to eighteen-year-olds in their area. They came about (the first was in Devon in 1970) as a particular response to the comprehensive reorganization of schools of the 1960s (DES, 1965) when some authorities divided responsibilities between schools for education up to age sixteen and tertiary colleges for those who were older.

The sixth-form colleges also owe their origins to the reorganization of secondary education in the 1960s. But, unlike the tertiary colleges, they catered mainly for full-time seventeen- and eighteen-year-olds studying for A-levels, who moved on to them mainly from comprehensive schools without sixth forms of their own. The sixth-form colleges were therefore squarely part of the school system working under local authorities to school regulations with the staff being qualified teachers paid on schools' salary scales. The first had opened in Luton in 1966, followed soon by Southampton and Scunthorpe and, by 1993, 116 colleges in 52 LEAs (admitting about a quarter of all sixth-form pupils) had been established. Many of the LEAs were upset at losing what they regarded as their showpiece schools to further education and their precipitate removal stopped secondary school reorganization along these lines in its tracks.

As well as the sixth-form colleges, there were other unlikely inclusions in the new sector. The Funding Council had placed within its ambit 35 agriculture/horticulture colleges, 13 art and design colleges, and 13 other colleges including two nautical colleges. The Workers' Educational Association was thrown in for good measure. The diverse origins and missions of the colleges not only made the purposes of the sector difficult to define, but meant that the Funding Council had to devise a unique method of allocating funds equitably (as Roger McClure, its originator, reports in Chapter 4). Whatever skill was brought to bear, however, the specialist colleges, like the sixth-form colleges, still remain as outliers and are particularly likely to be challenged by attempts to bring about convergence in funding.

The changed world of the colleges from 1 April 1993 is set out in Figure 1.1. From the protection of local authorities, they found themselves in the market-place. They had to adjust to running as businesses generating sufficient income in a system where money followed students. They found themselves in competition, not only with each other, but with schools and universities, and also private providers and in-house company training. Unlike the schools and the universities, they had no guaranteed markets, but had to work hard to hold on to what they had and open up new ones. It was a tenet of the prevailing ideology that the 'market' would result in demand-led adjustment of the supply of places and the quality of services. Although the theory implied a plurality of purchasers (which in the case of the colleges could include, besides the Funding Council, the Training and Enterprise Councils, the European Social Fund, employers, local authorities and people themselves), in practice the Funding Council has found itself in the position of being a near monopoly customer. The enterprise of the colleges has therefore often shown itself in ingenuous ways of maximizing their grant from the FEFC rather than extending their range of customers. As we shall be seeing, not all that imagination fell entirely within the bounds of the law.

Figure 1.1 The new sector

- Creation of sector with unified statutory framework, including sixth-form colleges which are no longer schools
- Colleges become corporate bodies having their own legal identity and responsible for their own financial affairs, staff and buildings
- Further Education Funding Council for England (another for Wales) to allocate funds, advise on reorganization, mergers and closures, and assess quality taking over from LEA inspectors
- Governing bodies to be reconstituted having the majority of their members from business though not necessarily anyone from the LEA
- FEFC to fund education and training towards qualifications, but non-examined adult education to remain with the local authorities
- Colleges expected to work closely with the Training and Enterprise Councils which are responsible for providing work-related education and training for unemployed young people and adults
- Colleges encouraged to earn money from a variety of sources and free to charge what private fees the market will bear
- Staff transferred to the new sector on existing pay and conditions, but direct negotiations between the colleges and staff, as employer and employee, to be encouraged

---

Source: Smithers and Robinson, 1993.

Trends since Incorporation

There is no doubt though that the great majority of the colleges have relished their freedom. In Chapter 3, David Melville (the Chief Executive of the Funding Council) and Deirdre Macleod give a quantitative overview of the trends since incorporation and the present position. The colleges currently provide for nearly 4 million students compared with 2.9 million when the sector was born. With the inclusion of the sixth-form colleges the sector now has more A-level students (though not entries) than the schools, and about half the sixteen- to eighteen-year-olds in full-time education study in the colleges. It also continues to be the main provider for adults with 15 per cent growth over five years. David Melville has turned up the remarkable statistic that the colleges now have more degree students than did the universities at the time of the land-mark Robbins Report (1963).

The physical estate of the colleges has also greatly improved. As George Edwards, of the property services division of the Further Education Funding Council reports in Chapter 9, one of the first tasks of the Council was to find out about the state of the property it was now overseeing. Things were worse than feared. The local authorities had enjoyed limited immunity from prosecu-tion under legislation governing the safety of buildings. On incorporation this was lost and some buildings had to be shut immediately as unsafe. Surveys conducted on behalf of the FEFC (1993) – the surveys by Hunter & Partners –

revealed that £128 million was required to make good possible breaches of legislation within one year and altogether £786 million would be required over five years to maintain the condition of the buildings. By offering grants and requiring the colleges to devote part of their income to the task, the most urgent problems were dealt with within sixteen months.

Many of the college buildings were not ideal for education and about 10 per cent of the floorspace was in any case temporary. During its first two years the Funding Council had little left over from essential remedial work to support improvements. The colleges were left to their own devices which included funding new buildings themselves, successfully arguing that it would be better to construct than repair, and bidding for European Regional Development Funds. But as the initial problems were brought under control the Council was able to offer limited capital support. By December 1998 colleges had committed half a billion pounds to 287 major projects agreed by the Council. Most of these were financed by reducing floorspace and since incorporation the net reduction has been more than a million square metres. Some of this has been freed by the amalgamation of colleges – compared with the 465 at incorporation there are 435 today. In inner London the number of campuses of the 12 colleges has been reduced from 80 to 68 with the target for 2001 being 40. But out of the more rational approach to accommodation made possible by the creation of the new sector, a number of the colleges have splendid new buildings – as are there for all to see.

Partnerships

The colleges in their new guise have also fostered all kinds of fruitful links with other organizations. Julian Gravatt and Ruth Silver in their chapter on partnerships with the community (Chapter 10) provide a very helpful listing of the forms it can take. They show that the colleges work with each other, with local education authorities to provide for disaffected fourteen- and fifteen-year-olds and adults, with schools to provide education and training for sixteen- to eighteen-year-olds, and with universities to provide higher education. They also are contracted by Training and Enterprise Councils to provide training for sixteen- to eighteen-year-olds and unemployed adults, and there are the New Deal programmes to help people into work. They are also involved in a variety of links with educational institutions in other countries through European Union funding. Gravatt and Silver tellingly suggest that partnerships are now so common that 'you can almost guarantee that, at any time of the day, at least one member of staff will be in communication with one of the college's partners'. Partnerships, as Gravatt and Silver point out, have the great advantage that they make it possible to deliver new programmes without the costs of setting up new organizations, and they can be dissolved as quickly as they can be formed. But the writers also caution that 'too many partnerships established too hastily with too many overlapping aims just add to the confusion and complexity that hampers education and training'.

As extensive as Gravatt and Silver's listing is, it does not really do justice to the colleges' links with employers. In Chapter 12, Patrick Coldstream recounts how the organization of which he was the founding director – the Council for Industry and Higher Education – painstakingly thought its way through to the realization that its real concern is with 'post-18 education' rather than just higher education. Although its members were perhaps less familiar with the contribution of further education they were every bit as dependent on it as that of the universities. In a report for CIHE (Smithers and Robinson, 1993), we urged that 'industry must learn to have high and intelligent expectations of the 465 newly independent colleges' and suggested a five-point agenda for any company wishing to work with colleges to extend their expertise and experience in developing employable skills. Coldstream in Chapter 12 shares that sentiment and extends the argument. He shows that employers work with colleges in five main ways: commissioning training, offering the workplace as a context for student learning, advising colleges, helping to train college staff and, through joint membership of bodies such as the Training and Enterprise Councils and Business Links, identifying local employment needs. The colleges, in turn, look to employers to play at least five distinct roles: as customers, as places of learning, as advisers, as joint planners and as subcontractors for learning 'franchised' by the colleges.

What Coldstream calls 'the web of interaction with employers' has both strengthened and become more elaborate since incorporation. Much of that growth has been through franchising. The House of Commons Education and Employment Committee (1998a) noted in its inquiry into further education that the proportion of FEFC students on franchised courses grew from 5 per cent in 1994–5 to 19 per cent in 1996–7. The FEFC's (1998) survey of 'collaborative provision' revealed that over half of all franchising (58 per cent) was carried out by just 20 colleges. Of that franchising about a fifth was with employers, nearly as much was with voluntary organizations, but over half was with private providers. Some employers, as the Select Committee (Education and Employment Committee, 1998a) found, received considerable subsidies towards their training costs through this means, with Scottish and Newcastle, for example, receiving £950,000 of public funding through its franchising agreement with Stafford College. The Committee heard that Scottish and Newcastle without that financial support would not offer National Vocational Qualification accreditation but would revert to in-house certificates.

Franchising has been controversial. The arguments for are that:

- it creates training opportunities in the actual workplace;
- it provides for the integration of education and training to consistent national standards;
- it is flexible and brings together many partners.

The arguments against are that:

- it pays for training out of the public purse which employers would be doing anyway;

- it can lead to schemes whereby employees are qualified for essentially going about their work;
- it severely distorts further education provision.

'Ross' Rospigliosi, Principal of Plymouth College, has been one of the leading critics of franchising and in Chapter 13 sets out his concerns. Through careful examination of the detail he shows that the NVQ Level 1 in Distributive Trades, which shelf-stackers at Tesco can be awarded through a national franchise agreement with Halton College, Widnes, contains little more than any employer would require all its shelf-stackers to do. He concedes that franchising may bring back into education and training those who have written themselves off at an early age, but argues that, in the context of a capped further education budget, money seeping away on such ventures will put at risk the high quality but expensive training, in engineering and construction for example, for which the colleges had become known. The colleges' own inspectorate did not find inherent weaknesses in franchised provision, but noted that problems could arise when the colleges were opportunistic, went beyond their expertise, took on too much and where the provision was too far away (FEFC, 1997b).

Inspection

With the creation of a further education sector, responsibility for inspecting the colleges passed to the Funding Council. In Chapter 14, Jim Donaldson (the chief inspector) describes how that inspectorate is organized: at arm's length from the other directorates and reporting directly to the Council. All colleges are inspected on a four-year cycle. In the first cycle reports were published on 452 colleges based on the inspection of 70,000 classes involving three-quarters of a million students. Over two-thirds of the provision was given the two highest ratings, but there were also 62 courses in 52 colleges which were deemed deficient and needing to make substantial improvement. All but two of these re-inspections were successful. The inspectorate's view is that the quality of the academic provision of the colleges has been holding up very well during a period in which funding per full-time equivalent student was being sharply reduced (by 21 per cent from 1993–4 to 1997–8).

In many ways therefore the liberation of the colleges can be counted a great success. They have enhanced educational opportunity by providing for many more students (including those who in the past might not have participated), they have according to the inspectorate maintained academic quality at lower cost, they have physically regenerated themselves and they have developed fruitful networks with the community, employers and other institutions. But there has also been a downside. Although the inspectorate's role is mainly to review academic quality it does also consider the college's governance and management. In some cases problems have been identified, as at Matthew Boulton College in Birmingham and Dewsbury College. The governing body of Hereward College, Coventry, resigned when it was given the lowest grade for 'governance and management'.

Governance

Hereward College is only one of a number of instances where colleges have strayed beyond the bounds of acceptability, as Michael Shattock reveals, in his penetrating analysis of the evolution of governance in the colleges since incorporation. The governors of Wirral Metropolitan College were allowed to resign in advance of a damning report. A special rescue team has had to be set up to decide what to do about Bilston Community College. When the Select Committee visited Stoke-on-Trent College it was told by the current management team of the 'unhealthy control exercised by the previous principal and chairman of governors' which ultimately resulted in the college having to repay large sums of money which had been inappropriately claimed. Before that there had been inquiries into Derby Tertiary College, Wilmorton (which had been chaired by Shattock) and St Philip's, Birmingham, whose provision has been transferred to South Birmingham College (FEFC, 1995).

More recently Halton College, the home of the shelf-stacking franchise, has come under scrutiny by the FEFC and the NAO (1999), and has been ordered to repay £7.3 million for making ineligible claims. This sparked an examination of another 117 colleges by the NAO (1999). The NAO recommended tighter controls on college credit cards, advice to governors on controlling the expenditure of principals and a 'whistle-blowers' charter'. 'Ross' Rospigliosi is led to comment in Chapter 13 that it is no wonder that at one stage further education seemed to be appearing as much in *Private Eye* as the *Times Educational Supplement*.

In some ways it is not surprising that the governance and management is taking a while to bed down. Notwithstanding the introduction of devolved management in 1990, the colleges were largely the creatures of the local authorities until, almost overnight in April 1993, they had to put in place the whole panoply of checks and balances that make for the healthy running of a large corporation. They were also let loose into a world of rampant competition where money had to be earned by attracting students working towards recognized qualifications. There was also an uncapped demand-led element to the funding through which colleges could earn a standard fee for every student recruited beyond targets agreed with the Funding Council. The unprecedented energy that was thereby released might have been containable had a secure qualifications structure been in place, but the newly emerging colleges were hit by the double whammy of a new funding methodology and a novel approach to qualifying people.

Funding and Qualifications

The key task for the new Funding Council when it was established in embryonic form in 1992 was to devise an equitable means of distributing money to the colleges. In Chapter 4 Roger McClure, who devised the scheme, for the first time gives us the insider's view of how it was arrived at. Faced with the great variety of methods favoured by the local authorities the Council decided to think out from first principles the best way of deploying the funding to achieve what it had been contracted to achieve by government. The local authorities had tended to fund on enrolments; the Funding Council wanted to fund learning. It decided that basing grants on just enrolments was illogical since it did not take into account the numbers actually on courses – from which the main expenditure arose. It also wanted to reward colleges for bringing students to successful completion. Accordingly, it devised a system of units – actually millions of units of just a few pounds – which colleges could accumulate through their activity. The actual value in units of any area of activity was decided by the Tariff Advisory Committee (TAC) made up of representatives of the sector.

A very flexible funding system had therefore been devised, recognizing the great diversity of further education. It was also very flexible in the sense that if a policy decision was taken to, for example, widen participation (see Annette Zera and Tom Jupp, Chapter 11) or precipitate changes had to be accommodated, as with the withdrawal of the demand-led element, the values of the units could be altered without changing the overall system. But it was also very flexible in the sense that it could be manipulated. The process of hoovering up tens of thousands of units to arrive at a college's funding from the Council left considerable scope for entrepreneurial imagination.

A college's financial returns depended on, among other things, very extensive and accurate keeping of the records of students, something the colleges had not had to do in the past when they were under the tutelage of the local authorities. An elaborate Individualized Student Record had to be put in place. This itself created difficulties and as the Principal of Stoke-on-Trent College (which found itself having to repay large sums) told the Select Committee 'we had all sorts of reasons why we could not submit them [the necessary data] and the Funding Council, if they are open to criticism, and I think that they accept they are, were too trusting' (Education and Employment Committee, 1998b). The funding system also encouraged colleges to acquire as many units as they could with the least effort, since it conferred benefits beyond the immediate cost savings through reducing the Average Level of Funding (ALF). Franchised units were generally much cheaper and hence the rush to this kind of provision. The funding mechanism also opened the way to 'unit farming', whereby colleges sold on units to private providers often at a distance and remote from their primary task. (Private providers were incidentally less liable to inspection since the new Training Standards Council which has responsibility for inspecting them only took office in April 1999.)

The funding system would have been less vulnerable to manipulation and less likely to have unintended consequences for the shape of further education if the qualifications structure had been secure. But, as Chapter 5 shows, this too was novel. Under the Further and Higher Education Act 1992, only students working towards a specified range of qualifications were eligible for funding. These included the new National Vocational Qualifications which were being introduced by the National Council for Vocational Qualifications established in 1986. These were devised on an outcome basis, so it did not matter what you studied or for how long providing you could do the things specified by the qualification. In the early days, the NCVQ was fond of using the analogy of the driving test, but unfortunately it did not put in place the system of independent examiners. Instead it relied on the candidate's supervisors to do most of the assessing. When the FEFC, and even more so the Training and Enterprise Councils' introduced forms of output-related funding, this became the equivalent of a driving test where the examiner was the person who taught you and who moreover would not get paid unless he passed you. The new NVQs were at five levels, the lowest of which was very rudimentary. This clearly opened the way to instances like the Halton franchising of a qualification for shelf-stackers, where the allegation is that the students were qualified for getting on with the job. Since there are numerous shelf-stackers and the challenge of the qualification is low, the potential for acquiring numerous funding units at little effort is obvious.

Funding problems have been exacerbated by the size of the pot available for further education. This was never over-generous and was squeezed in the first years of incorporation. In its evidence to the Select Committee, the FEFC showed that the total funding had been reduced from £3,168 million in 1993–4 to £3,039 million in 1997–8 (Education and Employment Committee, 1998b). Since over this period the student numbers in FTE terms had increased by about a third, this amounted to a reduction in the funding per student from £3,210 to £2,528 (−21 per cent). Not surprisingly a number of colleges have been experiencing financial difficulties. The FEFC (1998) uses three categories to assess financial health, the lowest of which is 'colleges that are financially weak and which are dependent on the goodwill of others or likely to become so'. In 1994 it placed 6 per cent of colleges in that category, but this had risen to 27 per cent in 1997. Overall it considered that over 100 colleges were experiencing financial problems and more were expected to do so following the withdrawal of the uncapped demand-led funding. More money has been found for further education by the Labour government elected in 1997, but whether it is enough is something we shall assess in the concluding chapter when we consider the prospects for further education in the new millennium.

Staff Relations

The financial plight of the colleges has hit staff relations very hard. Dan Taubman in Chapter 7 graphically describes the impact on staff from the union perspective. His view, which he amply illustrates, is that 'the revolution that has been the incorporation of the further education sector, cannot be seen from the perspective of college lecturers as the dawn of a bright new age'. He says it 'is a narrative of almost unrelieved misery'. As LEA employees, further education staff enjoyed generous nationally agreed terms and conditions (the 'Silver Book'), the case having been accepted that this was necessary in order to induce skilled craftspeople to give up their lathes for lecturing. It was recognized that things would change following incorporation, but it was never envisaged that the colleges would be squeezed so hard and they would react by, in turn, squeezing the staff very hard. Staff retaining their jobs have been employed on new contracts, the number of teaching hours for students has been reduced and the employment of part-time and agency staff has greatly increased. According to FEFC figures (Education and Employment Committee, 1998b), in 1995–6, 55 per cent of all staff in further education colleges, and 39 per cent of teaching staff, worked part-time. Roger Ward, the Chief Executive of the Association of Colleges and also its predecessor body, the Colleges' Employers' Forum (CEF), spearheaded the attack on the Silver Book and not unnaturally became the focus of the lecturers' discontent (hence some of the stories in *Private Eye*). This was heightened when it emerged that he had a connection with the only staffing agency for the sector to receive the endorsement of the CEF. The Select Committee claimed its first casualty when Roger Ward resigned, following an apology for misleading it over a register of interests (Education and Employment Committee, 1997).

Strategic Planning

The FEFC interpreted its remit to mean that it has primary responsibility for establishing financial and regulatory structures and that its role in strategic planning is limited. It did indeed during the early years receive less guidance in relation to areas of provision than, for example, the Higher Education Funding Council, where this is specified in the annual letter from the Secretary of State. In her report on widening participation for the FEFC, Kennedy (1997) refers to 'rich choices' but also 'a fair amount of chaos and confusion'. As we have seen in the arrangements that have emerged, the further education sector is allowed to take its shape amoeba-like in response to the funding units attached to qualifications. Kennedy's main proposal was that there should be a weighting of units towards disadvantaged students (identified by postcodes). This proposal has been adopted by the FEFC, but how it might work out in practice is interestingly explored in Chapter 11 by Annette Zera and Tom Jupp, respectively Principals of Tower Hamlets and City and Islington Colleges. They conclude that the funding methodology is 'far from transparent' and that in the case of the so-called Kennedy students may not have the consequences intended. They argue that there is 'a need to recognize the paucity of strategy to combat educational failure'.

Retrospect and Prospect

We shall return to the issue of strategic planning, particularly in the light of the importance the present government attaches to 'lifelong learning', when in a concluding chapter we consider what might become of the colleges in the new millennium. We do so on the basis of where they have got to now. After more than a century of being under-valued they suddenly found themselves thrust into the limelight. How have they been faring? This volume brings together many of the people in the best position to know – those who have taken the crucial decisions, those who have had the task of implementing them, those who have been on the receiving end, and those with an opportunity to reflect on the changes.

David Melville, the Chief Executive of the FEFC, with policy analyst Deirdre Macleod, outlines the colleges' present position. Roger McClure who was instrumental in devising the unique funding mechanism, George Edwards who initiated the 'Hunter' surveys of the physical estate, Michael Shattock who conducted the Derby Wilmorton inquiry, and Jim Donaldson, the chief inspector, consider how the emergence of the colleges has been shaped by funding (both recurrent and capital) and by governance and accountability. Richard Dimbleby (with his deputy Clive Cooke), Ruth Silver (with her registrar Julian Gravatt), Annette Zera and Tom Jupp, and Guardino Rospigliosi, as college principals, take a critical look at the curriculum and learning, community and partnership, widening participation, and franchising. Dan Taubman of the National Association of Teachers in Further and Higher Education describes the impact on staff and Patrick Coldstream, founding director of the Council for Industry of Higher Education, explores the web of interaction with employers. There are distinguished academic contributions from John Pratt on the history of the colleges and Geoff Stanton on the role of research. One of us (Alan Smithers) discusses the post-16 qualification reforms which have done as much as anything to influence the direction of the colleges since independence.

We chose the title of this chapter, and indeed the whole volume, very carefully. The colleges are still in the making; once more they are being re-formed. As their future emerges, so does ours.

References

DES (1965) *The Organization of Secondary Education*, Circular 10/65, London: DES.

Education and Employment Committee (1997) *Further Education, The Association of Colleges, Minutes of Evidence and Appendix, Tuesday 25 November 1997 and Tuesday 16 December*, London: The Stationery Office.

Education and Employment Committee (1998a) Sixth Report, *Further Education*, vol. 1, *Report and Proceedings*, 264-I, London: The Stationery Office.

Education and Employment Committee (1998b) Sixth Report, *Further Education*, vol. 2, *Minutes of Evidence and Appendices*, 264-II, London: The Stationery Office.

FEFC (1993) *Allocation of Minor Works Funds*, Circular 93/15, Coventry: FEFC.

FEFC (1995) *Council News* 25 (28 September), Coventry: FEFC.

FEFC (1997a) *Inspection Report: Halton College*, 25/97, Coventry: FEFC.

FEFC (1997b) Chief Inspector's Annual Report, *Quality and Standards in Further Education in England 1996–97*, Coventry: FEFC.

FEFC (1997c) *Annual Report 1996–97*, Coventry: FEFC.

FEFC (1998) National Survey Report, *Collaborative Provision*, Coventry: FEFC.

Kennedy, H. (1997) *Learning Works: Widening Participation in Further Education*, Coventry: FEFC.

NAO (1999) Report by the Comptroller and Auditor General, *Investigation of Alleged Irregularities at Halton College*, HC 357 1998/99 (15 April).

Robbins Report (1963) *Higher Education: Report of the Committee appointed by the Prime Minister under the Chairmanship of Lord Robbins 1961–63*, Cmnd 2154, London: HMSO.

Smithers, A. and Robinson, P. (1993) *Further Education in the Market Place*, London: CIHE.

2   The Emergence of the Colleges

John Pratt

It was in the last quarter of the nineteenth century that the system of further education as we know it today became established. Its creation owed much to the burst of state involvement and collectivism that, in contrast to some popular opinion, characterized the late Victorian period. A number of factors helped promote technical education. The 1867 Great Exhibition confirmed the urgent need for reform of technical and scientific education if Britain was to remain competitive. Various Royal Commissions and inquiries were set up. The City Parochial Charities Act in London helped release substantial funds which supported the development of technical education. But the taking-off point was major constitutional legislation in 1888 which paved the way for the establishment of local authority technical colleges.

The Local Government Act 1888 established competent local authorities with rate-raising powers, to which powers in education could be given: 'Upon this administrative change depended the expansion of technical education in the last two decades of the nineteenth century' (Burgess and Pratt, 1970). Technical education became the first educational activity to be supported by the new authorities. Two further pieces of legislation enabled this to happen. The first was the Technical Instruction Act of 1889, which empowered the new authorities to devote the product of a penny rate to 'supply or aid the supply of technical or manual instruction'. The second was something of a windfall. An enterprising MP, Arthur Acland, was able to slip into the Local Taxation (Customs and Excise) Act of 1890 sections empowering local authorities to spend money from additional taxation on spirits to support technical education. By the turn of the century, 'whisky money' amounted to nearly 90 per cent of all public expenditure for this purpose and by 1902 had helped build twelve polytechnics or technical institutions in London, thirteen elsewhere and more than one hundred science schools (Ministry of Education, 1951).

These developments meant that technical education was now supported by two different bodies at local level: the school boards and technical instruction committees. The school boards, under the aegis of the national Education Department and responsible for elementary education, were providing evening continuation classes and schools, which by 1899 had nearly half a million students. The technical instruction committees, under the Science and Art Department, ran a wide range of technical and sometimes secondary education in their areas, often supporting provision established by voluntary bodies of all kinds. Small wonder that the Bryce Commission of 1895 found the system wanting in 'coherence and correlation', with the authorities and agencies acting with vested interest.

The situation was resolved almost accidentally. A court decision in 1900–1 held that school board expenditure on evening continuation classes and higher grade schools was unlawful. The Cockerton Judgment, as it came to be known, helped to bring about the 1902 Education Act which abolished the school boards and the technical instruction committees and made local authorities responsible for all forms of public education. The 1902 Act did not itself bring about any immediate increase in the material facilities available for technical education (Ministry of Education, 1951). Its main concern was with secondary education and teacher training. In technical education there was mainly reform and reorganization of existing facilities, as civic enterprise built on the achievements of the local authorities at the end of the nineteenth century.

At this stage, much of what we would now recognize as further education still took place in schools. With their increased responsibilities for secondary education, local authorities began to establish trade or technical schools for pupils staying on beyond the compulsory age of thirteen and designed for artisan or industrial occupations or for domestic service. Some pupils stayed on in general education beyond compulsory school age in continuation schools or classes. In any local authority, all these might exist alongside technical or commercial schools or colleges. But the consolidation of responsibility in local authorities meant that they gradually established more rational provision in their areas and developed much of the pattern of the further education system as we know it today. Essex, for example, commissioned a survey of further and higher education in 1905, which recommended additional facilities in parts of the county (Burgess *et al.*, 1995). Later, in the 1930s, as its population expanded through the growth of the London suburbs, it reorganized its post-school education and built two new technical colleges at Walthamstow and Barking. One is still a further education college; the other is part of the University of East London.

Vocational Education

The precursors of current further education can be found in the apprenticeship system. From the Middle Ages to perhaps the end of the eighteenth century, most people acquired their education through apprenticeship (Wardle, 1970). In these years, educational provision of any kind was limited, and such schools as existed were run by the church (Sylvester, 1970). Apprenticeship education was more secular, predominantly vocational and industry-led, and according to Sylvester 'a highly effective system'. The system was run by guilds, companies and corporations based on trades or skills 'teaching in all such skill as belongeth to the craft' (Sylvester, 1970).

But with the emergence of new technologies in the early years of the

Industrial Revolution, apprenticeship declined in importance. The old organizations and guilds did not relate to the new technologies and skills, and mechanization reduced the need for skilled labour. Yet it was not until the beginning of the nineteenth century that significant steps were taken to introduce more formal provision for technical education to meet economic and social needs. It took even longer for the state to assist in these developments.

There had been numerous earlier attempts to introduce forms of vocational or technical training, although they were aimed at what are now school-age groups. Locke argued in 1697 for the establishment of 'working schools' for the children of labouring people (Barnard, 1947) and something of this idea was taken up in the eighteenth century in schools of industry, where pauper children were taught to spin, sew, cobble and learn other trades of the time. (Unkind parallels might be drawn with some of the youth training schemes of the recent past.)

Already, there was diversity of institution. Charity schools, started by the Society for Promoting Christian Knowledge in 1698, offered mainly religious education but also encouraged 'habits of industry' in children who were destined to become labourers or domestic servants. The Sunday School movement offered children – and some adults – mainly religious and social instruction, but included some manual work. These initiatives were few and sporadic. They relied mainly on individuals, often philanthropic, acting in a 'voluntarist' tradition (Glynn, 1998) which the governments of the time were only too anxious to promote. It took the development of the Industrial Revolution and the growing importance of science to economic advancement to prompt greater efforts in technical education. It had, however, to combat the class structure and social presumptions of the time (and of much of the next two centuries) of the superiority of liberal education and a distaste for manual labour, industry and trade, which have left their mark on the qualifications of today.

Not untypically, one of the main initiatives in English technical education came from Scotland, which already had a flourishing scientific tradition. As early as 1760, evening classes in science, which working men were encouraged to attend, had been offered by a professor at Glasgow (Barnard, 1947). At the beginning of the nineteenth century, George Birkbeck, Professor of Natural Philosophy at the university, found that the artisans who helped prepare his apparatus were so intelligent and eager to learn that he started a series of lectures and experiments 'for persons engaged in the practical exercise of the mechanical arts'. In 1823 the students organized the class into a 'Mechanics' Institute' whose purpose was 'instructing artisans in the scientific principles of arts and manufactures' (Barnard, 1947).

When Birkbeck moved to London in 1804, he took the lead in establishing a similar institute there, and soon there were institutes in most major cities. There were other precursors, such as the Mechanic Institution in Chester, proposed in 1810 and the Mechanical Institution in London founded in 1817 (Kelly, 1970). Not all the institutes were founded by patronage. Many were founded by working men themselves and some by local industries, such as that in Stratford, east London, established by the Eastern Railways Company for its workers (Pratt and Richards, 1998). Hudson (1969) records that by 1851 there were 610 institutions with over 100,000 members. They became the most widespread means of educating adults in England at this period. Many institutions can today trace their origins back to a mechanics' institute, including Birkbeck College, London, and my own University of East London.

Although the mechanics' institutes flourished and their numbers increased, their development was not always what the founders had intended and it reflected the baleful influence of social class structure on English education. The artisans were often replaced by the middle classes and in an early form of 'academic drift' (Pratt and Burgess, 1974) the curriculum increasingly resembled liberal adult education rather than technical education. Engels found that the education was 'tame, flabby and subservient to the ruling politics and religion' (Argles, 1964). The editor of the *Mechanics Magazine* (1845) wrote that 'the mechanics of London have long ceased to identify themselves in any way' with the London institute. Dissatisfaction such as this sometimes led to new initiatives. In 1852, artisans frustrated by middle-class domination of the Greenwich Society for the Diffusion of Knowledge – one of a number of voluntary organizations providing further education classes – founded the rival East Greenwich Institution, and five years later similar frustrations with this led to the foundation of the Greenwich Mutual Improvement Society (Crosswick, 1978).

Technical education at this time faced a number of problems, which have dogged much of its development since. First, technology was thought to be for the lower classes and though it related to the development of the economy it was provided fitfully and cautiously. 'We find in the country and town schools little preparation for occupations, still less for the future agriculturalist or mechanic' (cited in Argles, 1964). Industrialists were afraid of revealing commercial secrets to competitors. There were fears of raising workers above their station, though science and technical instruction – through their association with useful knowledge that might make better workmen – avoided some of the resistance to general education of the working class.

The national attitude towards education for the economy was largely one of complacency. Victorian England did not detect a pressing need to improve the education of its workforce. Labour was plentiful and the demands of the technology of the time could be mastered by the employees; Britain was industrially pre-eminent and education was not widely seen as necessary to meet competition. Even if technical education had merits in making the workers more efficient, science and engineering were not suitable subjects for study by gentlemen. Playfair lamented in the mid-nineteenth century (in terms that were repeated for most of the next 100 years) 'that France, Prussia, Belgium and Switzerland possess good systems of industrial education for the masters and managers of factories and workshops, and that England possesses none' (Roderick, 1967). England 'entered the fierce economic competition after 1870 with artisans the least trained and a middle class the worst educated in Europe' (Argles, 1964). Even at the end of the century 'it was widely held that

Great Britain was falling behind her industrial competitors abroad and that their advance was largely due to superior technical education' (Ministry of Education, 1951).

State Involvement

Much of the responsibility for the country's lagging in technical education lay with the government itself. Voluntarism was not able to develop and sustain systematic provision for technical education. As Glynn (1998) puts it: 'Institutional failure was much more likely than long- or even medium-term success and the record is littered with casualties'. State provision, as in education generally, was minimal. The first state grants to voluntary societies for education were not made until 1833. Efforts such as the mechanics institutes failed in part because of the failings of general education; more than a third of those marrying in 1841 signed the register with a mark (Pratt and Richards, 1998).

By contrast, France and Germany had established the foundations of national education systems by 1800. The Ecole Polytechnique in Paris had been established in 1793. It was forty years before the term 'polytechnic' was used to describe an English institution – the Cornwall Polytechnic Society at Falmouth in 1833 (Roderick and Stephens, 1972) – and another half century before a major institution of this kind (Regent Street Polytechnic in 1882) was founded. Those who warned of the dangers of such neglect were few and were often ignored. It was not until 1851 that the Great Exhibition provided undeniable evidence of the emergence of Britain's industrial competitors and supported the case for state involvement in technical and scientific education long argued by 'savants', such as Babbage, Playfair and Huxley.

Playfair, assisted by Prince Albert, was the most vociferous proponent of technical education in England and agitated Parliament sufficiently to establish – with surprising speed – the Science and Art Department in 1853. The creation of this department enabled central funds to be made available for technical education, although the government had already sponsored the establishment of schools of design in London and elsewhere (the London school later becoming the Royal College of Art). The Science and Art Department began by recognizing existing 'schools of science or trade' – the mechanics institutes were examples of these – and granting aid to them (Roderick and Stephens, 1972). But the funds were tiny – aid to science classes from 1853 to 1859 totalled less than £900 (Argles, 1964). In 1859, the Department changed its approach and introduced a scheme whereby any school or science class approved by the Department could apply through its managers for a certified teacher in certain subjects. It still was up to voluntary initiative to establish local committees to run the schools and classes, in suitable premises and with at least ten students. The teachers' salaries were augmented by payments based on the results of examinations set up by the Department.

The scheme embodied several features that were to characterize state involvement in technical and further education for more than a century.

Indeed, a departmental minute bears disconcerting familiarity to some political statements of the 1980s. It hoped that 'a system of science instruction will grow up among the industrial classes which shall entail the least possible cost and interference on the part of the State' (Roderick and Stephens, 1972). The minute thus makes clear the class basis of technical education: the middle and upper classes got their education elsewhere. It also demonstrates the parsimony of the government. In the reluctance of the state to involve itself directly, it sets out the tradition of 'partnership' which has typified further education – between local providers and the government undertaking a regulatory and inspectorial function.

Nevertheless, the influence of the state was strong, but not always beneficial. Its regulations and payment by results produced a curriculum emphasizing theory rather than practice or application, and 'stale and unimaginative teaching' (Argles, 1964). Others acted to remedy this. The Society of Arts started examinations intended for artisans in 1856 and introduced technological subjects in 1873. In 1876, the City of London Livery Companies decided to promote education, especially technical education, 'with the view of educating young artisans and others in the scientific and artistic branches of their trades' (Argles, 1964). The City and Guilds of London Institute was incorporated in 1880, took over the technological examinations of the Society of Arts, and went on to become a major examining body in technical and trade subjects. It also founded the first technical college in England, at Finsbury in 1881.

The state was acting elsewhere in education, too. It gradually recognized that voluntary provision was not sufficient for general or 'popular' education, at this time predominantly elementary education. The state aid initiated in 1833 continued and by 1858 it amounted to over £660,000 (Barnard, 1947). But many poor areas could not raise the matching funds needed and there were concerns about quality, despite (or perhaps because of) the system of payment by results. Eventually, in 1870, the Education Act set up local school boards empowered to fill the gaps left by voluntary provision, using funds raised by local rates. At last there was a system of general education available for the whole school population, on which later stages of education could build. Moreover, many of these boards began to provide evening continuation classes, offering both elementary and technical education for students up to the age of eighteen (later twenty-one). The stage was set for the 'heroic phase' (Argles, 1964) of English technical education from 1888 to 1902, with which this chapter opened.

National Certificate Scheme

The period from the 1902 Act and the next great educational reform in the 1944 Education Act was also one of considerable growth. Total numbers of students in technical and commercial education more than doubled, from under 600,000 in 1910–11 to over 1.2 million by 1937–8 (Ministry of Education, 1951). An important factor in this growth was the development of a national system of examinations that became the mainstay of further education colleges – the National Certificate Scheme.

The National Certificate Scheme arose out of an initiative by the government. When the old Science and Art Department was incorporated into the Board of Education in 1899, its examinations were reorganized. Part-time technical education was based on a grouped award instead of single subject examinations. Importantly, the Board endorsed the certificates issued by schools and colleges. This new approach was the basis of the National Certificate Scheme. In 1921, the Board initiated arrangements with two professional institutions by which national certificates and diplomas were to be awarded jointly by the Board and the institutions, for courses and examinations created internally and assessed externally. The awards were at two levels – ordinary (roughly equivalent to GCE A-level) and higher (described in those days as comparable to a pass degree but across a narrower range) (Burgess and Pratt, 1970). Certificates were awarded for part-time study, diplomas for full-time.

The principles embodied in this scheme became the distinguishing marks of further education in the ensuing years with significance for the development of the sector and beyond. They were based on 'partnership' (Venables, 1955) – between government, the colleges, industry and the professions. They offered the colleges academic independence – the ability to create syllabuses related to local needs and to examine their own students – combined with awards of national standing. At the time the technical colleges were free to do this, new university colleges established in many cities were obliged to offer the courses and examinations of the University of London in which they had little say. Moreover, the scheme enabled the colleges to offer professional and vocational awards that were recognized as higher education, with implications for both social mobility and institutional aspiration.

The scheme was not without its problems: innovation was limited and the joint committees overseeing the awards restrictive, but the awards were quickly successful. New subjects were added and by 1931 nearly 2,800 passes were gained (Argles, 1964). They became an important route for working and working-class people to gain higher level qualifications. The alternative of university education was generally available only to those with money and who had stayed on at school, or to the very bright who were able to obtain scholarships. University places were available in the 1920s and 1930s for less than 2 per cent of the age group (Robbins Report, 1963). Indeed there were about the same number of full-time students in each sector – around 40,000 (Robbins Report, 1963; Roderick, 1967) – though only a few in further education were on higher education courses. To these should be added the more than a million part-time further education students, though again only a minority on higher education courses.

University courses were, nevertheless, available in further education. In what Venables (1955) called one of the most 'unequal' partnerships in further education, the technical colleges were able to offer external degree courses of the University of London (and one or two other universities). Unlike the National

Certificate Scheme, the University controlled the syllabus and set the examinations. In a few colleges in the London area, suitably qualified teachers could be recognized by the University and internal University of London degrees offered. The external degree scheme was important for further education, since it offered the colleges qualifications at degree level. In the 1950s over thirty colleges awarded more than 1,100 external degrees. It helped to meet the aspirations of their students and, of course, to meet – and feed – those of the colleges themselves for status.

Advanced Further Education

The development of higher education (advanced further education, AFE, as it was later known) within further education became one of the key issues in policy for the sector for the rest of the century. Although AFE was always a minority provision, it dominated the development of the sector. There were those who thought the colleges were aspiring beyond their status or legitimate function. A Board of Education memo in 1935 proposed 'delimiting the frontier line a little more closely' between technical college and university work and 'keeping the University out of the Polytechnic' (Board of Education, 1935). In policy terms, further education's function as a route of social mobility was less important than its contribution to the production of technically qualified workers to enhance economic growth.

The issue was highlighted by two reports immediately after the Second World War. Both the Percy Report (Ministry of Education, 1945) and the Barlow Report (Lord President of the Council, 1946) expressed concerns about the shortage and quality of technologists. The war and the need for post-war industrial growth had drawn attention to the issue. The position appeared parlous. In 1943, according to the Percy Report, the annual 'national output' of civil, electrical and mechanical engineers was only about 3,000 – and the technical colleges produced, nearly all through National Certificates and Diplomas, more than half of these. The universities' contribution – about 1,200 – had not changed much for decades – and the report thought this was the limit of desirable expansion. Both Percy and Barlow advocated selection of a limited number of technical colleges in which new degree-level technology courses could be developed. With this, the reports began the debate that led to the 'binary policy' of the 1960s and which, in the end, led to the Further and Higher Education Act of 1992.

The post-war debates had recognized the contribution that further education was making in higher education. This was more than just a numerical matter – though with the expansion of higher education the numbers were to become more significant – but also one of the nature of education and its relationship to the economy and industry. Put crudely, the Percy and Barlow reports acknowledged that the universities were not interested in responding to pressing needs for practically oriented technologists, and it was the technical colleges which traditionally had responded and were increasingly pressing to expand this provision. Here, the reports echoed critics of the universities throughout the previous half century (see Roderick, 1967) (and anticipated some – for example, Robinson, 1968 – of the next). Although the government received the opposite advice from the Advisory Council on Scientific Policy (1949), it was eventually convinced of the need to designate eight Colleges of Advanced Technology (CATs) in 1956 (and two more later) to provide a full range and substantial volume of work exclusively at advanced level (Ministry of Education, 1956a).

The creation of the CATs had implications for all further education colleges, even though advanced further education was a minority activity. By far the larger part of further education was 'lower level' work, as it was disparagingly known. Of around 2,000,000 students in further education colleges in the mid-1950s, under 100,000 were on advanced courses and only about 10,000 of these were full-time. Nor did the CATs have all of it; they had fewer than 20,000 AFE students in 1958 and roughly the same number when the total in the sector exceeded 140,000 in 1964 (Burgess and Pratt, 1970).

Academic Drift

But the designation of the CATs reflected – and reinforced – a pattern of aspiration in further education. Further education was an important route for students to remedy deficiencies or exclusion from other forms of education. Colleges in turn sought to extend this opportunity to degree level (and even doctoral level) by offering external or internal university degrees. The CAT policy now granted status to institutions which had predominantly degree-level work. They dropped the lower level courses that led to it and were rewarded by university titles. In doing this, the CATs were merely following a pattern that had afflicted the technical colleges for the previous century. Many of the colleges founded in the nineteenth century in the technical college tradition had already turned into universities, and in some cases the pattern was repeated. In Manchester, the nineteenth-century Owens College became the University of Manchester, leading to the rise of the Municipal School of Technology. This in 1956 emerged as the University of Manchester Institute of Science and Technology. The Royal Technical College at Salford then became the leading non-university institution in the conurbation, but this became a CAT and subsequently Salford University. Later a somewhat similar sequence led to the establishment in 1992 of the Manchester Metropolitan University. Pratt and Burgess (1974) have called this historical process 'academic drift'.

It was, in part, an attempt to contain this process that led an incoming Labour government to introduce a binary policy in higher education and the designation of new 'polytechnics'. It was a recognition of the importance of the further education sector. It was a response to – and rebuttal of – the structural assumptions of the Robbins Report (1963). Robbins had seen higher education as broadly synonymous with university education. His recommendations for expansion included not only awarding the CATs university status, but a succession of upgradings of the leading technical colleges as they developed advanced work.

Anthony Crosland, the Secretary of State for Education and Science in 1965, explicitly rejected this 'ladder' system in higher education 'characterized by a continuous rat-race to reach the First or University Division', by 'constant pressure on those below to ape the Universities above' and 'inevitable failure to achieve the diversity in higher education which contemporary society needs' (Crosland, 1965). The binary policy would help meet the increasing demand for vocational, professionally and industrially based courses by recognizing the distinctive role of the technical colleges. No new universities would be created for ten years. The colleges would provide vocationally oriented degree courses, using the new Council for National Academic Awards to do so. They would meet the needs of thousands of young people for sub-degree courses and of 'tens of thousands' of part-time students seeking advanced courses. Very little was said about the rest – the majority – of students on non-advanced courses.

The binary policy was implemented through the creation of polytechnics. A White Paper (DES, 1966) announced the government's intention to create twenty-eight (later thirty) polytechnics from more than fifty colleges in the further education sector to head the 'public sector' of higher education. The first of the polytechnics was designated in 1968 and the final two of the initial thirty in 1973. They contained (in 1973) over 150,000 students, split almost equally between full-time and part-time study, and over two-thirds on advanced courses (Pratt, 1997).

The Remaining Colleges

The binary policy, of course, left the main body of further education colleges bereft of their star institutions and uncertain of their status and future. Policy documents were ambiguous about their aspirations. The 1966 policy was for concentration of full-time higher education outside the universities in the polytechnics, although it was 'not intended that they should have a monopoly of higher education within the further education system'. But the role for the 'other colleges' was mainly specified in terms of specialist provision or to meet local needs (DES, 1966). The White Paper implied other full-time higher education would transfer to polytechnics. Yet, in 1973 the 'other' further education colleges had almost as many advanced students (92,000) as the polytechnics (116,000) (Pratt, 1997). The polytechnic policy had the consequence of creating aspiration in the further education colleges for polytechnic status – a particularly ironic form of 'academic' drift. As with the CAT policy, advanced work expanded in the non-designated institutions as fast as in the polytechnics. By 1989, the polytechnics had 264,000 advanced students, the other colleges 230,000 (Pratt, 1997). In both cases, the numbers were influenced (as was the development of the colleges) by changes in teacher education.

In 1972, a White Paper (DES, 1972) had announced proposals that significantly affected further education colleges, although as in 1966 they were neglected as a sector. The White Paper announced a substantial reduction in numbers entering teacher training and proposed that, in effect, the colleges of education would have to find their own new futures. Over the next few years, the college-of-education sector disappeared, as over 150 colleges variously merged with polytechnics, universities, each other or further education colleges, or closed (Locke, Pratt and Burgess, 1985). Out of the process emerged a new sub-sector of around 50 colleges of higher education, effectively forming a second tier in the public sector. A few of these eventually attained polytechnic status and some acquired university titles after the 1992 Act. The remaining, larger group of further education colleges, mostly concentrating on non-advanced work for the 16–19 age group, plugged on apparently thanklessly. Yet the sector had managed to double in size since the end of the Second World War (Cantor and Roberts, 1986). By the early 1980s it consisted (in England and Wales), in addition to the 30 polytechnics, of some 70 colleges and institutes of higher education (most with substantial volumes of non-advanced work), 500 other FE colleges with mainly non-advanced work and over 5,000 evening institutes.

Steps to Independence

Government policy increasingly reflected the 'economic ideology of education' (Tapper and Salter, 1978) and further education was perhaps the sector where these aims were most evident. Policy reflected too, the government's view that education had become 'producer dominated' (Maclure, 1989). There was a welter of reports and policies on the education and training of young people (MacFarlane, 1980), including the Youth Opportunities Programme and training for jobs (MSC, 1981; DES, 1984, 1986; DES *et al.*, 1985), and the creation of National Vocational Qualifications (see Chapter 5) and the Training and Enterprise Councils, all of which affected the work of the colleges. Then, in the great spasm of policy-making of the 1988 Education Reform Act and the 1992 Further and Higher Education Act, the status of the colleges was irrevocably changed.

For the further education colleges, the 1988 Act was significant in three main ways:

1   It confirmed that they were a separate sector from the polytechnics and major colleges of higher education. These institutions were removed from local authority control and centrally funded (see Pratt, 1997, for details). The 'seamless robe' ideal of progression in post-school education in the public sector was rejected.

2   Further education was clearly defined as excluding higher education and more clearly linked with what had hitherto been regarded as adult education. The Act tidied up the legislative basis of further education, doubts about which had been raised (DES, 1981). The legal obligation on local authorities to provide further education was restated and clarified.

3   It introduced changes to the funding and governance of colleges, delegating greater powers to their governing bodies, similar to arrangements for local management of schools. Local authorities had to produce schemes of financial delegation and governing bodies had new powers and

duties to manage their colleges to be more market-oriented, entrepreneurial and efficient. The local authority no longer had a majority on governing bodies.

Under the 1992 Act, the local authority no longer even owned the colleges. With the brief experience of a few dozen polytechnics as independent statutory corporations to draw on, the 1992 Act granted statutory independence to the several hundred colleges of further education and sixth-form colleges. The colleges became independent corporations. Their governing bodies were again reduced in size and the proportion of members representing industry and business increased. The FEFC took over responsibility for funding them.

The 1992 Act was the final phase of evolution of the colleges in the second millennium. It established the basis on which they face the hazards and opportunities of the third millennium. The colleges are now seen as businesses, characterized by 'product lines', dealing with 'customers' and 'responsible for the quality and efficiency of their own provision' (Cantor, Roberts and Pratley, 1995). They have shown in the past that they can evolve in response to changing circumstances. All the signs are that in the future they will have to continue to do so to survive and flourish.

References

Advisory Council on Scientific Policy (1949) *Second Annual Report*, Cmnd 7755, London: HMSO.

Argles, M. (1964) *South Kensington to Robbins*, London: Longmans.

Barnard, H.C. (1947) *A Short History of English Education*, London: London University Press.

Board of Education (1935) *Memo: Mr Savage to Mr Eaton, 11 December*, London: Board of Education.

Burgess, T. and Pratt, J. (1970) *Policy and Practice: The Colleges of Advanced Technology*, London: Allen Lane/The Penguin Press.

Burgess, T., Locke, M., Pratt, J. and Richards, R. (1995) *Degrees East: The Making of the University of East London 1892–1992*, London: Athlone.

Cantor, L.M. and Roberts, I.F. (1986) *Further Education Today*, London: Routledge & Kegan Paul.

Cantor, L.M., Roberts, I.F. and Pratley, B. (1995) *A Guide to Further Education in England and Wales*, London: Cassell.

Crosland, A. (1965) *Speech at Woolwich Polytechnic*, 27 April (printed in full in Pratt and Burgess, 1974).

Crosswick, G. (1978) *An Artisan Elite in Victorian Society: Kentish London 1840–1880*, London: Croom Helm.

DES (1966) *A Plan for Polytechnics and Other Colleges*, Cmnd 3006, London: HMSO.

DES (1972) *Education: A Framework for Expansion*, Cmnd 5174, London: HMSO.

DES (1981) *The Legal Basis of Further Education*, London: DES.

DES (1984) *Training for Jobs*, Cmnd 9135, London: HMSO.

DES (1986) *Working Together – Education and Training*, Cmnd 9823, London: HMSO.

DES, ED and DTI (1985) *Education and Training for Young People*, Cmnd 9482, London: HMSO.

Floud, R. and Glynn, S. (eds) *London Higher*, London: Athlone.

Glynn, S. (1998) 'The establishment of higher education in London', in Floud and Glynn, 1998.

Hudson, J.W. (1969) *The History of Adult Education*, London: Woburn Press.

Kelly, T. (1970) *A History of Adult Education in Great Britain*, Liverpool: Liverpool University Press.

Locke, M., Pratt, J. and Burgess, T. (1985) *The Colleges of Higher Education: The Central Management of Organic Change*, Croydon: Critical Press.

Lord President of the Council (Barlow Report) (1946) *Scientific Manpower*, London: HMSO.

Maclure, S. (1989) *Education Reformed*, London: Hodder & Stoughton.

MacFarlane, N. (chair) (1980) *Education for 16–19 Year Olds*, London: DES.

Mechanics Magazine (1845), XLII (236), January–June.

Ministry of Education (Percy Report) (1945) *Higher Technological Education*, London: HMSO.

Ministry of Education (1951) *Education 1900–1950*, Cmnd 8244, London: HMSO.

Ministry of Education (1956a) *Circular*, 305, London: HMSO.

Ministry of Education (1956b) *Technical Education*, Cmnd 9703, London: HMSO.

MSC (1981) *A New Training Initiative: An Agenda for Action*, Sheffield: MSC.

Pratt, J. (1997) *The Polytechnic Experiment 1965–1992*, Buckingham: Open University Press.

Pratt, J. and Burgess, T. (1974) *Polytechnics: A Report*, London: Pitman.

Pratt, J. and Richards, N. (1998) 'Higher education and the London economy', in Floud and Glynn, 1998.

Robbins Report (1963) *Higher Education: Report of the Committee appointed by the Prime Minister under the Chairmanship of Lord Robbins 1961–63*, Cmnd 2154, London: HMSO.

Robinson, E.E. (1968) *The New Polytechnics*, Harmondsworth: Penguin.

Roderick, G.W. (1967) *The Emergence of a Scientific Society in England*, London: Macmillan.

Roderick, G.W. and Stephens, M.D. (1972) *Scientific and Technical Education in 19th Century England*, Newton Abbott: David & Charles.

Sylvester, D.W. (1970) *Educational Documents 1800–1816*, London: Methuen.

Tapper, T. and Salter, B. (1978) *Education and the Political Order*, London: Macmillan.

Venables, P.F.R. (1955) *Technical Education*, London: Bell.

Wardle, D. (1970) *English Popular Education 1780–1970*, Cambridge: Cambridge University Press.

3   The Present Picture

David Melville and Deirdre Macleod

There has been dramatic growth in the further education colleges since they were given their independence in 1993, and the sector now caters for nearly four million students of all ages and abilities. Seven years on, it is possible to claim that the sector is the largest provider of full-time education for sixteen-year-olds[1] as well as continuing to be their main route to part-time training (DfEE, 1998a), that it continues to play a key role in the education and training of adults[2] (FEFC, 1998a), that all this has been achieved at a time of great financial stringency[3] (FEFC, 1998a), while maintaining a good record on quality[4] (FEFC, 1998b).

In this chapter we look in particular at how the student population has grown and changed since the sector was incorporated in April 1993. We consider the key characteristics of the student population – size, age, social profile and patterns of qualifications obtained – in relation to the government's policies on growth and consolidation. We begin by briefly describing the colleges and the further education sector.

The Colleges and the Sector

In describing further education it is necessary to distinguish the colleges from the sector of which they form part. The colleges are a diverse collection of institutions, derived mainly from the institutions whose emergence was traced in Chapter 2, but also others. The sector is mainly what is funded by the Further Education Funding Council. Most further education takes place in or under the auspices of the colleges but, among other things, they can also offer higher education, and non-vocational and leisure courses funded by local authorities. Most of the FEFC's funding goes to the colleges but it also funds other things, including further education in higher education institutions. There can therefore be FE in HE and HE in FE.

The Colleges

There are now 435 colleges in the further education sector. The main group comprises 217 general further education and 63 tertiary colleges, both of which have broad vocationally oriented curricula. Another major component consists of the 107 sixth-form colleges which some local authorities established during comprehensive reorganization to provide sixth-form studies to pupils from 11–16 feeder schools, and which still offer mainly A-levels. But there are also 28 agriculture and horticulture colleges; 6 art and design colleges and a music college; and 13 specialist designated colleges, mainly catering for adults through evening classes. There is a range of types and sizes of colleges, with places for between a few hundred and tens of thousands of students. About 92 per cent of FEFC-funded students are in the general further education and tertiary colleges, 6 per cent in sixth-form colleges and 2 per cent in agriculture and horticulture, art and design or specialist colleges.

The Sector

Students may also enrol at 235 local authority maintained external institutions, which receive some of their funding from the FEFC, or in 52 higher education institutions, which also receive FEFC funding for the further education provision that they deliver. They cater respectively for some 310,000 and 50,000 students.

Overall, there are 4.5 million students studying in further education sector colleges, external institutions, higher education institutions and specialist designated institutions. Some 3.7 million of these students are funded by the FEFC. Of FEFC-funded students studying in sector colleges, 22 per cent are full-time and 78 per cent part-time.

While there is great diversity in the size, location and type of provision offered by sector colleges, they share a number of common characteristics. They are generally non-selective and offer learning opportunities for both young people and adults. A high proportion of the students are returners to learning.

Student Numbers

Given the diversity of routes and modes of study which students in further education follow, participation is most conveniently expressed on a full-time equivalent (FTE) basis – that is, the number of person-hours of full-time study to which the various routes amount. In the academic year 1997–8 the further education colleges provided for 1,349,000 FTEs, of whom 1,146,000 (85 per cent) were funded by the FEFC. (The others were funded from a variety of sources including the Training and Enterprise Councils, the Social Fund of the European Union, business, the local authorities and the students themselves.) The 1,349,000 FTEs were derived from 3,950,000 people of whom some 80 per cent were funded by the FEFC.

Figure 3.1 shows the increase in FTE students since the colleges became independent. Over the five years, the total has risen by 8 per cent, but this is made up of an increase of 15 per cent in FEFC-funded students and a decline of 21 per cent of those funded from other sources. The FEFC-funded component had in fact increased by 19 per cent to 1996–7, but following a change so

Figure 3.1 *Students as full-time equivalents*

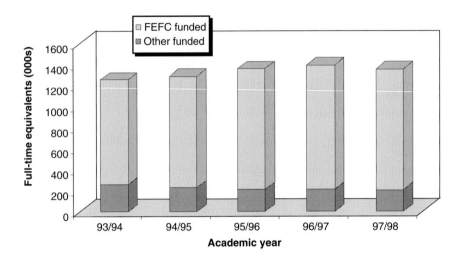

Source: *Unpublished data from the FEFC.*

that colleges were no longer rewarded for recruiting above agreed targets (the 'demand-led element', see Chapter 4) numbers fell back somewhat in 1997–8. Under funding plans announced in December 1998 (DfEE, 1998b), participation is due to grow considerably again. The plans provide for an additional 700,000 students by 2001–2, representing a growth in FTEs of 19 per cent. If this expansion is realized, students numbers will have increased by some 80 per cent since incorporation.

Within this overall pattern, there was differential growth by mode of attendance. Figure 3.2 shows that, in terms of actual people, from the last year of local authority control to 1997–8, full-time student numbers (including those not funded by FEFC) increased by about 6 per cent and part-time student numbers increased by a dramatic 42 per cent. The strong growth in part-time student numbers masks a decline in full-timers since 1995–6.

These patterns can be interpreted in terms of policy decisions. In his letter of guidance to the FEFC in July 1992, the then Secretary of State specified that the key aims of funding for further education should be to achieve growth in student numbers, to expand participation and to secure greater efficiency (FEFC, 1992). He made it clear there should be a direct incentive to colleges to expand by relating an element of the colleges' funding to actual student enrolments. In light of this, the FEFC was asked to develop a new system of funding that would reward expansion. The system did indeed include a number of mechanisms to encourage growth. Among these was a demand-led element, initially for full-time students only in 1993–4, but this was extended to part-time students in 1994–5. By this means, funding was provided at marginal rates

Figure 3.2 *Full-time and part-time students*

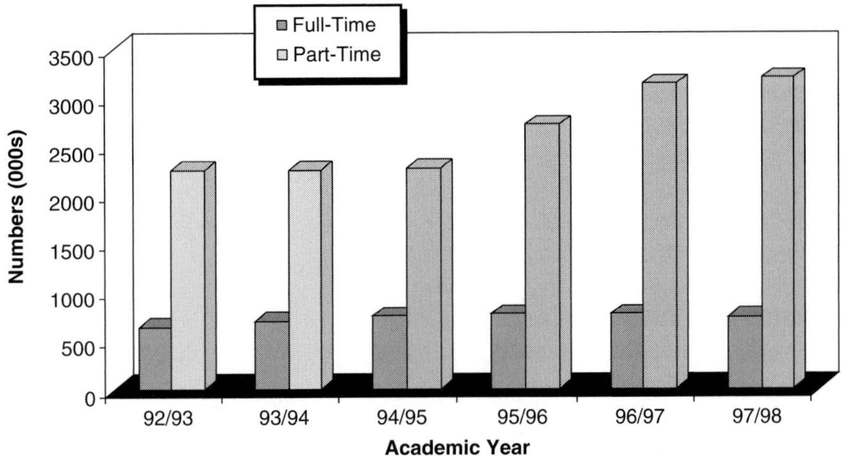

Source: *Unpublished data from the FEFC.*

over and above that for agreed targets. The introduction of these funding levels, as well as policy developments (such as allowing colleges to franchise to other providers), gave rise to the significant increase in FTE student numbers between 1994–5 and 1996–7. Within this, the major impact was on part-time numbers, although the demand-led element was also extensively used by sixth-form colleges to expand and bring down unit costs.

Participation Rates

In looking at participation it is convenient to consider sixteen- to eighteen-year-olds and adults separately.

Young People

In 1997–8, there were approximately 1.3 million sixteen- to eighteen-year-olds (that is, the three years after compulsory schooling) undertaking education and training by all routes – in schools, further education and work-based training – of whom approximately 1 million were in full-time education (DfEE, 1998a). These figures can be compared with the population figure of 1.8 million. About half of the sixteen- to eighteen-year-olds in full-time education were studying in further education colleges and together with the part-timers this makes the colleges the main provider of education and training for the age group. Further education's share of participation by sixteen- to eighteen-year olds has steadily increased over the last decade, although the rate of increase now appears to have slowed somewhat. In the Secretary of State's 1998 guidance (DfEE, 1998b), he indicated that he expects to see 50,000 more sixteen- to eighteen-year-olds in further education by the year 2002. The size of the age cohort is due to rise after 2002 and, if age participation rates remain the same or go higher, then the numbers of young people entering further education can be expected to continue to rise.

Adults

Levels of participation of adults in further education have almost doubled over the past fifteen years, rising from approximately a million in 1983 to nearly 1.8 million in 1997–8. Figure 3.3 shows the extent of the growth. Full-time numbers have almost quadrupled to 246,000, while part-time numbers have risen by 72 per cent to 1,488,000. The number of those aged nineteen and over is likely to increase still further as a result of the present government's desire to widen access. The Secretary of State's December 1998 guidance to the FEFC sets out his expectation that, by 2002, there should be an extra 650,000 adult students.

Student Characteristics

Nationally, a higher proportion of women than men are recruited into further education. This is particularly marked among the older age groups. For example, 60 per cent of the forty- to forty-nine-year-olds in further education are female.

There is also a higher proportion of students from ethnic minorities in further education than in the population generally. Among students aged sixteen to eighteen, about twice as many Bangladeshi, Pakistani and black

Figure 3.3 *Adults in further education*

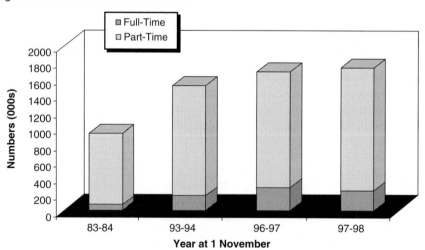

Note: *'Adults' here refers to students aged nineteen and over.*

Source: *FEFC (1998a) and unpublished data from the FEFC.*

African students are recruited as might be expected from the composition of the age group. Among adults, the proportions of black African and Bangladeshi students are over four times that to be expected from the national figures.

Students from socio-economically deprived areas have always been better represented in further education than other sectors of post-16 education and the participation of individuals from areas of socio-economic deprivation has increased since incorporation. The statistical evidence to the Kennedy inquiry (Kennedy, 1998) showed that there were proportionally more FEFC-funded students from areas of high deprivation, as defined by the Department of the Environment, Transport and the Regions' index of local conditions based on postcodes (DETR, 1998). This was true of both sixteen- to eighteen-year-olds and adults, with the effect being more marked among the latter.

Among sixteen- to eighteen-year-olds, students from deprived areas are more likely to go to general further education and tertiary education colleges than to sixth-form colleges. Figure 3.4 shows that there is also a difference in prior educational attainment. It in fact reveals a symmetrical relationship between GCSE performance and what the students do in the year following compulsory schooling. Students gaining at least five GCSEs at grades A*–C were to be found predominantly in schools and sixth-form colleges, while those with one to four A*–C or at least five D–G went on mainly to the general and tertiary colleges or into government-supported training. Those reporting no GCSE passes were also the least likely to be receiving further education or training.

It is also is worth noting the role of the further education sector in providing for students with learning difficulties and/or disabilities. While the FEFC does not keep records of such students, an indicative estimate of the numbers involved may be obtained from those receiving additional support. In 1996–7

Figure 3.4 *Participation and GCSE results*

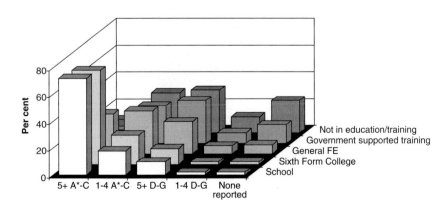

Source: *Unpublished data from the FEFC.*

there were 116,000. This may, however, also include students receiving additional literacy and numeracy learning support. In 1997–8, 2,034 students were funded by the FEFC to study in one of the 83 independent specialist institutions under the terms of the Further and Higher Education Act (Section 4) where provision within the sector is not adequate to meet an individual student's special needs.

Qualifications

In 1997–8, the 3.2 million students on FEFC-funded provision in colleges and external institutions were studying for 5.8 million qualifications. They take an enormous variety of awards. In fact, there are over 17,000 different qualifications available within further education colleges spanning general and higher education through to job-related training.

Remarkably, fewer than half (as Figure 3.5 shows) are for recognized general education (GCE A-level and GCSE courses), general vocational education (GNVQs and awards with similar aims), job-related training (NVQs) and access to higher education awards. The majority (55 per cent) are for 'other' awards – a wide range of college and occupationally specific awards outside the national framework. This is in addition to the non-vocational and leisure

Figure 3.5 *FEFC-funded qualifications*

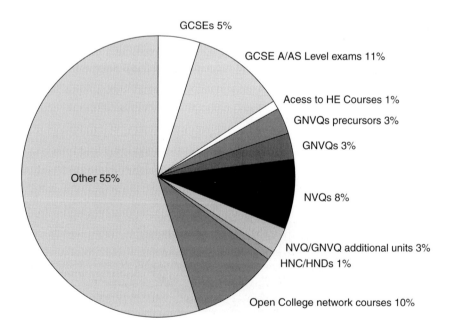

Source: *FEFC, 1998c.*
Note: *Figures refer to further education colleges and external institutions 1997–8.*

Figure 3.6 *Students on FEFC-funded qualifications by level*

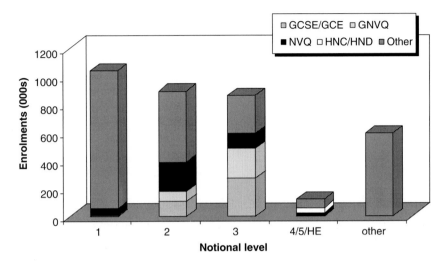

Source: *FEFC, 1998c.*

courses funded by the local education authorities or paid for privately, and higher education courses funded by the Higher Education Funding Council.

The national framework attempts to distinguish five levels of qualification (see Chapter 5 for details). When the awards are grouped into these levels, as in Figure 3.6, it can be seen that only at Level 3 (set to be equivalent to A-levels) do qualifications obtained in the colleges on the framework exceed 'other' awards. This in part reflects the contribution of the sixth-form colleges.

Higher Education

There are also higher education students in further education colleges. In 1996–7, there were 212,000, which is 13 per cent of the total of higher education students and 5 per cent of students in further education colleges. They mainly undertake part-time and vocational provision, often following progression from earlier further education courses, and related to local industrial and commercial needs. Approximately 11 per cent of these students are on provision franchised from higher education institutions. It is an astonishing fact that the number of higher education students in further education colleges now exceeds the total number of students who were studying in universities and colleges of education at the time of the Robbins report on higher education in 1963 (estimated at 183,000).

Qualification Trends

There has been a substantial increase in all programme areas. However, between 1994–5 and 1997–8, the highest growth rates have occurred in health and community care (120 per cent) and sciences (120 per cent). The lowest growth rates during the period have been in construction (3 per cent), humanities (3 per cent), art and design (9 per cent), and engineering (13 per cent). These differential rates may be accounted for, in part, by a significant increase in the provision of short Level 1 course qualifications in the areas of health and community care, and sciences.

Growth in health and community care may also be explained by a number of factors including increased demand created by the expansion of care in the community and in the provision of childcare; a wider range of, and greater industrial demand for, courses offered in the hairdressing and beauty sub-programme area; and the impact of new government health-and-safety regulations which require increased numbers of employees with first-aid or food-hygiene qualifications in the workplace. Growth in the sciences area is associated with increased numbers of students on information technology courses. In the construction programme area, it appears likely that lower growth reflects the downturn in the construction sector as a whole. In the engineering sector, the pace of technological change is rapid and the relatively high cost of equipment may be a limiting factor for colleges. The relatively slow growth reflects the decline and restructuring of the UK manufacturing industry and parallels a similar picture in higher education.

Modes of Delivery

The ways in which students learn have also changed markedly since incorporation. While the traditional mode of delivery (that is, classroom teaching) is still dominant, students are increasingly learning through a variety of innovative methods. Provision is increasingly being delivered on a more flexible basis to accommodate part-time, temporary or shift workers; those who are unemployed; and those who cannot study during normal hours owing to personal circumstances. In addition to the normal evening opening, many colleges now open at weekends. Students are more frequently learning within the community by open and distance learning; through resource centres; in the workplace and through franchising.

During the past four years, further education colleges have developed their resources to support information technology. Many colleges have worked together in consortia to develop technology-based curriculum materials. These have played an increasingly important role in ensuring that opportunities for study can be offered in ways that suit the students' needs and promote information technology skills. Most colleges have developed learning resource centres which bring together library provision and information technology, and many offer open and distance learning using information and communications technology.

Conclusions

In the seven years since incorporation, the further education sector has developed both diversity and inclusiveness. While growth (particularly in part-time numbers) has been dramatic, opening up education and training to many who would not otherwise have gained access to learning, international comparisons show that participation and success at the first three levels of the framework are still below most of our industrial competitors. The government has already set out its priorities for further education over the next three years: higher standards, wider participation and skills development (DfEE, 1998b). These are considerable challenges for the further education sector and ones which are likely to bring about further far-reaching changes in the size, structure and shape of further education in the early years of the millennium.

Notes

1   DfEE (1998a) figures for 1997 show that about 85 per cent of sixteen-year-olds (the year beyond compulsory schooling) were participating in education and training. Of the 69.3 per cent in full-time education, 34.3 per cent were in schools (27.9 in state and 6.4 in independent) and 34.9 per cent in further education. In addition, 9.8 per cent were on government-supported training, 2.2 per cent on employer-funded training and 4.6 per cent in other education or training. For 7.6 per cent of the age group this part-time training was provided by the further education colleges.

2   FEFC evidence to the Education and Employment Committee (FEFC, 1998a) reports that 'in 1995–96, 79 per cent of students on Council-funded provision were adults, studying a diverse range of qualifications many of which were provided in the workplace'.

3   FEFC (1998a) evidence to the Select Committee also seeks to demonstrate that further education since incorporation has had to cope with efficiency squeezes greater than any other part of the education service, despite starting from a low financial base. It claims that public funding for FE is now significantly below that for schools and TECs. Drawing on DfEE (1997) figures for 1996–7 it shows that sixth-form colleges received only 80 per cent and general FE colleges 85 per cent of the public funding paid to local and voluntary aided schools for a student completing three GCE A-levels over two years. FE colleges received only £3,900 for an NVQ Level 3 compared with £8,900 for TEC training providers.

4   The FEFC inspectorate in 1997–8 (FEFC, 1998b) assessed some 65 per cent of the 8,800 lessons observed as good or outstanding. This represents a slight improvement on the previous year, continuing a trend which has emerged over the last five years.

References

DETR (1998) *Index of Local Deprivation, Regeneration Research Summary No. 15*, London: DETR.

DfEE (1997) *Public Funding Costs of Education and Training for 16–19 Year Olds in England 1995–96*, London: DfEE.

DfEE (1998a) 'Participation in education and training by 16–18 year-olds in England', *DfEE News*, 335/98, 30 June.

DfEE (1998b) *Further Education Funding for 1999–2001*, Letter of Guidance to FEFC, December.

Education and Employment Committee (1998) Sixth Report, *Further Education*, vol. 2, *Minutes of Evidence and Appendices*, 264-II, London: The Stationery Office.

FEFC (1992) 'Letter of guidance to FEFC from the Secretary of State, July 1992', in *The Establishment of the FEFC*, Circular 92/08, Coventry: FEFC.

FEFC (1998a) 'Towards an inclusive learning society in the new millennium – the contribution of further education', in Education and Employment Committee (1998), Appendix 4.

FEFC (1998b) Chief Inspector's Annual Report, *Quality and Standards in Further Education, 1997–98*, Coventry: FEFC.

FEFC (1998c) *Statistical First Release*, 22 December.

Kennedy, H. (1998) *Widening Participation in Further Education: Statistical Evidence*, London: The Stationery Office.

NAO (1997) *The Management of Growth in the English Further Education Sector*, London: HMSO.

4   Recurrent Funding

Roger McClure

To have their funding switched from local authority control to national funding arrangements was a very significant transition for the colleges. With most of their money at stake it is not surprising that the means of its distribution should have become a major preoccupation. In a sector that was generally under-funded before incorporation and faced increasing financial pressure soon afterwards, the funding methodology has taken on an almost mythical significance, being held responsible for nearly every woe, real or imagined, and always controversial. And yet it has survived five years and three major reviews without a better alternative being found. The latest indications from the FEFC are that it will continue at least until 2000–1, a venerable age in the world of funding systems.

Funding before Incorporation

Some consistency of approach was introduced into college funding a few years before incorporation by the introduction under the 1988 Education Reform Act of local management of colleges and schools (LMC and LMS). Each of the 107 LEAs with FE colleges and fifty-two LEAs with sixth-form colleges was required to have funding arrangements, approved by the Secretary of State for Education, which conformed to a given pattern. The bulk of the college budgets was built up from a formula whose basic unit was the full-time equivalent student (FTE). Each LEA had a scheme for agreeing the number of FTEs it would fund each year at its colleges and the amount of money it would attach to each FTE. In most schemes, FTE numbers in different subject areas were weighted differently to reflect perceived differences in the cost of providing each subject. Although each was required to have such a scheme, LEAs were allowed considerable discretion over key variables such as the way part-time student numbers were converted into FTEs, the number of subject areas funded differentially and the size of the weightings applied in each area. When the non-formula elements and other more *ad hoc* adjustments were taken into account, these schemes, although following a common approach, in practice produced a huge variety of detailed calculations which in turn led to a wide range of levels of funding for apparently the same courses (FEFC, 1992a)

Other significant influences on colleges' preparedness for incorporation were that LEAs provided much of the administrative apparatus for their colleges, including financial, personnel and information services, and there were relatively few colleges in any one LEA. This meant there could be a comparatively intimate relationship between the LEA and each college with again a large variety of approaches to key matters such as following up actual recruitment against target recruitment, consequent funding adjustments if any, negotiations for additional resources throughout the year, and a college's understanding of the make-up of its expenditure and the income generated by its activities. For example, in the case of income, many colleges were quite unaware of how grants from the European Social Fund were being attracted by their LEA, perfectly legitimately, on the basis of students enrolled at the college.

In summary, then, there were in effect over 100 different funding methodologies operating; there was always the hope, if not the realization, that additional funding could be negotiated during the year; and a college, as an integral part of its local authority, could not formally become bankrupt. Most seriously, the majority of colleges had only a sketchy knowledge of their finances. This was hardly the best springboard from which to manage the leap to a national sector.

Funding in Transition

Colleges were incorporated on 1 April 1993. At that point they began to receive their main funding from the Further Education Funding Council which had been established in an embryonic form just over a year earlier. The first major headache for the Council was to decide how to allocate funding for that inaugural year 1993–4. Colleges needed to be able to plan their expenditure for the coming year and this left no time for the working out of a new national methodology to replace the variety of LEA ones. The Council quickly decided to guarantee each college funding equivalent to the amount it had received from its LEA the previous year, plus an amount for inflation, plus the offer of some growth funds, depending on the outcome of the Public Expenditure Survey (PES) in November 1992. Because some local authorities had reduced their colleges' funding significantly in 1992–3 in anticipation of independence, the Council made an alternative offer of 95 per cent of a college's 1991–2 equivalent funding if that were greater.

This approach was intended to be straightforward to understand and equitable, while ensuring financial stability during the transition to independence. In reality, it was extremely difficult to put into practice. Well before any bottom-up analysis of college budgets could be completed, the PES timetable required the Department for Education (as it was then) to agree with the Treasury the amount of funds to be transferred to the FEFC from the local authority element of the Department for the Environment vote. Meanwhile, each college was attempting to understand its budget, including elements of college expenditure which had been previously carried out by the local authority with little or no reference to the college: central services was one key example. The fledgling FEFC orchestrated a nationwide 'baseline budgets' exercise in which every potential recipient of funds from the Council, including the colleges, some 550 local authority institutions and over 50 higher education institutions offering FE courses, were required to decode their local management (LMS or LMC) or other budgets to establish a fair baseline for setting their 1993–4 allocation from the Council. This was an immensely complex and arduous task. The up-side for the colleges was that they became acquainted with the detail of their financial inheritance, something essential to their independent existence. The down-side was that the information they needed was mostly held by their local authorities, who in many cases appeared to believe that they were being asked to provide the evidence for their own further impoverishment. It was nerve-wracking for the FEFC because there was no particular reason why the sum of all the college baseline budgets should match the transfer already agreed at government departmental level in the PES negotiations.

In the event, there was enough money to go round in that first year. The situation was helped by the government's policy of seeking to expand the sector by some 25 per cent in its first three years and providing additional resources for this to happen. The FEFC was able to allocate to each institution a roll-forward of its previous year's total 'local authority' income (or the alternative where it was greater) and the offer of up to 8 per cent growth in weighted FTEs at a fixed price of about 60 per cent of the average funding level in the sector. Simplified standard methods for calculating FTEs and assigning a limited number of weights to the different courses were established after brief consultation with the sector. Most colleges accepted in full the offer of additional funds for growth.

That first year saw also the introduction of some features in recurrent funding that were new to the sector. Translated from higher education came the concept of a funding 'agreement' in which the Council set out for each college a statement of the amount of funds being provided for the year, the purposes for which they could be used and the sanctions that would apply if the college failed to deliver at least the number of FTE students for which it had been contracted. The last meant, in particular, that funds corresponding to any shortfall in recruitment would be clawed back the next year. As far as the Council was concerned, the funding agreement was the end of the story for that particular year, subject to correcting any errors that could be substantiated: the Council allocated as much funding as it could, well in advance of the coming year, and then it was up to the colleges to manage within their allocation and any other funds they could raise. At least, with independence, the colleges were able to keep all the income they could generate and at last had a real incentive to diversify their sources of income.

One such incentive was a new element of public funding which had been foreshadowed in the White Paper, *Education and Training for the 21st Century* (DES and ED, 1991), and came to be known as the 'demand-led element' or DLE. The idea was to promote efficient growth in the sector by offering colleges a standard payment for each additional student recruited above the annual target agreed with the Funding Council. The sector and the Council were told that this additional funding was not to be subject to the normal cash-limit control that applied to most government funding. Instead, the only limit on the amount of DLE funds that could be earned was the number of additional students that a college could enrol on approved programmes. The reality of this apparently generous and enlightened concession by government was to be put to the test within three years when the extra bills for the colleges' additional efforts began to come in. At that point, amid much acrimony, the DLE was withdrawn.

In the first year, the Department for Education insisted that the DLE should be available for full-time students only. This was curious for at least two reasons. First, the great majority of further education students attended part-time and, second, the concept of full-time had been breaking down for many years so that, already by incorporation, the Department's own student record allowed colleges to decide themselves whether students attending a course for between fifteen and twenty-one hours per week and for at least seven sessions were full-time or part-time. It was no surprise that in 1993–4 many of these students who had previously been classified as part-time were reported as being on full-time courses (see Figure 3.2, p. 29, for the relative growth of full-time and part-time students).

Notwithstanding the complexity and difficulty of the transfer from LEA funding to the FEFC, the first year's allocations did succeed in starting the sector on a reasonably stable footing while, at the same time, providing a stimulus for growth which matched the prevailing mood of optimism. The FEFC was also able to make specific allocations to each college to fund equipment and minor building works. For many, these were the most welcome benefits of incorporation since capital had been scarce or non-existent in most local authorities in the run-up to independence.

Developing a New Recurrent Funding Methodology

While the FEFC was working with colleges to implement the stop-gap funding arrangements for the first year, it was also hard at work developing a new allocation method appropriate to the complexity and diversity of the sector. In June 1992, a working group with a broad membership drawn from colleges, higher education, LEAs, the National Council for Vocational Qualifications, the Training and Enterprise Councils, the validating bodies, employers and the appropriate government departments, had its first meeting (FEFC, 1992a). By December that year, it had met nine times and considered a wide range of papers written by members of the group and commissioned from others. It heard evidence from specialists on provision for students with learning difficulties and/or disabilities and adult learners. The meetings were quite a journey: there was much, often passionate, argument; there was an increasing understanding of what mattered and what did not; and there was always the shared belief that here was a rare opportunity to devise arrangements which were appropriate to the labyrinthine world of further education and which positively encouraged good practice in the provision of learning opportunities to increasing numbers of students. On 22 December, the Council was able to issue the results of the group's work in the consultation document *Funding Learning* (FEFC, 1992a).

The title was carefully chosen. The group considered but rejected the current conventional funding methods which, in effect, funded the presence of students rather than the objective of their presence – to learn. It knew only too well that drop-out rates after the annual census date – near the beginning of the year, in early November – were unacceptably high and that funding levels paid no heed whatsoever to whether any student ever achieved anything while enrolled, largely at public expense. Indeed some months after *Funding Learning* was published, the Audit Commission and Her Majesty's Inspectorate issued a joint report under the title *Unfinished Business* (AC and OFSTED, 1993) which converted the drop-out rates and low achievement rates into estimates of 'wasted' public money. These very large figures made headlines in the national press. The climate of the times was for some more targeted funding system with employers in particular pressing for 'payment-by-results' through an approach similar to the training credits that were being piloted by some TECs for sixteen- to eighteen-year-old part-time trainees.

So retention and achievement were at the top of the agenda. These were outcomes that could be influenced by what a college did once a student was on a course. The group also recognized, however, that the processes which led to the student being on that course were of crucial importance too. Put simply, if students were placed on unsuitable courses – for example too difficult, or unin- teresting, or inaccessible – they would be much more likely to lose interest and drop out or fail, and public funds could be said to have been wasted – at least to some extent. Bringing these ideas together, the group argued that all of the varied learning programmes in further education could be analysed into three generic elements: entry, on-programme and achievement:

- 'Entry' was all the processes such as marketing and outreach, diagnostic assessment, and guidance and counselling, which ideally should ensure that each student's needs were appropriately met;
- 'On-programme' was all of the activities required to deliver the chosen programme, including teaching, support, facilities, assessment and so on;
- 'Achievement' was quite simply whether or not students achieved the learning goal they agreed with the college.

The group saw that these elements were different in nature and therefore could be funded differently.

Entry

The entry processes would be broadly the same for the great majority of students, whether full-time or part-time, whatever their subject and however long the course. The exceptions would be students seeking very short specific courses of a few hours only, and students with learning difficulties and/or disabilities who were likely to require specialized assessment. These exceptions aside, a standard rate of funding would be appropriate to cover 'entry' for most students.

On-Programme

On-programme activities, on the other hand, would vary a great deal from student to student and so would their costs to the college. The intrinsic costs of teaching one subject as opposed to another could differ significantly depending on the number of students that could be managed per member of staff and the amount and cost of consumables, equipment and space. In addition, attending full-time or part-time would impose differing loads on the college in any given year. It seemed clear that the on-programme element would require different levels of funding, the key variables being the cost of the programme and the length of time that was required to deliver it.

Achievement

The third element, achievement, was different from the first two in that it did not of itself cause a college to incur any cost. The college would in effect have incurred all its costs in respect of a student's programme or a part of a programme at the point where the student was undergoing their final assessment for the programme or part programme. Consequently any funding paid to the college for the student's success would be by way of a reward or bonus for the college's effective efforts in helping the student to succeed. Seeing how to pitch such a bonus at the right level raised some interesting and, in the end, unanswerable questions. It seemed obvious that the prize for helping a student to succeed in a one-year humanities course should not be any less than for a one-year engineering course. But a college helping a low-achieving student to pass one A-level, albeit with a low grade, might in reality be a much greater achievement both for the individual and the college than a high-achiever getting three As. It would be extremely difficult and complex, however, to incorporate such considerations in a funding system: the search for value-added measures robust enough to bear the weight of funding decisions has been a long and so far inconclusive one. As a compromise, the group suggested a proxy, namely that the length of a programme was some sort of measure of the effort required to be put in by the college and therefore the achievement element should be a standard percentage of the time-related costs of the on-programme element. Accordingly, a two-year programme successfully completed would bring twice the reward of a one-year programme, irrespective of the subject content.

Tracking Students

This analysis of the components of a student's learning programme shifted the emphasis of funding away from courses and firmly onto the individual student. The LEA schemes had identified an amount of funding for having a student enrolled on a given course or more commonly a group of courses with similar costs. The shift to the individual student was of major significance not least because of the step-change in management information systems that would be required to track each student's progress. But the group was convinced that the ability to perform such monitoring was essential to improving the educational performance of the sector. Few in the sector were prepared to disagree. When the FEFC asked a sample of colleges for their drop-out rates by course or even on average, none had readily available or reliable information to draw on. Because the national record counted enrolments on courses, nobody knew how many individuals were participating in FE.

The switch to making the individual the basis for funding was reinforced by the Funding Group's analysis of the funding required to support students with learning difficulties and/or disabilities. LEA schemes invariably had a course category labelled 'special needs' which generally attracted the highest levels of funding. To qualify for this funding, colleges had to bring students with learning difficulties together onto identifiable special needs courses. The group was advised by its expert witnesses that this was often detrimental to the students concerned since they had a very wide variety of needs. While the needs of some were so specialized they would be met best in discrete groups, many others would benefit from integration into mainstream classes provided their individual support needs could be met. Again the emphasis was on the individual, and the Group was led to propose that on entry to a college, all students should be assessed individually to identify not only the most suitable course but also their particular support needs. These individual needs could then be costed and funded separately.

Quality

While student support needs were reasonably tangible, the quality of provision was not. The Secretary of State had asked the Council to maintain and enhance quality by relating funding to its assessments of quality (FEFC, 1992b), but this posed at least two major difficulties. First, what was meant by quality? The term was broadly used to mean the content of a programme, the standards of skill and knowledge it was intended to confer, and also how well it was delivered. The first two of these were largely the responsibility of awarding and examining bodies rather than the institutions and so could not be influenced by funding decisions of the Council. As to the third, the group concluded that beyond a certain threshold level of resources, the organization and training of staff, the management of programmes and supporting services, and the ability of staff to motivate and communicate with students would have a greater impact on learning outcomes than increased funding. This was supported by evidence from the former polytechnics and colleges sector which showed no obvious correlation between institutions' inspection results and their average levels of funding. The second major difficulty was that it would be some four years at least before the Council would have comprehensive inspection results for the whole sector.

Notwithstanding these difficulties, the group considered four possible funding approaches to encourage institutions to improve their programme delivery. One was the 'carrot' approach by which a monetary reward would be given for good performance. This would be a simple bonus unrelated to the costs of provision but always likely to be effective in a leanly funded sector. The counterpoint to the carrot was the 'stick' approach, by which funding would be withdrawn as a penalty for poor performance. This too would be effective for the same reasons as the carrot approach. A third possible approach was that used successfully in higher education, that is, to allocate more funded places to the institutions gaining the best assessments, thus creating increased access to centres of quality. The group concluded, however, that this was more appropriate to higher education where the majority of students were full-time and freer to move to institutions with strong reputations. Most further education centres served students living close by them. More appropriate would be to make specific short-term investments in institutions which were found to be failing, to bring them up to at least an acceptable standard.

The Group also considered a great many other issues which were or might be relevant to funding and set out its arguments in *Funding Learning*. For example, besides students with learning difficulties and/or disabilities, it debated the needs of adult learners, people with low incomes and groups in the population who were not participating in education notwithstanding an apparent need to do so. These different client-groups were not mutually exclusive. In each case the group tried to analyse how their needs could be assisted through a new funding methodology. The group also considered the case for a factor to take account of the large differences in character and scale among the institutions the Council was to fund. It concluded that the Council's role should be to fund student programmes as equitably as possible without regard to type of college. To do otherwise would be to risk ossification of the system and the perpetuation of inherited unfairnesses and inefficiencies.

Strategic Planning

A final major debate was the issue of strategic planning. Colleges were used to being part of their local authority's plans and different authorities attempted to plan and coordinate their provision of education to differing extents. Now the colleges were on their own. The question was how they could be effective responders to the needs of people in their localities while being part of a sector funded on a national basis. There were calls for the FEFC to exercise not only its statutory funding role but to adopt a strategic planning role as well. To some extent these calls reflected a lack of confidence on the part of some principals that they would be able to hold their own in a world of free competition. Others believed that provision could only be economical and effective if it was carefully planned and coordinated with each institution being assigned its place by the central planning body.

The Council took a different view. It did not have any confidence that it could plan effectively for the myriad different circumstances at the local level. It had no wish to become what some dubbed 'the biggest LEA in the world'. It saw its role as providing a financial and regulatory framework that would be equitable and would encourage, and in some cases require, colleges to manage themselves effectively. The key drivers would be the need to attract students in order to obtain the funding necessary to remain solvent and develop; and external inspections of quality by the Council's inspectorate which were to be published and could lead to funding consequences. The latter meant that simply doing less to achieve gains in efficiency was not an option. With these thoughts in mind, the Council rejected any notion that it could operate like a merchant bank reviewing each college's business plan and allocating funding accordingly. Quite apart from the risk of second-guessing and thereby undermining local management competence, it would have been an administrative nightmare to review so many plans and then explain, let alone justify, the consequent funding decisions to the rest of the sector.

Implementing the New Approach

The closing date for responses to *Funding Learning* was 2 April 1993, the day after the new sector became independent. The level of response from the sector was both high and enthusiastic. Many responses were received also from bodies and individuals with an interest in further education. Much positive and constructive commentary emerged on the analysis of the issues in *Funding Learning*, but the consultation tended to boil down to which of the six funding options set out in the document would gain the endorsement of the sector. The options included conventional student-number-driven formula approaches, as well as an approach based on vouchers. Most attention was focused, however, on 'Option E' which was the most radical.

Option E

The fifth option was based on the three elements of a learning programme: entry, on-programme and achievement. It proposed that instead of measuring quantity in terms of FTE student numbers there should be a new common currency – the funding unit – and a tariff in which all the funding aspects of providing courses could be set out and ascribed a value of units on the basis of their relative costs to the institution to provide. There would be units for the entry element, for the on-programme element – in this case reflecting the costs of the particular course – and for achievement. A total of units could be built up as a student progressed through their programme, which measured the relative funding value of providing that student's programme as opposed to another student's. Adding up all the units generated in a year by all of the students enrolled at a college would give a measure of the total fundable output of the college for the year and thereby a means for comparing the volume of fundable activity between colleges, even though their character and scale might be very different. The reliability of such a measure would rest entirely on the construction of the tariff and the values put into it. It was proposed that these tasks should be entrusted to a Tariff Advisory Committee (TAC) made up mainly of practitioners from colleges and other providers funded by the Council.

The concept of the tariff enabled the method of annual allocation to institutions to be greatly simplified and also helped to resolve the local-versus-central planning conundrum. Each allocation could be expressed in terms of £x to provide y funding units of provision in support of the institution's strategic plan. A variety of methods could be used to determine each year what the values of x and y would be for each college. While the Council could and subsequently did take steps to strengthen institutions' planning processes and satisfy itself that they were planning their development in a rational and orderly manner, it did not seek to approve the content of their plans: that was a matter for the institutions themselves acting competently to identify and choose how to respond to their local needs. The separation of the annual allocation procedure (the values of x and y) from the measurement mechanism (the tariff) made Option E potentially very flexible. The tariff could be refined and developed each year without disturbing the allocation procedure or, alternatively, the allocation procedure could be changed without altering the tariff. (This flexibility was to prove invaluable later, in 1996–7, when the Council was able quickly to introduce a new allocation procedure in response to the urgent financial pressures arising from the eventual withdrawal of the demand-led element in that year.)

Finally, Option E included the so-called 'core and margin' approach to funding which had previously been adopted in higher education funding. Each institution would be allocated, as baseline funding and units, 90 per cent of their previous year's allocation. This would be their 'core funding' and 'core units'. The '10 per cents' and any new funds made available by the government in the year in question would then be allocated among institutions by whatever procedure was agreed. This was the 'margin' funding and units. The purpose of this procedure was to recognize that colleges needed a certain amount of financial stability from one year to the next if they were to maintain their commitments to students on courses longer than one year and if they were to plan effectively. The core and margin approach simply made explicit the maximum reduction in funding that the Council believed a college could tolerate in a single year (10 per cent) and this was used as a starting point for its allocations.

When the vote was taken, the sector was overwhelmingly in favour of the radical new approach, Option E. This may have been partly because the FEFC showed greatest enthusiasm for it (not least in an explanatory video targeted at college governors), but there was undoubtedly also the feeling of it being a new beginning, specially formulated for further education, and an approach that really did attempt to relate funding to student learning. The Council decided at its meeting on 29 April 1993 to adopt Option E as the basis of its new methodology and work began in earnest on sorting out the details and making the system work for the college year 1994–5. The aim was to provide institutions by Christmas 1993 with all of the guidance necessary to operate the methodology.

The work proceeded in dialogue with the sector. Four crucial circulars (FEFC, 1993a, 1993b, 1993c, 1993d), each dealing with a key aspect of the method, were announced and issued in sequence to all providers. Responses were sought on specific proposals and also more general comments. Summaries of the responses were fed back to the sector as the dialogue progressed. Fortunately for the Council, a high level of consensus was achieved on nearly every key point, both from the sector as a whole and from the different types of colleges and other institutions.

Tariffs

The TAC was established at an early stage under the independent chairmanship of Sir Roy Harding, an experienced and canny campaigner in the education world, and began to collate the collective knowledge of the practitioners making up most of its membership. It was empowered to commission research into specific matters that would help it to advise the Council on the items to be included in the tariff and the unit values to be assigned to them. It was also required to consult all providers before making its recommendations to the Council.

Despite the tightness of the timetable, the work stayed on track and the various components of the methodology were gradually chosen and refined. The annual procedure for allocating the margin funds was to be by bids, each institution applying for additional units above their core units at a standard price set by the Council in the light of the funding made available to it and the growth target set for it by the Secretary of State. The criteria for selecting bids were established in advance, again after consultation with the sector. They included checks to ensure a bid was valid (such as consistency with a college's strategic plan) and assurance that the bid if accepted in full could be physically accommodated. Selection was mainly based on performance against the previous year's funding agreement; the contribution the bid was making to achieving the rapid growth sought by the government; and the institution's average level of Council funding per unit – its ALF. This last was to become a prominent feature in the further education world. The acronym had a friendly colloquial air which belied the fact that it was a crucial measure of a college's performance and a key determinant of its success in winning additional funds. Provided the tariff was correctly recognizing the relative and relevant costs of provision, the ALF was in effect an institution's price to the public purse for each standard unit of provision.

As requested by the Secretary of State, quality as measured by the Council's inspectorate was also to be a significant criterion. At that stage, the Council could not adopt the 'carrot' approach of giving a cash bonus for good performance because it did not have assessments for all institutions. On the other hand, it could not ignore bad inspection results as they became known. It therefore implemented the 'stick' approach by which poor performance was to be penalized. In doing so, it drew on the experience of the former polytechnic and colleges sector which showed that quality assessments were reliable for funding purposes only at the extremes – 'poor' and 'very good' could be discerned with some confidence but not gradations around the average. It also made little sense to withdraw funding immediately from a struggling institution, because that would only make matters worse for the students already there. Instead, the institution would be put on notice to correct the deficiencies identified by the inspectorate and would not be allowed to take any additional students into the area in question until it had achieved a satisfactory assessment. Timescales for re-inspection would be agreed and the institution's funding would be maintained while it was taking the necessary corrective action. Perhaps inevitably in a sector offering a variety of sports qualifications, this became known as the 'yellow card' approach to funding quality. In the event, it proved highly effective. In each of the dozen or so cases identified per year, the institutions concerned were able to achieve satisfactory or better results on reassessment or, in the few instances where acceptable improvement could not be achieved, the Council reached agreement with the institution to withdraw from the subject in question, there being alternative provision of at least acceptable quality elsewhere in the locality.

By the December meeting of Council, the TAC had completed its initial work and, having consulted the sector, made its recommendations on the tariff for 1994–5 to the Council. Besides clarifying the detail on the three programme elements, the first tariff introduced a number of innovations. Consonant with the rise of the student as 'customer' and the government's introduction of a student charter, the end of the entry phase for each student was to be marked by the signing of a learning agreement by the institution and the student. The agreement was to spell out the learning goal or goals (normally one or more nationally recognized qualifications) that had been agreed with the student and confirm that the student had been assessed and given appropriate guidance on their choice of programme. The units for the on-programme element were as far as possible set as standard values for each named qualification. The standard value could be claimed however the qualification was delivered, thereby leaving institutions free to decide how best to deliver the programme. This was intended to reward efficient and innovative institutions which had found better ways of helping their students to learn while providing an incentive to the less efficient to catch up. In addition, the on-programme units were to be claimed on a termly basis thus providing a strong incentive to institutions to improve as far as they could their retention of students.

A range of values of units could be claimed for the costs of providing additional learning support to students with learning difficulties and/or disabilities, subject to the evidence of the assessment being available. The relevant value of units was also available to compensate institutions which remitted their tuition fees in full in respect of students with low incomes, typically those in receipt of a means-tested state benefit and their dependants. A small extra achievement bonus was included where the achievement of a qualification contributed to the National Targets for Education and Training and certain incentives were also built in for any student enrolled on an adult basic education course. For each item in the tariff, the audit evidence that would be required to support institutions' claims for funding units was specified. It was a testimony to the care and effort taken by the TAC that all of its recommendations for the first tariff were accepted in full by the Council. With the last piece of the jigsaw in place, *How to Apply for Recurrent Funding 1994–95* (FEFC, 1993e) was duly despatched to principals on Christmas Eve 1993.

Theory into Practice

Much hard and in some instances tricky work remained to be done in 1994, however, both by institutions and the Council. The latter had to decide what price to assign to the margin units that institutions were about to bid for. This had to be based on an estimate of how many units the sector had generated in 1993–4, a judgement of how much of its funds it could make available for the margin, and the growth target set for the coming year by the Secretary of State. The Council also had to work out in detail how it was going to process over 1,000 bids in a sensible and defensible way that would allow the Council members to decide the allocation to each bidder. Institutions, on the other hand, had to calculate in detail the value of units they each generated in 1993–4 so that the Council could determine the number of their core units which would be the baseline for their bid. For most institutions this was another major exercise and another learning experience. In theory, it meant a complete analysis of the progress of each student through their individual programmes and the identification of any additional units generated, for example, through additional learning support and the remission of fees. The Council suggested a number of shortcuts and proxies to reduce the burden of this task, but many colleges chose to use it as an opportunity to really get to grips with their student number data.

Late in the day, agreement was finally reached with the Department for Education as to how the demand-led element (DLE) would be incorporated into the new methodology. The Department was persuaded that the scope of the DLE had to be extended beyond full-time students if it was to be a really effective incentive to the sector to expand. After debating various half-way house options, it was agreed that the DLE would apply to each funding unit at the rate of £6.50 per unit or just under a third of the average level of funding in the sector. This was an enlightened decision since it meant that institutions could earn £6.50 for each unit they generated above the number allocated by the Council, however those units were arrived at. For example, additional funds could be earned by improving retention or achievement rates, even if the number of the student body remained constant.

The bids of 494 colleges and higher education institutions were received by 21 April 1994. Local authority institutions offering Council-funded programmes were given longer to prepare their bids and funds were set aside for them. The first task for the Council was to test the validity of each bid and, in particular, whether it appeared to be broadly consistent with the bidder's strategic plan. Second, the Council evaluated special particulars that each bidder was given the opportunity to provide to ensure that funding decisions were not taken purely mechanistically, in ignorance of matters that would be pertinent. The special particulars included an explanation where the institution had failed to achieve its previous year's target and any exceptional circumstances which the institution thought the Council ought to take into account in reaching its decision. The Council developed a small number of criteria which it applied rigorously to these two tasks and, where it considered that a sound case had been made, it intervened as necessary to ensure that the allocation was appropriate. Such interventions have never exceeded twenty cases in the five years the methodology has been used.

Once the groundwork was done, there remained the question of the Council members making the actual allocations. It would have been impossible for a group of 'non-executive directors' to have reached rational judgements while attempting to grapple with the paperwork needed to set out the salient facts and figures of over 1,000 bids. Chaos and loss of confidence would quickly have ensued. Fortunately, information technology came to the rescue. All the relevant data were held in a massive computer spreadsheet that could be displayed on a large screen and manipulated by an operator present at the meeting. The centrepiece was a scattergraph which displayed all of the bids in two dimensions: the size of the bid (expressed as the increase sought in core units) and the bidder's ALF (effectively the institution's price). Each bid appeared as a small anonymous diamond on the scattergraph. The pattern of the diamonds gave an immediate overview of the scale and pattern of growth being sought and how that related to each bidder's funding level.

The demand for margin funds far exceeded the funds available and so it was necessary to devise a rationing mechanism that would systematically and fairly distribute the available funds according to the Council's criteria. A simple algorithm was established in the spreadsheet, which allocated a percentage increase in core units which varied in an inverse relationship to the value of the ALF. The application of the algorithm was displayed on the scattergraph as a line cutting through the pattern of diamonds. A bid appearing on or below the line would be accepted in full; a bid appearing above the line would be trimmed back to the percentage increase indicated by the line for that particular value of ALF. A second, vertical line indicated the ALF at which the margin of funds ran out so that any bid beyond it would be wholly rejected. The precise relationship between growth and the ALF could be varied by entering different parameters: in effect, the two lines on the scattergraph could be moved around at the suggestion of Council members until a position was found which appeared satisfactory in terms of the different amounts of growth allocated to different institutions and which was within budget.

The spreadsheet had other functions built into it, including most importantly a series of reports which could be displayed on screen or printed out, quickly photocopied and distributed to Council members. These reports allowed members to see the effect of particular decisions on, for example, the distribution of growth by all institutions and by type of institution, the allocation of units and funds by region, and the details of the institutions that were the greatest losers. Institutions were only identified by an anonymous number.

These facilities enabled the members to function as intended, that is, as a strategic body, able literally to shape the allocations for the sector as a whole and to check their decisions at the macro level without delving down into the special pleading of individual institutions. Over the years this computer model became more refined so that it offered members considerable flexibility in applying the agreed selection criteria while always allowing them to test the effect of their decisions before confirming them.

The first allocations under the new methodology were notified to colleges on 29 April 1994. They were accompanied by a full explanation of the mechanics of making them and colleges were invited to comment on whether the data used were correct and on any other aspect which they considered should be reviewed. The allocations were finalized at the next meeting of Council in the light of these comments. Again, a rigorous line was taken: technical errors were corrected without hesitation but claims for special treatment and requests to provide new information were for the most part rejected. The same approach was adopted in finalizing the allocations to local authority institutions and higher education institutions which followed a few weeks later. While there remained a longish tail of problem cases, mostly with inadequate data, the vast majority of the allocations were made on schedule. The new approach had been made to work in practice as well as in theory. In due course, a full descrip-tion of the process and the resulting allocations to each institution was published, the first of a series of such publications which opened up the key decision-making of the Council to scrutiny by institutions and others with an interest in further education (FEFC, 1994b, 1994c).

Evolution and Reflection

Each year after the introduction of the new method, the TAC met regularly and bit by bit it refined the tariff, adding some items and adjusting the values of others, always after consultation with the sector. The full implications of the tariff were complex, reflecting the diversity and complexity of further educa-tion itself, and there was a steady stream of calls for it to be simplified. Curiously, the specific requests from institutions for changes to the tariff were invariably for the addition of some further detailed items that they considered would make it fairer (to them). A review of the tariff by Coopers and Lybrand (1995) concluded that there would always be a trade-off between complexity and fairness and that the Council had got it about right.

Franchising

Nevertheless, the correctness of the tariff was crucial to the methodology. This was to be thrown subsequently into sharp relief by the issue of 'franchising', a new controversial form of curriculum delivery in which colleges made arrange-ments with others, including employers, to deliver programmes on the provider's premises. This is not the place to debate the merits of franchising (see Chapter 13), but it grew rapidly and in a variety of forms, some of which were relatively inexpensive for the partners to provide. The implications of these new forms were not immediately apparent and, for a year or two as franchising was emerging, the tariff did not include appropriately lower values to reflect the lower costs of some of this provision. As a consequence, a small group of colleges moved fast to set up large-scale franchising contracts which boosted their income from the non-cash-limited DLE. By 1997–8, this imbalance was being corrected. The experience demonstrated very clearly how the tariff and the DLE could provide powerful incentives which led, in the case of franchising, to the first major innovation in programme delivery for many years.

Individualized Student Record

A second funding-related issue was management of information and in particular the new Individualized Student Record (ISR) introduced by the Council. The statistical steering group set up by the Council and again consisting mostly of members from the sector concluded at an early stage that the Department for Education's existing course-based record was no longer adequate to support the management of students' learning. The record should be based on the individual student thus allowing institutions to track each student's progress and to identify where they were being successful and also where they were not. An individualized record would also be needed to support the new funding methodology with its emphasis on the individual student. It was recognized that the switch from courses to students would bring a step-change in complexity and there was some nervousness in the Council as to the ability of colleges to cope. At last it was decided the ISR was the only sensible way forward and the sector embarked on yet another major management exercise (FEFC, 1994d).

Like the baseline budgets exercise the year before, this task was painful and prolonged for many colleges but it was ultimately therapeutic since eventually (in some cases after two or three difficult years) it gave all colleges a powerful management tool that will enable them to deliver their core activities more effectively. The pain of the development was to some extent exacerbated by deficiencies in the software the Council had commissioned to help colleges convert their ISR data into funding units for the funding methodology. Conceived as a useful tool to help the sector, it was rushed out before all of its bugs had been detected and as a result it added considerably to the tension and frustration of many managers trying to comply with the funding timetable.

In this exercise, as in all of the major tasks undertaken by the sector, disparities in the management skills of the different institutions were apparent. Given its scale and diversity, it is no surprise that, in educational parlance, it constituted a 'mixed ability group'. Many colleges completed all the tasks relatively easily and effectively and within the timescales set by the Council; others struggled with nearly every task and took years to manage them effectively. The Council's response to this situation was to press ahead at the rate which the better-managed colleges could cope with while providing many seminars, much informal support and a flexible approach to deadlines for their weaker brethren.

Convergence

The third and perhaps sharpest controversy arose over a Council policy that came to be known as 'convergence'. Even before the new funding system was introduced with its tariff enabling comparisons among institutions, the Council had identified that there was a wide range of inherited levels of funding for apparently the same work. Once each institution's provision was expressed in funding units it was immediately clear that some were receiving over four times as much funding per unit than others: if the tariff was 'correct' – and that was an important 'if' – then such disparities could not be justified. Certain groups of colleges stood out as being relatively generously funded: for example, certain of the agriculture and horticulture colleges – but not all of them – and most of the big colleges in inner London. There was at least anecdotal evidence to suggest that these colleges had been funded previously at relatively high levels but there remained a lingering concern that some subtle ingredients might be missing from the tariff.

After consultation with the sector, the Council declared an objective to converge in three years the range of average levels of funding (ALFs) to a band that was plus or minus 10 per cent of the median ALF. This was still quite a wide range but it left room for any need that might emerge to revise the tariff. The main drivers to convergence were the preference given to institutions with lower ALFs in the annual bidding round and the encouragement of the DLE to institutions to expand beyond their targets. Significant convergence did occur in the three years from 1993–4 to 1996–7, with the proportion of colleges within the band increasing from 42 per cent to 70 per cent. However, it was during this period that government finances came under increasing pressure and the promised reasonable annual increases to fund the government's expansion objective were gradually whittled away. Increasingly, institutions became concerned about their funding allocation and whether they would be able to meet their costs, many of which were effectively fixed in the short run. The publication by the Council of all the details of the funding allocations meant that every institution could see how every other one was faring. It was not long before the colleges with ALFs below the median began to demand that convergence should be speeded up, preferably to a single common value rather than a band, while those with ALFs above the median protested that convergence was already being required at a faster rate than they could reasonably manage. While the 'low ALFs' campaigned for instant convergence, the London colleges set out to demonstrate that they did indeed face certain higher costs that were not adequately recognized by the tariff. The Council set up a London costs group to settle the issue.

Demand-Led Element

The funding squeeze came to a head with the DLE crisis of 1997. The reckoning of the amount of DLE earned by the sector necessarily lagged by at least a financial year because it had to wait for the final annual ISR return of each institution to be submitted and validated. In the early years, there were many delays as institutions struggled to establish effective information systems. In 1997, an outstanding bill of some £84 million was recognized covering the previous periods. A public row ensued with charge and counter-charge: the size of the bill should have been made known earlier (there was insufficient information to do so); the DLE was not really non-cash-limited (endless ministerial statements had claimed credit that it was); and so on. In the end, additional funds were found to meet most of the outstanding bill but the DLE was summarily withdrawn and as a consequence, a cut of some £100 million was imposed on the sector. At a stroke, the government removed the most cost-effective weapon yet deployed to expand education and widen participation – and at a marginal funding cost that was about a third of the average funding level in the sector.

Now the clamour for convergence intensified and the justification for delay diminished. The Council declared a new objective to converge average levels of funding to a single value by 2000–1. To ensure this happened it introduced a revised allocation procedure in which it determined each institution's ALF and target units over the three-year period by formula so as to bring the sector to convergence. Bidding by institutions was restricted to special initiatives, such as widening participation, for which the Council set aside a specific budget. Additional funds were immediately allocated to the low ALF colleges to bring their ALFs up to the chosen convergence level for the sector. The London costs' study concluded that the Council's London weighting factors ought to be increased, while the widening participation factor introduced following the Kennedy review (1997) particularly benefited the inner London colleges since it was based on measures of deprivation. These moves took much of the immediate heat out of the convergence debate and the election of the new government, with its emphasis on education, training and lifelong learning, created a relative calm of anticipation that funding overall would be increased.

Reviews of the Methodology

When it introduced the new methodology, the Council said that it would review it after three years. In the intervening period, it made minor refinements and improvements, particularly in the tariff, but the basic structure and procedures remained remarkably stable. This was part of a deliberate policy to give the sector plenty of opportunity to understand and respond to the implications of the new approach, while maintaining as much stability in its regulatory environment as possible. Before the Council could conduct its review, however, the new method was scrutinized in 1995–6 by the National Audit Office (NAO, 1997a). The NAO's investigation included not only a thorough analysis of the workings of the system – the NAO even sat in on some of the meetings when bids were being validated and claims for exceptional circumstances being evaluated – but also a survey of college opinions about the new approach. The NAO found no fault with the basic concepts and procedures and the results of the opinion poll were very positive, somewhat in contrast to the impression that tended to be portrayed on occasions in the press. It did, however, point to practical problems such as the difficulties many institutions were having with their management information systems and concluded that it was too early to tell whether the method was producing the intended educational benefits such as improved retention and achievement. The NAO (1997b) examined the methodology again in its inquiry into the management of growth and was positive about the incentives, but drew attention again to the familiar problems of data collection.

The Council's own review got underway in September 1996. The work was conducted in two phases, the first (re-examining the basic principles) by a joint Council–sector working group under the chairmanship of Helena Kennedy, QC (FEFC, 1997). The first phase review report concluded that 'the methodology works' and that 'in general, the new methodology has been an improvement on former methods and other current methods in other sectors, and has resulted in tangible benefits to the education and training of students.' The report also drew attention, however, to some continuing concerns, in particular, its complexity and management information burden. It also identified the blurring, frequently made by principals and others, of two crucial distinctions: between the methodology as an instrument of policy rather than a policy in its own right; and between the methodology as a mechanism for sharing out the money made available to the sector by the government and the size of the quantum available for distribution. The real test of the method would be whether it could continue to work while transmitting more directive policy steers and during a period of contraction as well as expansion. In the present climate, the latter looks unlikely to be put to the test for some time. The report set an agenda for the second stage review, but none of the issues called for fundamental change.

The basic approach to funding came under scrutiny once again when the Education Sub-Committee of the parliamentary Education and Employment Committee conducted a review of further education in 1997–8 (Education and Employment Committee, 1998). It broadly endorsed the conclusions of the earlier reviews: it was necessary to clarify funding policy and use the method more directly to support policy aims; the sector was under-funded both in recurrent and capital funding; the method should be simplified wherever possible; convergence should continue but to a 5 per cent tolerance band rather than a single value (to recognize that the tariff could never be exact); the FEFC's conclusions on London were supported; and harmonization of funding between the various sectors offering 16–19 provision was recommended, but along FEFC rather than the local authority lines.

The Future

The various reviews of the Council's funding approach have all pointed to emerging policy issues and asked whether the funding methodology would be able to accommodate them. The obvious examples are widening participation (the so-called Kennedy agenda), lifelong learning and regionalization. In each case, they would involve recognizing certain characteristics or specific factors to which funding was to be targeted. There are generally two ways this could be done: either by introducing new factors into the tariff or by 'top-slicing' an increasing proportion of funds for distribution as special initiatives outside the methodology. It is likely the Council will deploy both options. It has already added a widening participation factor to the tariff while inviting bids from institutions for funding for collaborative projects to target specific problem areas.

Special initiative funding seems likely to be given greater emphasis by the government's desire to see any additional money provided to the sector being used to achieve quite specific national policy objectives. Special initiative funding is not new, and was used by both the University Grants Committee and the National Advisory Body (on polytechnics and colleges) in the 1980s. It is attractive to the policy-maker because it seems to guarantee that the chosen policy will be implemented. Actual practice, however, was not so positive. The costs of bidding were usually very considerable, particularly to the unsuccessful bidders (who lost not only on the administrative overheads but also on their share of the funds diverted to the initiative), and the success of the initiatives rested entirely on the central policy-maker coming up with an appropriate idea. Where this is something which well-managed institutions have not already chosen to do, the central policy-maker is in effect second-guessing local management. That the latter often remain unconvinced was demonstrated by the number of these initiatives which fizzled out when the specific funding dried up. It was in response to such disappointing outcomes that the 1990s saw a shift to a more market-driven approach.

Perhaps the most far-reaching development to affect funding methodologies will be the drive to lifelong learning. This will inevitably require further unitization of the curriculum, greater flexibility in modes of attendance and, in the information age, new modes of delivery which could change the conventional costs paradigm dramatically. These things will happen because the customers will demand that they do. When they do, the tariff could, in theory, incorporate any number of additional items and the FEFC methodology could carry on more or less as now. Changes in the relative costs of provision could continue to be identified by the TAC and incorporated in the tariff so that it followed educational developments. It is a good thing that such changes to the tariff inevitably lag behind changes on the ground since the 'over-pricing' gap which may be temporarily opened up provides a necessary financial stimulus to the pace-setters.

Substantial further unitization of the curriculum would mean, however, another step-change in the complexity of the student record and in college management information systems. The implications of this are hard to predict: again, in theory, computer systems ought to be able to cope and they would be recording increased complexity which would have to be managed in any case on the ground; but how well managers would be able to cope and whether the administrative overheads would be acceptable are less clear. The introduction of the ISR was a three- to four-year struggle. Wisely, the Council is proceeding cautiously and is proposing to run a pilot-study of funding part-qualifications in 1998–9.

Postscript

In his inaugural letter of guidance to the Council in 1992, the Secretary of State stated that the key aims of funding should include *inter alia* greater efficiency, expanded participation, further development of flexible and part-time approaches to learning, and enhanced quality (FEFC, 1992b). After five years (1993–4 to 1997–8), the figures speak for themselves:

- the number of funding units generated for each pound of public money up by 40 per cent;
- the number of students on approved courses up by 64 per cent from 1.9 million to nearly 3.2 million;
- part-time and part-year numbers up by 88 per cent from 1.3 million to 2.5 million;
- some 8 per cent of provision now delivered outside colleges on premises more convenient for learners;
- open and distance learning up by over 50 per cent, albeit from a low base;
- the percentage of classes assessed by the inspectorate as being in the top two grades of its five-point scale up by 18 per cent, while the percentage of classes achieving grades 1–3 has remained at 96 per cent.

These improvements have been achieved in a climate of financial stringency. Table 4.1 shows that since incorporation the colleges have had to make substantial 'efficiency gains'. The planned intake increases have had to be made against real-terms reductions in the amount of money received for each student (in full-time equivalents) of between 4.5 and 6.5 per cent a year until the policy was ameliorated for 1998–9. This was a tough time for many colleges as the FEFC's financial monitoring clearly showed. It is not surprising that the colleges were keenly interested in how the sector's funding was shared out each year. We will never know whether a different methodology would have delivered better results, but there seems little doubt that the FEFC's approach has been effective.

It has also demonstrated how carefully constructed mechanisms can play a role in bridging the gap between the policy concerns of the public sector and

Table 4.1 *Government funding and planning numbers*

	1992–3	*1993–4*	*1994–5*	*1995–6*	*1996–7*	*1997–8*	*1998–9*
Funding (£m)	2,664	2,808	2,924	3,014	3,047	3,063	3,165
% change		5.4	4.1	3.1	1.1	0.5	3.3
Planned nos (000 FTE)	833	891	951	995	1,044	1,072	1,095
% change		6.9	6.7	4.7	4.9	2.8	2.1
Per FTE (£)	3,834	3,662	3,446	3,290	3,080	2,932	2,890
% change		−4.5	−5.9	−4.5	−6.4	−4.8	−1.4

Note: *Per FTE (£) is given in 1998–9 prices.*

the business efficiency of the private sector. For example, the national funding framework promotes the equitable distribution of taxpayers' money for further education (a public-policy concern) while encouraging providers to respond differentially to their differing local conditions and demands (closer to a private-sector market approach). The identification and use of the average-level of funding (ALF) to drive funding decisions has introduced a quasi-market price in the distribution of resources to a substantially publicly subsidized service. Using the equivalent of standard pricing in the tariff has promoted innovation by giving the pace-setting providers the opportunity to 'beat the market', albeit temporarily. And just as significant, but a good deal less glamorous, the audit requirements in the funding framework have introduced to the discharge and management of a complex service a rigour not always associated with the public sector.

In the end, however, the single factor that will impinge most forcefully on colleges, their managers, staff and students is the total funds available to support their activities. In practice, this continues to mean the amount of funds made available by the government of the day. If that is too little, there is no way any funding system can improve matters. As a former chairman of the University Grants Committee was wont to remark: 'if the cake is too small to start with, there is no satisfactory way of dividing it up'. Towards the end of the second millennium, it is encouraging that the present government appears seriously intent on baking a bigger cake.

References

AC and OFSTED (1993) *Unfinished Business: Full-time Educational Courses for 16–19 Year Olds*, London: HMSO.

Coopers & Lybrand (1995) *The Costs of Further Education*, Coventry: FEFC.

DES and ED (1991) *Education and Training for the 21st Century*, Cmnd 1536, London: HMSO.

Education and Employment Committee (1998) Sixth Report, *Further Education*, vol. 1, *Report and Proceedings*, 264-I, London: The Stationery Office.

FEFC (1992a) *Funding Learning*, Coventry: FEFC.

FEFC (1992b) 'Letter of guidance to FEFC from the Secretary of State, July 1992', in *The Establishment of the FEFC*, Circular 92/08, Coventry: FEFC.

FEFC (1993a) *Recurrent Funding Methodology 1994–95*, Circular 93/14, Coventry: FEFC.

FEFC (1993b) *Recurrent Funding Methodology 1994–95: Allocation Mechanism*, Circular 93/16, Coventry: FEFC.

FEFC (1993c) *Recurrent Funding Methodology 1994–95: Funding Categories*, Circular 93/20, Coventry: FEFC.

FEFC (1993d) *Recurrent Funding Methodology 1994–95: Tariff Values for 1994–95*, Circular 93/32, Coventry: FEFC.

FEFC (1993e) *How to Apply for Recurrent Funding 1994–95*, Coventry: FEFC.

FEFC (1994a) Chief Inspector's Annual Report, *Quality and Standards in Further Education in England 1993–94*, Coventry: FEFC.

FEFC (1994b) *Funding Allocations 1994–95*, Coventry: FEFC.

FEFC (1994c) *How to Apply for Recurrent Funding 1995–96*, Coventry: FEFC.

FEFC (1994d) *Individualized Student Record Data Collection*, Circular 94/10, Coventry: FEFC.

FEFC (1997) *Fundamental Review of the Funding Methodology*, Circular 97/31, Coventry: FEFC.

Kennedy, H. (1997) *Learning Works: Widening Participation in Further Education*, Coventry: FEFC.

NAO (1997a) *The Further Education Funding Council for England*, London: HMSO.

NAO (1997b) *The Management of Growth in the English Further Education Sector*, London: HMSO.

5   The Qualifications Framework

Alan Smithers

Unlike the universities the colleges have never had a qualification of their own. As we have seen in Chapter 2, they began by offering the vocational qualifications of such bodies as the Royal Society of Arts and the City and Guilds of the City of London, and the ordinary and higher national certificates and diplomas which became BTEC awards. But gradually, through initially offering a second chance at GCE O-levels and, on the back of this, A-levels, they have become more and more involved with academic qualifications. They also took the overspill from the universities in the aftermath of the Second World War and got a taste for teaching degrees which has fuelled the process that Pratt and Burgess (1974) have dubbed 'academic drift'. The whole range of qualifications, including many certificates and diplomas particular to certain colleges and employers, are represented within further education. As Melville and Macleod report in Chapter 3, the FEFC has so far counted no less than 17,000 different awards.

The colleges therefore have a considerable interest in qualifications structures and they are not entirely satisfied with what exists. Currently an attempt is being made, led by the City College, Birmingham, to establish a College Diploma (Mager, 1999), which it is hoped will in time become what the degree is to universities. The reasons for the colleges' discontent are various. At heart, there is the feeling that qualifications depending on examinations at the end of one-year or two-year courses are not entirely appropriate to the needs of college students, particularly adult part-time learners. There is also the belief that the present three strands of study – academic, applied and occupational – form a distinct hierarchy to the disadvantage of the vocational.

The attractions of a modular system to the sector are understandable. The opportunity of clocking up credits towards some overarching qualification would not only be more flexible and more of an incentive to the students, but there is the hope that if A-levels and vocational qualifications were all dissolved into modules the status differences would go away. There is also the colleges' growing experience of operating a unitized funding mechanism. Given the Labour government's commitment to lifelong learning there were reasons for believing that policy formulated in the light of the Dearing (1996) review of qualifications for sixteen- to nineteen-year-olds would deliver a unitized qualifications structure. But in the event, although there have been some concessions, for the time being at least they have been dashed. In order to understand why this has been the outcome and why a unitized framework might not be the panacea it is taken to be, we need to look more closely at the nature of the qualifications which colleges offer.

A-levels

With about half the A-level candidates now in the colleges (Smithers and Robinson, 1993), it is easy to lose sight of the fact that the colleges have taken over a qualification designed in another place and for a specific purpose. At their inception in 1951, A-levels were the last of three hurdles – the others being the 11-plus and O-level – intended to pick out a small proportion of the age group (initially less than one in twenty) who could be educated in the universities to a high standard in a short time with few drop-outs. Even with the enormous expansion of the universities which saw the capacity being doubled following the Robbins Report (1963) and more than doubled again since (Smithers and Robinson, 1996), A-levels have retained that function adapting, along the way, but intrinsically unchanged.

Performing, as they have, this selective function has led to A-levels being regarded with a certain ambivalence, fondly remembered by those who they sped on their way (the few) but treated with suspicion by those whom they cast aside (the many). Some of the charges against A-levels have been unfair. It is sometimes said that they bear little relation to degree success, but that is to forget that we are only dealing with, even now, relatively thin slices off the top of the ability range (Smithers and Robinson, 1989). It is just the same in tennis or golf, for example, where there is a fair amount of interchangeability among the top performers, but it would simply be no contest with the average club player. It is also said that A-levels are a barrier to progress, which of course they are, because they were designed to be selective. But this is merely, as it were, to shoot the messenger since they are performing a necessary function.

The selectivity of A-levels also explains some of the confusion surrounding the supposed status differences between the academic and vocational. There is nothing intrinsically superior about studying a subject for its own sake compared with studying a field defined by a particular area of employment. Medicine and law, vocational studies, are among the most prestigious of degrees. What gives status to a qualification is what you can do with it. Hence the high standing of classics at a time when it was the gateway to the Civil Service. The reasons for the different statuses attached to A-levels and voca-tional qualifications are therefore less to do with their subject matter or the way they are taught, than where they lead. Successful A-levels, by and large, take people on to university and the attractive range of jobs which this can open up; vocational qualifications taken at an early age usually lead off from a lower branch of the qualifications tree towards areas of employment with more limited horizons.

A common qualification at eighteen would need to be capable of taking people in different directions according to their abilities, interests and aspirations, and it is highly probable that, as with the French 'bac' or the German *abitur*, definite pecking orders would soon emerge. A-levels can be criticized as being too specialized because with a norm of just three subjects they represent a considerable narrowing down from the ten subjects of the national curriculum. But they do have the considerable advantage of leaving the choice to individuals in what is, after all, the period beyond compulsory schooling. People can specialize or combine a variety of subjects according to what it is they want to do. Students have been increasingly mixing science and arts/social science A-levels (Smithers and Robinson, 1988) and the proportion has now reached almost 40 per cent. A-levels do therefore have a flexibility, which will be increased by the new half-A-level which gives the opportunity of taking five subjects (DfEE, 1999a, 1999b). They would thus seem to meet the needs of further education students aiming for university. An overarching or grouped award, like various 'bacs' which have been proposed (Finegold et al., 1990; David and Jenkins, 1996; Raffe et al., 1998) would be more restrictive since it would impose areas of study and not leave the choice to individuals.

Vocational Qualifications

Vocational qualifications have not been valued as much in Britain as perhaps they should, and certainly they are not held in the same esteem as by our continental neighbours. We have already discussed some of the reasons for this, but a view which was widely held at one time was that they were not sufficiently visible. In the early 1980s the Reverend George Tolley (1986), principal of what was then Sheffield Polytechnic, led a campaign to set up a national framework to rival the well-established academic ladder of O-levels, A-levels and degrees. The government responded by setting up the De Ville Committee (1986) and accepted its recommendation for a National Council for Vocational Qualifications to oversee a national system.

The NCVQ was charged (DES and ED, 1986) with securing the necessary changes 'to develop the NVQ framework and to ensure standards of competence are set'. It developed a matrix of five levels across eleven categories of work. The five levels of qualification were set at the equivalent of not doing very well at GCSE (Level 1) to above degree standard (Level 5). The areas of work ranged from 'tending animals, plants and land' to 'developing and extending knowledge and skill'. Thus it is possible to have NVQs distinguished by level or area: for example, there are Levels 1 to 4 in administration; and there are Level 2 awards in administration and engineering production. Altogether there are some 900 different qualifications, offered by awarding bodies ranging from the Association of Accounting Technicians to the Waste Management Industry Training and Advisory Board. NVQs were intended to be specifically workplace qualifications and there has always been some doubt about whether colleges could or should offer them through simulated settings (CBI, 1994), but in fact further education has become the main provider.

In addition, in 1991 the NCVQ was asked to oversee the development of General National Vocational Qualifications (Smithers, 1993). Unlike NVQs,

GNVQs were not tied to specific jobs, but were intended to consist of learning applied to practical activities. They were envisaged as a way of incorporating the main awards of bodies like Royal Society of Arts, City and Guilds and the Business and Technology Education Council into the national framework. Nevertheless NCVQ insisted that they should be on the same groundplan as NVQs. Over a period of seven years they have been introduced in fifteen areas at the first three levels of the framework called, in this instance, 'foundation', 'intermediate' and 'advanced' (said to be equivalent to two GCE A-levels). Currently, there are forty GNVQs altogether, twelve at foundation level and, with the addition of media and of retail and distribution, fourteen each at the intermediate and advanced levels (management, the fifteenth, has been dropped).

Since they were introduced, over two million NVQ certificates have been awarded (in fact 2,223,523 by 30 September 1998, according to QCA, 1999a). There has also been an upbeat presentation of GNVQ results within the year to 31 July 1998, with the Joint Council of National Vocational Awarding Bodies (1998) reporting that more students than ever before – 92,036 – had gained an award at one of the three levels. There are doubts, however, whether the new national framework has been as successful as might have been hoped (Smithers 1993, 1998; Robinson, 1996). Tellingly, Melville and Mcleod's Figure 3.5 (see p. 32) shows that the majority of FEFC-funded qualifications still lie outside it. To have achieved Tolley's aims, they should by now be within it.

There are many reasons why they are not, but perhaps the most important factor is that the NCVQ adopted a restrictive view of what could count as an NVQ. It interpreted its brief literally and turned 'standards of competence' into a search for competencies that could define qualifications. It required that qualifications, in order to be recognized, had to conform to a particular analytic model. Each award was to consist of a number of units subdivided into elements (see Figures 13.1 and 13.2, p. 155 for examples), which were further subdivided into performance criteria. The candidate has to collect evidence, usually in the form of a portfolio, that the performance criteria have been met over certain ranges. This became something of a Procrustean bed on which many employers refused to lie – partly because they were comfortable with their own ways of doing things and partly because, better than most, they could see the flaws.

Although superficially plausible, setting out the requirements in this way has meant that the content of the qualifications has not been clearly specified nor has there been any assessment of overall performance. Without programmes of study this has meant that there could be no guarantee that the students have been taken beyond what they know and can do already. Leaving the assessment mainly with the individual supervisors has meant a complicated and expensive system of checks which still have not been enough to ensure reliability. The government of the time heard some of the early criticisms and responded to the Capey (1995) review of GNVQs and the Beaumont (1996) review of NVQs by instituting a number of changes to curb the worst excesses. It also took the opportunity of the quinquennial review of NCVQ's performance to merge it into the School Curriculum and Assessment Authority (SCAA) as the Qualifications and Curriculum Authority (QCA). The QCA (1999b, 1999c) is currently consulting on further improvements to NVQs.

Attempts have also been made to repair the lack of training specifications in NVQs through the introduction of Modern Apprenticeships and National Traineeships. Modern Apprenticeships were piloted in 1994 to provide a work-based route to the skills and qualifications needed at craft, supervisory and technician level in industry and business. They led to an NVQ at Level 3 or above, but with the training specified in frameworks developed in partnership with employers and Training and Enterprise Councils by the National Training Organization (NTO) for the relevant sector (NTOs established to date range from the Association for Ceramic Training and Development to the Voluntary Sector; see DfEE, 1998).

Modern apprenticeships were originally aimed primarily at sixteen- and seventeen-year-olds, but were extended in 1995 to eighteen- and nineteen-year-olds through an accelerated scheme for those with higher attainment on entry. The concept was also extended in September 1997 to National Traineeships with training programmes leading to NVQs at Level 2. The training for Modern Apprenticeships, which generally lasts for 2–3 years, is provided mainly in the workplace, but there can also be off-the-job training provided by the further education colleges. Employers tend, however, to be reluctant to pay for this (Hillage et al., 1998; Economic Research Services, 1998). The current target is to have 60,000 new apprenticeships per year (DfEE, 1999c) though in the past there have been difficulties in filling all the places.

The NVQ system as it has emerged (QCA, 1999a) is in some respects in embryonic form the unitized system the FEFC would like to see for all qualifications (except perhaps degrees). The QCA seeks to ensure that the NVQs meet particular criteria and are broadly comparable across the different sectors. It accredits proposals from awarding bodies, and quality assures and audits their activity. The awarding bodies both develop NVQs and accredit centres that wish to assess them. In developing the qualifications the awarding bodies must work to standards laid down by the NTOs. Colleges and other providers work within this framework to help candidates achieve these qualifications. Financial support to the providers may come from the FEFC, the TECs or the employers themselves.

Qualifications Structure

The findings of the Capey (1995) and Beaumont (1996) reviews were fed into the Dearing (1996) review of qualifications for sixteen- to nineteen-year-olds. Dearing accepted that there were three kinds of study appropriate to that age range:

1 *Academic*, where 'the primary purpose is to develop knowledge, understanding and skills associated with a subject or discipline'.

2 *Applied education*, 'where the primary purpose is to develop and apply knowledge, understanding and skills relevant of broad areas of employment'.

3 *Vocational training*, 'where the primary purpose is develop and recognize mastery of a trade or profession at the relevant level'.

He offered the Conservative government of the time essentially three options:

1 To develop those three kinds of education and training through the existing qualifications of A-levels, GNVQs and NVQs.

2 To underline the equivalence of those qualifications by incorporating them into an overarching certificate which could be awarded on the basis of any A-levels, GNVQs or NVQs, or combination of them, meeting the minimum requirement.

3 To specify a pattern of study through an advanced diploma which required a combination of a science and maths (later separated), an arts subject, a modern foreign language and a social science, plus key skills.

The Conservative government was inclined towards the first, but when a Labour government was elected in May 1997, it put the proposals out to further consultation (or rather the first two, since the advanced diploma – the one imposing combinations – was quietly dropped; see DfEE, 1997). The responses were analysed by QCA which made its recommendations to government in March 1998. Most of these were accepted, but there was a delay in announcing policy because, one suspects, of a difference of view within the government itself. As it has emerged, A-levels and GNVQs are to be further developed, but in ways which will make it easier for them to come together. They are to be repackaged in the same-sized modules with qualifications based on groups of three, six and twelve units. The new half A-level will comprise three modules; a six-unit GNVQ is to be developed. There are also to be further attempts to give the elusive key skills some substance in a new qualification. Although limits on coursework in A-levels have been raised to 30 per cent, there will continue to be a strong element of terminal (called 'synoptic') assessment. Grading is to be introduced into the new GNVQs. In neither case will the qualifications be dissolved into their constituent units. A-levels are also to be strengthened by the introduction of 'new world-class tests' for high achieving sixteen- to nineteen-year-olds which will be based on the same content as A-levels, but ask more demanding questions (DfEE, 1999b).

The subtlety of the new policy is that it allows the qualifications to grow together if that is what is wanted, or they can remain apart. It is entirely up to students, schools and colleges to show what they want by what they do (rather than by what they say which, as Dearing acknowledged, is sometimes different). The opportunity for the academic and vocational qualifications to come together has been enhanced by the mergers between the academic and vocational awarding bodies which the Conservative government encouraged.

BTEC, for example, merged with the University of London Examinations and Assessment Council (ULEAC) to become EdExcel.

Unitized Framework

Many within further education, including the FEFC itself, have been disappointed by the apparent caution of the qualifications policy of the present government. With the awarding bodies merged and the QCA as the one qualifications authority, it had been anticipated that a unitized framework leading to a common qualification would be embraced. Such a policy would have had the support of the House of Commons Education and Employment Committee (1998a, 1998b). In its further education inquiry it commented: 'We welcome the government's intention to seek further advice from the QCA on the feasibility of a unit-based system. This, we believe, is central to providing for the needs of students in further education.' By implication, it would like to see it apply to the whole 16–19 qualifications structure since it also said it did not want to see young people and adults treated differently.

But there are those of us who are pleased that the government is 'under no illusions about the potential difficulties, both conceptual and practical, to which [a unit-based credit system leading to a common award] could give rise' (Blackstone, 1998). Among the chief difficulties are those of manageability and affordability. A fully unitized system, in effect, replaces existing qualifications by (in the case of an A-level) six smaller ones. If a new qualification built up from these units is to have the same rigour as existing qualifications, all the paraphernalia to ensure consistency, authenticity and fairness will have to be transferred down to the unit level, multiplying the work if not actually by six then by something approaching it. It is sometimes argued that you would need fewer modules than qualifications since they can be shared (Stanton, 1997), but that is to assume a degree of interchangeability which is difficult to realize in practice. Simply labelling a unit 'maths' and giving a credit value at a particular level does not mean that it will be the right kind of maths for the training in question – plumbers learn maths best in the context of plumbing, electrical installers in the context of electrical (Smithers, 1993).

Another major concern is not a necessary feature of a modularized system, but is often associated with it. That is, the attempt to state the requirements in the form of outcomes. Experience has shown that outcome-statements alone are not sufficient to specify a qualification: there must, as in the National Curriculum, also be some statement of the ground to be covered and the level of performance to be expected. In practice, this will be exemplified in the tests to be administered. The great weakness of NVQs, as they were first formulated and even now, is that they specified neither content nor external assessment. They could therefore be something or nothing, or – to put it another way – they were fundamentally unreliable. With FEFC funding tied to qualifications, this opened the way to some of the abuses which other contributors to this volume have identified (see, for example, Chapters 8, 13 and 16).

The third doubt is whether credits and values can be assigned meaningfully. In accepting the NCVQ framework of levels we sometimes forget that A-levels, GNVQs and NVQs have their origin in qualifications designed to take young people in quite different directions – to degrees, to supervisory and technician posts, and to the shopfloor. The Ordinary National Certificate (ONC) – a fore-runner of the advanced GNVQ – achieved a kind of parity with A-levels when the Colleges of Advanced Technology became universities, carrying with them their recognition of ONCs as satisfying the admission requirements. But, as we can see from the contrasting GCSE performance of those going on to A-levels and other qualifications (see Figure 3.4, p. 31), this does not justify the wholesale equating of the awards. If those with at least five good GCSEs predominantly take one type of award (A-level) and those who do not, another (GNVQ or NVQ), it makes little sense to try to treat these awards as equivalent. Universities know this and will, where they have a choice, admit on good A-levels. (Where they do not, they tend to ply the rhetoric of access.) In spite of the evident illogicality, the admissions service (UCAS) has been struggling for years to come up with a convincing tariff system applying the same weighting to different awards. Its latest offering (Cassidy, 1999) is unlikely be any more successful than its previous ones (less, in fact, because there are now to be points for literacy, numeracy and computer skills). The obvious thing to do, of course, is to recognize that the quali-fications are distinctive and make sure they work in their own terms.

Experience of Other Countries

Other countries, most notably New Zealand, have attempted to bring in a full-blooded unitized credit-accumulation qualifications framework. In New Zealand it ran into difficulties leading to the issue of two Green Papers (New Zealand Ministry of Education, 1997a, 1997b). In a review of the New Zealand Qualifications Framework, Smithers (1997) pointed out that as a structure it rested on many untested assumptions including those that:

- one size fits all kinds of learning;
- it is possible to state clear and unambiguous standards;
- it is possible to assign level and credit values meaningfully;
- the students' own teachers could be relied upon to make dispassionate judgements in high-stakes assessment;
- aggregating a number of pass/fail judgements will enable a qualification to differentiate adequately.

The review argued that there was no short-cut solution which would enable New Zealand to put in place qualifications that would perform all the functions expected of them, and that it would be better to concentrate on getting in place good academic, applied and occupational learning – in fact, Dearing's three categories – rather than trying to develop an all-encompassing framework.

To some extent this advice was heard. In response to the consultation the New Zealand government (New Zealand Ministry of Education, 1998) decided that it would after all keep its equivalent of GCSE and A-level (school certificate and university bursaries). It also decided it would continue to develop an overarching certificate (the National Certificate in Educational Achievement) towards which the school certificate and bursaries could count, but to which other units could be added. It was proposed also to have different kinds of modules for conventional and non-conventional school subjects (as they were referred to), and there would be exams as well as internal assessment for all components. The FEFC (Mager and Tait, 1998; FEFC, 1998a) have contended that many of the criticisms of the New Zealand framework do not apply to this country – for example, the over-reliance on outcome statements. Nevertheless, there would be, by definition, similar fragmentation leading to the need to keep track of and validate numerous components. A framework will also involve the difficult task of trying to establish numerical equivalences between kinds of learning which are intrinsically different and attract students of different abilities.

Within the United Kingdom, Wales is proposing to emulate New Zealand in establishing 'a single seamless path' to bring together, in this case, GCSEs, A-levels, AS-levels, GNVQs, NVQs and Higher Qualifications (Welsh Office, 1998). This will be a flexible credit-related qualifications framework post-16. Credit for learning achievements will be given whether they be at college, school, university, adult education classes, or through workplace training or voluntary work. Like New Zealand, Wales is putting its faith in the view that an all-embracing qualifications framework will be easier to put in place in a small country but, as New Zealand has found, the success of the venture depends less on geography than on how well the structure embodies the dual functions of a qualification system – to recognize achievement and to differentiate. A unitized system is likely to be strong on chalking up credit, but not good at making distinctions. Events in Wales, however, are likely to prove to be a very useful test-bed for England, which makes the government's cautious approach all the more sensible.

Qualifications and Funding

The FEFC (1998b) is very keen to see the development of a unit-based credit framework. Its Schedule 2 Qualifications Group with college, TEC National Council, DfEE and QCA representation has advised it that it 'is a key priority for the further education sector'. The somewhat tortuous title of the task group hints at both the attractions and risks of such a system. Schedule 2 refers to the particular section of the Further and Higher Education Act 1992 that links qualifications to funding. With the transfer of the colleges from the LEAs to the Funding Council only courses leading to recognized qualifications were eligible for funding (the rest were left with the LEAs but on severely reduced funding). In the preceding chapter, Roger McClure interestingly describes how the FEFC tackled its task through the development of a unitized funding framework. Since Schedule 2 ties funding to qualifications, it might seem logical therefore for this to be unitized also.

It is certainly logical for funding and qualifications to be considered together. They are two of the main forces shaping the further education sector and, as we have seen, they are linked by law. But their development, impacting on the colleges at a crucial phase in their history, has proceeded in isolation from each other. Just as the NCVQ was introducing an individualized qualification system where assessment depended on dispassionate judgements, and reliability was always going to be a problem (Jessup, 1991), so the TECs and (to a lesser extent) the FEFC were moving to a system of output-related funding. The new vocational qualifications were simply not robust enough to withstand the pressure of, in essence, only paying for training if those doing the training passed the candidates. The Select Committee (Education and Employment Committee, 1998a) hinted at the problem: 'in FE, much more than in other parts of the education system, the funding received by institutions is closely related to the qualifications sought and achieved by individual students', but was unwilling to go further because it had not taken evidence on this point. Beaumont (1996), however, in his review of NVQs was more forthright: 'funding by outputs brings a potential for conflicts of interest' and he recommended 'funding programmes and policy should be harmonized with qualifications systems'.

Output-related funding is not the only issue. The new qualifications contained no indication of the training time that might be involved. However, in the FEFC's unitized funding framework the lion's share of the units go to on-programme costs for which time is taken as a proxy. Funding by time for qualifications making no mention of time, left the colleges free to be inventive. Laxity in both training and qualification assessment requirements coupled with unitized funding invited the kinds of fraud that some private providers have perpetrated – for example, qualifying people who did not know they were on courses (Smithers, 1998). It also opened the door for the over-charging by colleges, like Halton and Bilston, which has led to them having to repay very large sums to the FEFC (see Chapter 8). The unitized funding framework of the FEFC has thus contributed to the problems.

McClure, in Chapter 4, has spoken enthusiastically of the advantages of the unitized funding framework and it is true that it has the potential for fairness and flexibility. But a major weakness is the very small value of the unit – about £17 – which means that the colleges have to accumulate a very large number to arrive at their income of perhaps several million pounds. Earning units depends on a very detailed process of record-keeping of the qualifications that are being worked towards and obtained. Qualifications are thus meant to hold all of the activity together rather like the magnetic cage in nuclear fusion. But the new vocational qualifications have not been equal to the task. As yet, they are only modularized, not unitized (that is the units are not free-standing). Imagine what would happen if they went the whole hog, dragging A-levels with them. The complexities of the unit funding arrangements would be multiplied by the complexities of the units of the qualifications framework: a problem squared rather than halved!

Conclusion

The argument for a unitized qualification framework for the colleges must therefore rest on something other than numerical tidiness. As Smithers (1997) has argued, a key issue for any qualifications system is how to cater for the differentiation that employers and those at the next stage of education often need, while at the same time providing something worthwhile for everyone to aim at. That is, how to marry up qualifications *for* something with qualifications *in* something; how to bring together passports and badges. Although most qualifications embody elements of both, the emphasis can be very different. A-levels have, for example, been primarily about selection for university and have their roots in university entrance examinations; NVQs have been primarily about recognizing competence. Inevitably, they would not fit together easily in the one qualification.

Moreover, there is a difference with where the candidates have got to in their lives. Qualifications at the end of schooling are a passport to the next phase of education or employment. There they have an important differentiating function resembling the branches of a tree. Qualifications worked for and gained later in life are more badges of achievement and, to continue the tree metaphor, are the twigs and branches. It is conceivable therefore that we could have different qualification structures for sixteen- to nineteen-year-olds and for lifelong learning, with in the one case a development of A-levels and GNVQs and, in the other, a unit-based credit-accumulation framework. Such a distinction is implicit in the wish of some colleges to develop a distinctive College Diploma.

The dual approach has its attractions but, as the Select Committee (Education and Employment Committee, 1998a) observed, it runs the risk of the two types of qualification being valued differently and 'we would not wish to see different perceptions of the worth of qualifications achieved by young people compared with those achieved by adult learners'. To some extent, I fear, that is inevitable – for example, Open University degrees, while of the same standard, tend to be valued less those of other universities – because the degrees of young people have an important differentiating function for employers which they may not have later in life (Smithers, Hill and Silvester, 1990). But the point is taken and we need to guard against the unnecessary proliferation of qualifications.

No doubt the qualifications debate is set to run and run. In the next chapter, Richard Dimbleby presents further arguments for a unitized framework from a curriculum and learning perspective. My own view is expressed in *The New Zealand Qualifications Framework* (1997): there is no 'philosopher's stone' that will resolve all qualifications issues. The difficult question that always has to be faced is: what is the prime purpose of the qualification? It is an easy assumption, and perhaps a weakness of present government policy, that qualifications are seen as good in themselves. Most of life's learning does not have to be captured in qualifications. People seem less keen to stay on at school or buy into lifelong learning than politicians sometimes anticipate, perhaps because they ask the pragmatic question: what is this going to add to our lives? The essence of a good qualification is that it adds something to a person's life: perhaps opening the door to a desired career; perhaps celebrating some achievement. It may not be possible to encompass the whole range of qualification purposes within the one structure and we should be wary of seeking an over-tidy solution. Government policy as it has emerged in response to *Qualifying for Success* (DfEE, 1997) may be the best compromise that is possible between the need for qualifications that differentiate and, at the same time, have the flexibility to accommodate the needs of adult learners.

References

Beaumont, G. (1996) Report to the DfEE, *Review of 100 NVQs and SVQs* (no publisher given).

Blackstone, T. (1998) *Oral Evidence*, 11 March, in Education and Employment Committee, 1998b.

Capey, J. (1995) *GNVQ Assessment Review*, London: NCVQ.

Cassidy, S. (1999) 'UCAS updates points', *Times Educational Supplement*, 16 April.

CBI (1994) *Quality Assessed: Review of NVQs and SVQs*, London; CBI.

David, J. and Jenkins, C. (1996) *The Welsh Baccalaureate Cymru*, Cardiff: Institute of Welsh Affairs.

Dearing, R. (1996) *Review of Qualifications for 16–19 Year Olds*, London: School Curriculum and Assessment Authority.

DES and ED (1986) *Working Together: Education and Training*, Cmnd 9823, London: HMSO.

De Ville, H.G. (1986) *Review of Vocational Qualifications in England and Wales: A Report by the Working Group*, London: HMSO.

DfEE (1997) *Qualifying for Success: A Consultation Paper on the Future of Post-16 Qualifications*, London: DfEE.

DfEE (1998) *National Training Organisations, Prospectus 1999–2000: Strategic Guidance*, London: DfEE.

DfEE (1999a) 'A-level curriculum will guarantee standards', *DfEE News*, 125/99, 19 March.

DfEE (1999b) 'A-level curriculum will be rigorous and demanding: Blackstone', *DfEE News*, 132/99, 25 March.

DfEE (1999c) Education and Training 16–25, http://www.dfee.gov.uk/etb/chapter3.htm

Economic Research Services (1998) *Evaluation of Modern Apprenticeships: 1998 Survey of Employers*, London: DfEE.

Education and Employment Committee (1998a) Sixth Report, *Further Education*, vol. 1, *Report and Proceedings*, 264-I, London: The Stationery Office.

Education and Employment Committee (1998b) Sixth Report, *Further Education*, vol. 2, *Minutes of Evidence and Appendices*, 264-II, London: The Stationery Office.

FEFC (1998a) *Unitization: New Zealand*, Briefing note for Education and Employment Committee, not printed but referred to Education and Employment Committee, 1998a, p. lvi.

FEFC (1998b) *Further Memorandum*, Appendix 54, in Education and Employment Committee, 1998a.

Finegold, D., Keep, E., Miliband, D., Raffe, D., Spours, K. and Young, M. (1990) *A British Baccalaureate: Overcoming Divisions Between Education and Training*, London: Institute for Public Policy Research.

Hillage, J., Atkinson, J., Kersley, B. and Bates, P. (1998) *Employers' Training of Young People*, London: DfEE.

Jessup, G. (1991) *Outcomes: NVQs and the Emerging Model of Education and Training*, Lewes: Falmer Press.

Joint Council of National Vocational Awarding Bodies (1998) *GNVQ Completion Rates Up*, Press Release, 5 November.

Mager, C. (1999) *A Signature Qualification – the College Diploma*, Working Document, Further Education Development Agency.

Mager, C. and Tait, T. (1998) 'Credit where it's due', *Guardian Education*, 3 February.

New Zealand Ministry of Education (1997a) *A Future Qualifications Policy for New Zealand: A Plan for the National Qualifications Framework*, Green Paper, Wellington, NZ: Ministry of Education.

New Zealand Ministry of Education (1997b) *A Future Tertiary Education Policy for New Zealand*, Green Paper, Wellington, NZ: Ministry of Education.

New Zealand Ministry of Education (1998) *Secondary School Qualifications Improved and Updated for 21st Century*, Media Release, 5 November.

Pratt, J. and Burgess, T. (1974) *Polytechnics: A Report*, London: Pitman.

QCA (1999a) *DATA News*, Issue 10, London: QCA.

QCA (1999b) *Consultation on Flexibility within the National Qualifications Framework*, London: QCA.

QCA (1999c) *Improving the Value of NVQs and other Vocational Qualifications: Consultation Documents*, London: QCA.

Raffe, D., Spours, K., Young, M. and Howieson, C. (1998) 'The unification of post-compulsory education: Towards a conceptual framework', *British Journal of Educational Studies*, 46, 169–87.

Robbins Report (1963) *Higher Education: Report of the Committee Appointed by the Prime Minister under the Chairmanship of Lord Robbins 1961–63*, Cmnd 2154, London: HMSO.

Robinson, P. (1996) *Rhetoric and Reality: Britain's New Vocational Qualifications*, London: Centre for Economic Performance.

Smithers, A. (1993) *All Our Futures: Britain's Education Revolution*, London: Channel 4 Television.

Smithers, A. (1997) *The New Zealand Qualifications Framework*, Wellington, NZ: Education Forum.

Smithers, A. (1998) 'Improving vocational education: NVQs and GNVQs', in Shorrocks-Taylor, D. (ed.) *Directions in Educational Psychology*, London: Whurr.

Smithers, A. and Robinson, P. (1988) *The Growth of Mixed A-Levels*, Manchester: Carmichael Press.

Smithers, A. and Robinson, P. (1989) *Increasing Participation in Higher Education*, London: BP.

Smithers, A. and Robinson, P. (1993) *Further Education in the Market Place*, London: CIHE.

Smithers, A. and Robinson, P. (1996) *Trends in Higher Education*, London: CIHE.

Smithers, A., Hill, S. and Silvester, G. (1990) *Graduates in the Police Service*, Manchester: CEER.

Stanton, G. (1997) 'Patterns in development', in Tomlinson, S. (ed.) *Education 14–19 Critical Perspectives*, London: The Athlone Press.

Tolley, G. (1986) 'Putting labels on people: The qualifications business', *Royal Society of Arts Journal*, no. 5363 (October).

Welsh Office (1998) *Learning is for Everyone*, Green Paper, Cmnd 3924, Cardiff: Welsh Office.

6   Curriculum and Learning

Richard Dimbleby and Clive Cooke

Alongside the management changes occasioned by incorporation, and sometimes resulting from them, there have been changes in curriculum thinking and
learning paradigms. The previous experiences of students coming into colleges,
their current expectations and future ambitions are also changing. Similarly,
the expectations of employers, parents, funding agencies and contractors are
changing. 'Change' therefore seems to be the operative word, but there are also
indications that, when it comes to the point, change is in fact resisted.

A simple generalization of the current and continuing trends would be that
there is a concerted attempt to move towards a model of learning emphasizing
outputs. We would characterize this as a shift from a teacher-centred style to a
learner-centred style. The current language of further education which is in
terms of, among other things, individual learning programmes, primary
learning goals and personal training plans reflects this thinking.

The main purpose of all education and training is to enable students to
learn. 'The need to remind ourselves of something as obvious as this' says
something, as Bloomer and Hodgkinson (1997) suggest, about 'the policy
climate in which FE has had to work in England and Wales throughout the
1990s'. It becomes a moot point therefore whether the recent changes in qualifications and curriculum design have had the desired effects on student
learning. We know that the reality of education for learners is their experience
of the teaching/learning interface. Has this changed at an equivalent pace to
post-16 curriculum rhetoric, or has the rhetoric merely ruffled the margins of
further education without significantly impacting on learning – the very core of
our business?

National Context

In its Green Paper, *The Learning Age: A Renaissance for a New Britain* (DfEE,
1998), the new Labour government is seeking to commit us all to lifelong
learning. The general wish seems to embody at least five aspirations:

*   provision of opportunities for everyone to develop personally through
     learning;

- social inclusion of the currently disaffected or excluded;
- promotion of the national skills agenda for ensuring economic development and competitiveness;
- development of the use of information and communication technology;
- raising standards.

The constant challenge for further education is to develop curricula and modes of learning which attract individuals and enable them to learn and to continue learning. In support of the colleges, the FEFC has established three committees, Learning and Technology, Widening Participation, and Learning Difficulties and/or Disabilities, each of which has recently produced influential reports. The Higginson (1996) report made recommendations on the use of educational technology in further education, including measures to improve the effectiveness of students' learning. The Kennedy (1997) report got widening participation firmly on the political agenda with implications that are fully discussed in Chapter 11 and recur throughout this volume.

But perhaps the most salient report for the curriculum and learning is the Tomlinson report, *Inclusive Learning* (1996). Although concerned principally with learning difficulties and disabilities, its core argument applies to all students:

> Central to all our thinking and recommendations is the approach towards learning, which we term 'inclusive learning', and which we want to see adopted everywhere. We argue for it because it will improve the education of those with learning difficulties, but believe it is also true that such an approach would benefit all and, indeed, represents the best approach to learning and teaching yet articulated. When we tested our approach in a number of colleges, that is what we were told.
>
> Put simply, we want to avoid a viewpoint which locates the difficulty or deficit with the student and focus instead on the capacity of the educational institution to understand and respond to the individual learner's requirement. This means we must move away from labelling the student and towards creating an appropriate education environment; concentrate on understanding better how people learn so that they can better be helped to learn; and see people with disabilities and/or learning difficulties first and foremost as learners.

This emphasis on the individual learner has been taken up in the public statements of government policy. Michael Bichard (1998), the Permanent Secretary at the DfEE, was recently authorized to include in an address to the Society of Education Officers the following:

> This Government's programme of education reform will have at its core the needs of the individual learner rather than the convenience of institutions, of authorities, of agencies, or of departments of state. It will reflect a

conviction that excellence can exist without elitism, which is a must if the Government is to deliver what it wants most of all: a modern, inclusive, competitive society.

It also appears in the mission statements of the colleges. That of our own, Bournemouth and Poole College, for example reads:

> To enable individuals and organizations to realize their potential through high quality and innovative lifelong learning accessible to the whole community.

While, however, colleges have some freedom in local delivery designed to meet local needs, they have to operate within the context of national policies. Policies which impact most are those on funding and qualifications. The formation of the FEFC in 1992 led to the introduction of funding arrangements whose implications for the organization of learning have already been explored in Chapter 4. The Conservative government's decision in 1996 to bring together the Departments for Education and of Employment as the DfEE paved the way for more coherent thinking and planning across the erstwhile divide of education and training. This was reinforced in 1997 by the merging of the School Curriculum and Assessment Authority and the National Council for Vocational Qualifications to become the Qualifications and Curriculum Authority. Following the Dearing (1996) report, the qualification structure post-16 has developed in the ways discussed in Chapter 5.

Curriculum and Qualifications

It is our contention that the emerging framework does not yet provide for accessible lifelong learning. Within the new structure qualifications are still grouped into the three categories of 'general' (GCSE and A-level), 'vocationally related' (GNVQ and National Diplomas) and 'occupational' (NVQ). This merely reframes the threefold split of the 1956 White Paper on Technical Education: 'technologists, technicians and craftsmen' (Ministry of Education, 1956). Tripartite separation, in the view of many of us in further education (Stanton and Richardson, 1998), tends to shore up the academic/vocational divide and constrains freedom of choice for students. Qualifications are *de facto* the way of defining the curriculum.

Unfortunately, our national thinking with regard to curriculum and qualifications is still tied to nineteenth-century views of intelligence and ability. We thus perpetuate unhelpful notions of status and hierarchy, and a limited view of the potential of individuals. The work of Gardner (1993) and others, such as Goleman (1996), suggests we need to get away from a one-dimensional view to accept that there are different kinds of intelligence. These ideas have manifested themselves in qualification structures as 'key skills'. But given our current framework of thinking about curriculum and qualifications, key skills continue to present a problem in both conception and execution. The sad history of liberal studies, general and communication studies, and communication skills reflects our inability to break free of the rigid division into academic, technical and craft. We currently conceptualize key skills as literacy, numeracy and use of IT – with personal development, teamwork and problem-solving also included, but even harder to pin down. All of these reflect aspects of our intelligence and talents (and requisites for living) which should not be seen as bolt-ons to the main business of acquiring a qualification.

Individual Learning Programmes

We would also argue that while the world of education is beginning to think in terms of individual learning programmes to meet a person's particular needs, it is not yet acting as if it has done so. A much-used word has been flexibility. Flexibility is another way of describing individualized learning programmes available when, where and how individuals wish to access them. Such flexibility presents difficult management and resource problems for the colleges, particularly as the units of resource per student have been so drastically reduced in recent times. We would contend that to achieve true flexibility there must be a credit-accumulation and unit-based qualifications system. Many of us consider that this is essential to the achievement of a culture of lifelong learning. We recognize that qualifications have to maintain quality and standards, but believe a credit-based system can be designed which will not jeopardize them.

A qualifications framework for the future needs to allow students to tailor-make programmes of study that can be undertaken when and where it suits them. This is best served by validating learning in small parcels. A system for credit accumulation and transfer would accredit each one as a discrete unit/module of learning which in turn would be part of a larger qualification. This would allow learners to build qualifications to meet their own needs and interests. It would be a significant step forward in the pursuit of lifelong learning for everyone. It would also help to widen participation and enable colleges to be inclusive organizations.

A major stumbling block to this attractive scenario could well be GCE A-levels. A truly flexible credit framework would have to encompass these also. New Labour, however, seems anxious to avoid appearing to pose any threat to 'the gold standard' of A-levels. The eventual policy outcome of the Dearing (1996) review has been that while A-levels have been repackaged as modules they are still to retain their integrity. That is, while the qualification can be taken as components, the components are not free-standing. This compromise runs the risk of reinforcing the divisive education system which still persists in this country. It is also a blow to the quest for parity of esteem between academic and vocational qualifications. Inclusive learning cannot be delivered if we continue to think of qualifications as ways of excluding people from progression. Even if we maintain three pathways in our qualifications' philosophy, there must be the possibility of individuals moving across the pathways at various points in their lives, according to their personal and career needs.

Curriculum

Unlike schools, colleges do not have a national curriculum. A strand within colleges may resemble school sixth-forms and, indeed, sixth-form colleges were once schools. But, in England, our tradition has been to end broad-based general education at the age of sixteen to allow students to specialize. This will need to change if individuals are to gain the versatility needed for the 21st century.

The college curriculum is currently based on a range of models reflecting different academic and vocational cultures, and the traditions and qualifications that go with them. Schedule 2 of the Further and Higher Education Act of 1992 is our funding licence. The programmes of learning and experiences which are negotiated with our students must lead to qualifications listed in that schedule or provide a foundation for progression into them. It is tempting to suggest that the college curriculum is purely instrumental – that it just delivers qualifications for individuals. However, like schools, many colleges provide enrichment activities for full-time students enabling them to broaden their personal horizons through, among other things, sports, arts, international visits and work placements. We should not, however, confine our thinking to full-time students. The vast majority of students in colleges are part-time – on day, evening or flexible programmes – where the curriculum is defined by the qualification aim. As we move increasingly to individualized learning programmes, we must ensure that the curriculum is designed to contribute to the development of the whole person.

Further education is not a compulsory sector. Students and trainees of whatever age choose to come to the college, or perhaps their employer or training provider has made the choice for them. The students are there mainly to achieve qualifications that will open doors for them or add something to their lives. The instrumental view engendered means that enrichment activities are unlikely be embraced unless they are incorporated into the qualifications. Part of the continuing debate about key skills reflects this tension. GNVQs have had key skills built into them: other qualifications, whether academic or vocational, have not. One of the successes of Modern Apprenticeships has been the requirement by Training and Enterprise Councils for key skills to be part of the trainee's programme.

If we were to try to identify a distinctive further education curriculum it would centre on the practical application of knowledge to gain levels of understanding, skill and competence. The requirement to define competence within five levels of occupational standards has been a preoccupation since the mid-1980s (see Chapter 5). However defined, gaining competence and practical skills have been a key motivating factor for many students in colleges, who have not responded successfully to the requirements of schooling. The availability of a range of vocational and access qualifications has enabled individual students to identify new talents and potentials. Provision has, however, been fragmented and an overarching certificate would create greater coherence.

Learning Experiences

A curriculum model based on developing the broad talents of each individual leads to a range of learning models. Certainly many colleges continue to teach groups of students in fairly traditional-looking classrooms. Few of these class-room activities could be characterized as lectures and it is somewhat anachronistic that college teachers are still styled lecturers. 'Learner-centred' must be our watchword. Kolb's (1985) work on the learning cycle stresses the importance for individuals to review and action-plan from their personal expe-rience to ensure effective learning. Whatever is happening, whether in classroom, workshop or learning resource centre, we would want to see the materials, the content and the style meeting the needs of the individual learner.

Bayliss (1998) has recently offered a redefinition of schooling in a discussion paper prepared as part of the Royal Society of Arts' project on redefining work. She calls this her challenge to a closed society:

> Consider the strong grip of the conventional teaching model: when and how, and who does it. The model is a Platonic one; the teacher as the fount of knowledge passing on information to his pupils. The concept is hard to reconcile with the availability, electronically, of floods of information; chil-dren may access more than their teachers. School management is hierarchical, still based on the command-and-control model fast disap-pearing from the business world. The school day channels learning for all pupils into the same hours. And the school year still matches the rhythms of an agricultural society.

Anyone working in a college can decide how far her description of this traditional pattern still applies. Such criticisms have been heard for several decades. More than a quarter of a century ago, Taylor (1972) was making the same point:

> Children learn in part from 'being told', in part from 'an active personal interaction with people and things' (which we call 'play' when children are tiny, and 'discovery' or 'experience' as we grow older). For severely prac-tical reasons schools in the past have emphasized the 'being told': if children are in any case to be gathered together into schools, what cheaper than that their supervisors should talk to them, or more orderly than that they should sit attentive in desks? We have established a teaching-based system of learning. If we were instead to arrange things for 'active, personal interaction with people and things' we'd have a resource-based system of learning.

Although there are examples of colleges that have remodelled their accommo-dation to deliver resource-based learning (Theodossin and Pitcher, 1995), many it seems are still *talking* about it rather than *doing* it (and this applies just as much to schools). As we enter the 21st century, it is high time we made it

Figure 6.1 *The learning process*

- Initial information about possibilities at the college
- Information and guidance processes
- Diagnostic assessment for potential
- Negotiation and design of a learning programme
- Agreement on the learning goals and qualifications to be sought
- Help with study skills, personal and social education, career choices via a 'personal tutor'
- A programme of learning consisting of agreed weekly activities
- Access to additional support
- Availability of learning centres and learning resources
- Access to practical facilities and resources
- Work placements and work experience
- Development of key skills and personal interests
- Assistance with progression

happen rather than continually harking back to the models of bygone eras. The future for colleges is the inclusive learning agenda. In Figure 6.1 we attempt to characterize what this might mean.

Such a listing may currently reflect a full-time learning programme, but it can be applied to all learners – people who will not necessarily come to a college campus but will have opportunities to learn in a variety of settings, including libraries, pubs, shops, sports clubs, leisure centres and on-line at home. What distinguishes formal learning from what people pick up in their day-to-day lives is that an effective professional teacher will be on hand, directly or indirectly, to deploy a range of resources and skills to facilitate that learning. Currently the Further Educational National Training Organization (FENTO, 1998) is attempting to set out the standards for each key area of the learning domain shown in Figure 6.2.

In our view a flexible and unit-based qualifications framework is essential to delivering true learner-centred education and training.

Conclusion

The innovations in further education over recent years have been plentiful, but have they led to transformation? The importance of this distinction was emphasized by Kay McClenney (1998) in her keynote speech to the USA's League for Innovation in the Community College (roughly the American equivalent of further education):

> Innovation falls short because we keep creating innovations and reforms that focus on everything but learning. We have reforms dealing with

Figure 6.2 *Mapping the learning domain*

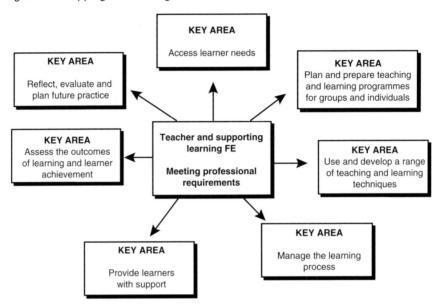

structures, organizational charts, administrative processes, faculty, teaching, business partnerships, TQM, and one hundred other things. To transform learning requires: first, clarity about what is to be learned; second, regular assessment of learning; and especially, third, a willingness to look at what those data tell us about the learning that is or is not occurring. Despite the rhetoric and exhortation of the past decade, much to our surprise and perhaps soon to our downfall, you cannot find many colleges where this is actually happening.

Let us ensure that we don't just busy ourselves tinkering with the details while ignoring the whole picture. If we are going to transform further education then we should not lose sight of our number one priority – the promotion of student learning. All innovations should be geared to this and success determined by whether we achieve real change. We can only succeed as colleges and as local, regional, national and international communities if we pursue excellence for each individual.

References

Bayliss, V. (1998) *Redefining Schooling: A Challenge to a Closed Society*, Discussion Paper 6, London: Royal Society of Arts.

Bichard, M. (1998) Speech to the Society of Education Officers, published in *Education Journal*, 25 (July/August).

Bloomer, M. and Hodgkinson, P. (1997) *Moving into FE: The Voice of the Learner*, London: FEDA.

Dearing, R. (1996) *Review of Qualifications for 16–19 Year Olds*, London: School Curriculum and Assessment Authority.

DfEE (1998) *The Learning Age: A Renaissance for a New Britain*, Green Paper, Cmnd 3790, London: The Stationery Office.

FENTO (1998) *National Standards for Teaching and Supporting Learning in Further Education in England and Wales*, London: FENTO.

Gardner, H. (1993) *Frames of Mind: The Theory of Multiple Intelligences*, 2nd edn, London: Fontana Press.

Goleman, D. (1996) *Emotional Intelligence: Why It Can Matter More than IQ*, London: Bloomsbury.

Higginson, G. (1996) *Report of the Learning-Technology Committee*, Coventry: FEFC.

Kennedy, H. (1997) *Learning Works: Widening Participation in Further Education*, Coventry: FEFC.

Kolb, D.A. (1985) *Experiential Learning: Experience as the Source of Learning and Development*, Englewood Cliffs: Prentice Hall.

McClenney, K. (1998) *Community Colleges Perched at the Millennium: Perspective on Innovation, Transformation and Tomorrow*, Mission Viejo, CA: League for Innovation in the Community College.

Ministry of Education (1956) *Technical Education*, White Paper, Cmnd 9703, London: HMSO.

Stanton, G. and Richardson, W. (eds) (1998) *Qualifications for the Future: A Study of Tripartite and Other Divisions in Post-16 Education and Training*, London: FEDA.

Taylor, L.C. (1972) *Resources for Learning*, 2nd edn, Harmondsworth: Penguin.

Theodossin, E. and Pitcher, T. (1995) *Altered Images: Transforming College Estates for a Learning Revolution*, London: FEDA.

Tomlinson, J. (1996) *Inclusive Learning: Report of the Learning Difficulties and/or Disabilities Committee*, London: The Stationery Office.

7   Staff Relations

Dan Taubman

The revolution that has been the incorporation of the further education sector cannot be seen from the perspective of college lecturers as the dawn of a bright new age. Rather, they see it as largely a retrograde and probably unnecessary upheaval. In creating a new national sector from the 'Cinderella' service that was local authority FE, everything was changed: the structures, the political control and accountability, the funding, the curriculum, governance, and (most of all) the industrial relations environment. Very little of this, from the view-point of college staff and NATFHE members, was change for the better. Jim Donaldson, the Chief Inspector and Director of Audit at the FEFC, publicly admitted to the House of Commons Education and Employment Committee (1998) that 'inspection findings suggest that the morale of teachers is low'.

Incorporation may have established further education for the first time as a national sector, but this was underpinned by the particular ideology of the then Conservative government which brought a semi-privatized bureaucratic market model to education and training. In part, this arose from long-standing concerns about the performance of the further education sector in terms of servicing what was, in fact, a declining and confused UK industry. These were crystallized in the *Unfinished Business* report (AC and OFSTED, 1993), which showed a diverse, incoherent patchwork of different models of post-16 educa-tion and vocational training.

Incorporation, as it emerged, became a particular and rather peculiar mix of competitive market forces combined with increased central control exercised by bureaucracy and audit. It created an almost monopolistic market in which the state, through the FEFC and also the Training Enterprise Councils (TECs), was the only buyer of any consequence. The 'modernization' has left almost nothing untouched and much of the sector is still in turmoil and a state of flux. Other chapters in this volume have discerned, discussed and analysed the impact of the changes on the main sets of relationships that define the sector. Here, as an officer of NATFHE, I want to consider the consequences for the staff.

The story of staff relations is a narrative of almost unrelieved misery. It is an indication of how bad industrial relations became during the first phase of incorporation that for two years running in the mid-1990s further education had proportionally more days lost to strike action than any other sector of the

British economy. While this may indicate as much about industrial relations in general as it does about further education, it is still a remarkable fact that demonstrates the depths to which this set of relationships had sunk. But industrial relations in further education cannot be divorced from the general context of industrial relations in the 1990s. The long period of Conservative rule saw the introduction of six pieces of trade union legislation which have largely hamstrung the unions' ability to resist management attacks on both wages and conditions of service. The new 'hard' human resource management was seized upon with alacrity by many of the new colleges. They embraced the redefinition of collective bargaining – in both the public and private sectors – away from the national level to that of the organization, even the plant.

The industrial relations situation at incorporation in colleges was fairly stable. There had been a relatively long period of national negotiations between the local authorities as employers and the main unions representing the academic staff, first in the FE sub-committee of the Burnham Committee and then later as a National Joint Council. Conditions of service were governed by a national agreement known as the 'Silver Book'. This gave good conditions of service to lecturers, including a thirty-hour week, fourteen weeks' holiday and no more than twenty-one hours a week teaching for a main grade lecturer. Pay scales were also national, although, by and large, through the 1970s and 1980s lecturers' pay had slipstreamed that of schoolteachers. The relatively favourable conditions resulted from negotiations in the 1970s when colleges, unable to offer salaries sufficiently attractive to induce skilled craftspeople to enter lecturing, were anxious to provide incentives. Even before incorporation, the local authority employers had been sniffing around the Silver Book conditions. They achieved a major breakthrough in 1988 when NATFHE, the main academic staff union, accepted in a ballot new definitions for a lecturer's duties and a division of academic staff into main grade lecturers and senior lecturers, with management grades for the rest. This latter group received a substantial cut in their leave entitlement. More importantly a breach had been made in the ramparts of the Silver Book and the teaching workforce had been divided.

NATFHE went into incorporation in a relatively strong position. Union membership was high, with union density at around 80 per cent. Union organization (almost uniquely among education unions) was based on the workplace branch and in most colleges was strong. Indeed, NATFHE activity was almost a prerequisite for recruitment to college management. But, by the late 1990s, a survey commissioned by NATFHE (Burchill, 1998) found that membership had fallen to an all-time low. National pay bargaining was in tatters, staff were being restricted to narrow bands within national scales and national pay rates had been largely abandoned. Very few staff remained on Silver Book conditions and there had been vast job losses. By 1999 over 20,000 further education lecturers had left. Among the reasons given were an atmosphere of 'oppression' from college managers, no sign of partnership between managers and staff, increased disciplinary procedures, victimization of union activists, low staff morale and 'further education [being] a system under serious strain' (Burchill, 1998). All of this a result of an almost continuous dispute lasting for over six years.

Incorporation for NATFHE started on a relatively high note when it obtained a landmark judicial decision on the contractual position of staff contingent on the transfer of employer status to the new corporations. This protected staff from an immediate assault on their conditions of service. Of course, the old national bargaining machinery was swept aside with incorporation but a new apparatus was set up with the new employers' association, the Colleges' Employers' Forum (CEF). The appointment of 'champagne' Roger Ward as the CEF's new chief executive, fresh from taking on NATFHE in the polytechnic sector, meant that the colleges would be pursuing a hard line with the unions. Given the way that incorporation had been accompanied by a tight squeeze on costs, and that almost three-quarters of all expenditure was on staff, a battle was inevitable.

The dispute started almost as soon as the colleges became incorporated. There was a breakdown at national level over conditions of service. The CEF, spurred on by the government holding back a percentage of funding until the lecturers' conditions of service had been changed, proposed in May 1993 to increase the working week, teaching hours and the working year. NATFHE responded with a ballot in which 62 per cent voted in favour of strike action and a further 8 per cent in favour of industrial action short of a strike. But an actual walkout was stopped at the last minute by a college going to law. This left the powers of the union even further diminished. The judgement held that the union must supply to the employer a list of all those to be balloted. If just one name proved incorrect, as in all probability it would given the general level of accuracy of union membership records, then the ballot could be declared invalid. This, combined with the fact that each college was now a separate employer, made coordinated national action by NATFHE extremely difficult.

Through 1994 the great further education contracts dispute began to resemble something akin to the trench warfare of the First World War. Neither side could make a substantial breakthrough. Instead there was a series of local and bitter disputes as colleges sought to pressurize staff into signing new contracts with diminished conditions of service. Where union organization was strong, these moves could be resisted. Where union organization was weak, the new contracts could be imposed. NATFHE embarked on a process of attempting to bypass national negotiations and achieve new negotiated contracts at local level. Given the government was sticking to the hold-back on college funds until changes had been achieved, it is difficult to see what other strategy the union could have adopted. The CEF had meanwhile taken a position whereby they were offering a teaching-hours ceiling of 1,000 hours per year – an increase of 30 per cent. Throughout 1994 NATFHE and the colleges as employers slugged it out at local level. Colleges offered cash inducements to staff who would accept the new contract. Those promoted and newly appointed were all put on to new contracts. As NATFHE negotiated local deals, fewer and fewer lecturers remained on the old Silver Book conditions.

By 1995 a new threat to lecturers' security was emerging. As the financial crisis in colleges began to bite, so the numbers of redundancies and resignations rose steeply. Some 1,500 full-time posts and over 8,000 part-time jobs were lost. NATFHE's troops were beginning to weary of the struggle. The 1995 Week of Action saw only fourteen colleges taking part. However, the number of local disputes did not diminish, with over 200 recorded in 1995. A third of colleges negotiated local agreements. These included some of the largest colleges. For the 1995 pay round, the Employers' Forum offered nothing to those staff remaining on Silver Book contracts.

At national level the hiatus continued through 1996. Redundancies were accelerating. Another 3,500 full-time staff posts were lost and staff morale was reaching rock-bottom. Pay rates were falling behind those of schoolteachers. Increasingly, colleges were abandoning national pay scales and resorting to narrow pay bands and spot placements on the pay scales. Being a NATFHE activist seemed a sure way of getting fired. More and more activists and national leaders felt they were being victimized by their colleges. Part-timers were frequently being used to fill the gaps left by full-time staff leaving or being made redundant. There was also an upsurge in the numbers of non-teaching staff being used in quasi-teaching roles such as instructors or demonstrators.

Further education colleges have always been more dependent on part-time teaching staff than other sectors of education. Part-time staff have historically been treated as little more than casual employees, with few rights and very little employment protection. However, following a historic House of Lords decision on part-time workers' rights in March 1994, the CEF began advising colleges to explore the possibility of using third-party providers of temporary lecturers. The government also recommended that colleges consider the use of agency staff in a letter to the Chair of the CEF Board announcing the 1995 hold-back conditions. The increases in the use of part-time and casual staff have now grown to an alarming extent (NAFTHE, 1998).

The contracts dispute was still at stalemate in 1997. Over half (55 per cent) of college staff were on locally negotiated contracts, but casualization had increased to the point where 45 per cent were on non-permanent contracts. That year the number of redundancies grew by 5,000. NATFHE switched some of its energies to a more political approach, campaigning on the need for increased funds for the sector and to preserve national bargaining. It fervently hoped that the arrival of the new Labour government would mean that these were achievable goals.

The start of 1998 saw new national leaders in both NATFHE and the Association of Colleges (AoC), as the CEF had become. NATFHE had a new general secretary, Paul Mackney, whose stated aim was to resolve the long-standing dispute. The new leaderships made fresh efforts to achieve some kind of settlement over the summer of 1998. A minimum national framework was worked out between NATFHE and the AoC. This allowed for up to twenty-seven hours teaching a week. However, in the autumn it was narrowly rejected by a postal ballot of NATFHE members. At the time of writing, it is still unclear whether the two sides will be able to put aside their disagreements over the amount of teaching time lecturers will have to undertake, so that they can talk over a number of the other unresolved issues. NATFHE is continuing to press for a national framework on conditions which will ensure minimum standards for lecturers in all colleges.

So at the turn of the millennium, 1993 has been the only year since incorporation when there has been a universally applied national agreement on pay for all grades of academic staff, and that was the very first agreement of the colleges' independent existence. Subsequently no lecturer on a Silver Book contract has received a pay award and recommendations from the national employers' body have been increasingly ignored by the colleges. A survey conducted by NATFHE in September 1997 found that fewer than half had implemented the national employers' recommendation on a pay award for 1997–8. Yet the salaries of principals rose consistently post-incorporation by around 11.6 per cent (Reeves, 1995). An earlier NATFHE survey in 1996 found that half of the lecturers responding earned under £20,000 a year. Nearly 16 per cent of the respondents earned between £15,000 and £19,000 a year. Less than £15,000 was earned by 20 per cent and 13.3 per cent were paid less than £10,000.

The same survey found that poor pay levels were a factor in lecturers wishing to leave the profession. Issues of low morale and unacceptable levels of stress are causing widespread concern, especially when further education is increasingly being seen as having a crucial role to play in opening up opportunities for disadvantaged groups and improving the nation's skills base. An independent survey of NATFHE members (Kinman, 1996) found that 35 per cent of respondents were actively seeking work outside the profession, 60 per cent were considering leaving the profession and 80 per cent said they would seriously consider early retirement if offered. The heavy administrative demands of the FEFC were commonly cited as one of the main stresses for teaching staff. The increasing obsession with measurable indicators of success removed what lecturers saw as their prime function – to facilitate learning and develop potential. Quantitative measurements, usually related to administrative and organizational arrangements, mean pedagogy seemed to be consistently undervalued and, with it, the role of the educator. The ever present threat of redundancy, together with the new pension arrangements that came into force in April 1997, made it virtually impossible for lecturers over fifty to access their pension should they have to leave the service before reaching pensionable age. This further depressed morale. Many of the most highly skilled and experienced teachers left before the pension change. Yet others were made redundant, leaving huge gaps in colleges and placing an ever greater burden on those remaining.

Burchill (1998) in his survey *Five Years of Change* has encapsulated the situation thus:

> Since incorporation, FE has probably been placed under more pressure than any other part of the public sector, particularly in terms of its system of industrial relations. The attack on pay structures and terms and conditions seems to have taken an extreme form in the FE sector. Many of these proposals can be seen as part of the process of creating a 'competitive market/customer' rather than 'student/service' orientation.

FE had been well and truly 'modernized'. As Reeves (1995) describes in his short book on the sector, the FE lecturer had moved from a position of being a craftsperson with enormous autonomy in the classroom to that of a Fordist production-line worker by whom the teaching of so many units could be achieved by the through-put of a standardized curriculum and qualifications. Industrial relations in the sector – in their bitterness and mutual suspicion – resembled something like Ford's own industrial relations of the 1930s.

The great experiment that was the incorporation of further education and the process of its modernization cannot be said to be a great success, at least from the point of view of its lecturers. The disruption to every aspect has been enormous. The costs in resources, energy and spirit have been debilitating. What may have been a backwater of the educational world has been remoulded into a national sector, but it has come with a high price.

The market model created at incorporation, however, contained within it the seeds of its own demise. With little vision or sense of purpose, the sector has spun out of control. Significant sections of further education – working and management practices and the curriculum principally – have been radically recast. However, they were found to be seriously wanting when it came to producing the kind of quality provision that the country was expecting from it.

With the election of a new government, there are glimpses of a different reality. In many ways it seems more palatable than the previous one, although its shape seems to move in and out of the shadows and, in doing so, at times seems to offer promise and at others to feel like more of the same misery. Set in a context of lifelong learning, further education's future could be bright as it attempts to become a major instrument of regeneration. The worst excess of incorporation have been curbed. The changes in working practices have made its services more flexible. There are still enormous reservoirs of talent and commitment among its staff that can be harnessed to an agenda which is potentially liberating.

Yet there are also huge barriers of cynicism and suspicion among college staff to overcome. The destruction of so much of the infrastructure and stability in the sector means that there is an increasing contradiction between the government's agendas of raising standards and quality, on the one hand, and widening participation on the other. To achieve both will be hard, especially as participation rates for post-school education are such that those who will have to be brought into colleges to meet the government's targets will find it the hardest to achieve and attain. This is especially so when the curriculum and its reform still focuses on the preoccupations of academic elitism. The Chief Inspector's Annual Report 1995–6 (FEFC, 1996) noted that 'early results of an analysis by inspectors of public examination performance indicate that a significant proportion of those failing is amongst those groups who have underpinned the recent expansion of further education'.

The twin goals certainly will not be achieved by a demoralized, underpaid, stressed workforce. A necessity will be a thorough re-evaluation of conditions of service and salary structures in the sector. This will need to be both independent and impartial. Only by this means can a settlement be reached in the sector and a new foundation laid on which lifelong learning can be securely built.

References

AC and OFSTED (1993) *Unfinished Business: Full-time Educational Courses for 16–19 Year Olds*, London: HMSO.

Burchill, F. (1998) *Five Years of Change: A Survey of Pay, Terms and Conditions in the Further Education Sector Five Years after Incorporation*, London: NATFHE.

Donaldson, J. (1998) *Oral Evidence, 11 November 1997*, in Education and Employment Committee, 1998, p. 33.

Education and Employment Committee (1997) *Further Education, Association of Colleges, Minutes of Evidence and Appendix, Tuesday 25 November 1997 and Tuesday 16 December 1997*, London: The Stationery Office.

Education and Employment Committee (1998) Sixth Report, *Further Education*, vol. 2, *Minutes of Evidence and Appendices*, 264-II, London: The Stationery Office.

FEFC (1996) Chief Inspector's Annual Report, *Quality and Standards in Further Education in England 1995–96*, Coventry: FEFC.

Kinman, G. (1996) *Occupational Stress and Health Among Lecturers Working in Further and Higher Education*, London: NAFTHE.

NATFHE (1995) *Managing to be Independent, Evidence to the House of Commons Committee of Public Accounts*, in Public Accounts Committee, 1995.

NATFHE (1998) *Evidence to the House of Commons Education and Employment Committee*, in Education and Employment Committee, 1998, Appendix 53.

Public Accounts Committee (1995) *Management and Financial Control at Colleges in the Further Education Sector*, London: HMSO.

Reeves, F. (1995) *The Modernity of Further Education*, Bilston: Education Books in partnership with The Community College.

8   Governance and Management

Michael Shattock

Born out of its belief in the efficiency of the market in raising educational standards and its dissatisfaction with local government, the Conservative government of the time removed the further education colleges from local authority control, with effect from 1 April 1993. In doing so, it launched one of the most ambitious and risky innovations in public administration in the eighteen years it was in power. It was risky because the colleges were not experienced in self-management – even after the introduction of devolved management in 1990 LEA staff remained available for advice and support and the local authority retained the ultimate legal responsibility. The tradition of interested and committed governance in schools had only patchily been translated into further education colleges. That these risks have not been realized, except in some well-publicized cases, owes a great deal to the operational framework laid down by the new Further Education Funding Council (FEFC).

It is worth, in looking back from the vantage point of 1999, remembering that further education had been looked upon as the 'Cinderella' sector in the previous decade and had not been particularly well managed or well led. Yet the 1992 Act projected some 460 colleges into independent corporate status with a funding regime that encouraged a competitive approach to student recruitment and the replacement of a service philosophy by one akin to entrepreneurialism. Governing bodies and college principals were required to change their *modus operandi* almost overnight and it is not surprising that so many failed to do so, and that others took the new agenda to extremes. An example of the former is contained in the inspection report of West Cumbria College (FEFC, 1998g):

> [Governing body] members have not conducted a rigorous review of the college's mission nor played a full part in shaping its strategic objectives. The corporation is not paying enough attention to monitoring and evaluating the quality of the college's provision. Vacancies and lengthy absences, some approved by the corporation, have reduced the average attendance at the last five corporation meetings to nine.

Newby's (1998) review of complaints against St Austell College states:

It has been a particular feature of this case that the governing body of the college played a limited and reactive role as events, including actions taken by the principal, unfurled. In principle, I cannot accept an argument which concludes, in effect, that the governors were unable to exert any influence over this matter.

An obvious example of a governing body and a principal taking corporate powers to an extreme could be found at Derby Tertiary College, Wilmorton, where an inner group of governors behaved in a wholly arbitrary manner in removing dissenting governors from membership of the governing body and where the principal and governors ruthlessly restructured the management of the college in defiance of appropriate procedures (Shattock, 1994). Another example was at Stoke-on-Trent College where the House of Commons Education and Employment Committee (1998) quoted evidence 'of the unhealthy control exercised by the previous principal and chairmen of governors working together without informing the governing body of their actions'. The White Paper, *The Learning Age*, refers to problems in the emerging governance and management structures:

Since the incorporation of further education colleges there have been concerns about the style of working and remoteness of governing bodies. Some have encouraged a confrontational management style which is unacceptable for publicly funded bodies.

(DfEE, 1998a)

In the five years since incorporation there have been many press headlines about badly managed or badly governed colleges. Financial mismanagement, fraud, false claims over student numbers and misbehaviour by chairmen, principals and other senior officers have emerged with distressing regularity, and have damaged the sector's image. The sagas of Huddersfield, Portsmouth and Glasgow Caledonian Universities, and of the Swansea and Southampton Institutes, have similarly damaged the reputation of higher education. But when it is remembered how many colleges were transferred from local education authority control to corporate independence, and the pressures on them to behave in an aggressively competitive and market-orientated way, it should not be a matter of surprise that some of them failed to measure up to the standards that Whitehall and the Public Accounts Committee looked for. It is much more worthwhile to recognize the very significant number – some hundreds of colleges – which made the transfer to corporate independence without difficulty and which realized the high hopes that the government invested in the 1992 Act.

The period between the incorporation of colleges in 1993 and 1999 has nevertheless seen a considerable change in the manner in which colleges are governed and managed. Partly this reflects a growing scepticism about reliance on a purely market-driven approach, a scepticism reinforced by the change in government; partly it results from public pressure arising out of the institutional failures in governance or management which required much greater attention to be given to accountability and transparency issues. The resulting procedural changes have had a significant impact on college governance. How far these changes should be seen as evolutionary and how far engineered or imposed by DfEE or FEFC in the light of particular reports must be a matter of opinion. Certainly these central authorities have led the changes, especially where questions of public accountability have been involved, but there is little evidence that they have been acting other than with the general consent and support of the sector as a whole. Without such central leadership there is no doubt that there would have been widespread foot-dragging at institutional level but, at the same time, on many issues the central bodies were responding to pressures for change from the sector itself and from other outside forces.

Membership of Governing Bodies

Perhaps the most important change, at least in a formal constitutional sense, is in the membership of governing bodies themselves, implemented from 1 August 1999. Although the changes have been promulgated by government, they reflect an unease in the sector itself over the ideological bias of the previous membership arrangements and the extent to which they were, in practice, effective. Behind the 1992 Act lay a philosophy that suggested that a governing body dominated by members drawn from a business background would impose a proactive market orientation on colleges that had previously been reactive and bureaucratic. While this philosophy was far from being realized in most colleges it certainly played an important role in those colleges where the 'confrontational style', referred to in the White Paper, was apparent.

Table 8.1 compares the constitution determined by the 1992 Act with that of the Modification Order which came into force on 1 August 1999. Before being agreed, the modifications were subject to an extensive consultation process, and the publication in summary form of the views expressed by colleges and other organizations provides a valuable insight into the maturity of the sector (DfEE, 1998b, 1998c). The changes could be seen as relatively cosmetic, but in fact they

Table 8.1 *Membership of the governing body*

1992		1999	
Independent members	13	Business members	7
Co-opted members	5	Co-opted members	3
TEC member	1		
Staff members	2	Staff members	1–3
Student members	1	Student members	1–3
Community members	2	Nominated by local community bodies	1–3
		Nominated by local authority	1–3
Principal	1*	Principal	1
Number permitted	10–20		12–20

* Depending on whether the principal opted for membership.

reflect a different view of further education to that taken by the previous government.

Overall they represent a shift away from the business-led, free market approach, back towards a more local, community-based membership without, however, any weakening of the colleges' legal independence. The DfEE was at pains to emphasize the important role that the business community should play in the running of colleges, but said that 'no single category should be able to control proceedings'. The title 'independent members' was changed to 'business members', but the new regulation permits a wide interpretation of 'business' to include the professions and any field of employment 'relevant to the activities of the institution'. A further important change was to bring the appointment of the business members under the sole authority of the governing body itself, instead of (as previously) the governing body being only able to approve the appointment of an 'independent member' if the appointment was approved by the existing 'independent members' acting as a group. This removed the special membership status accorded to independent/business members. These changes were welcomed in the consultation process.

The Kennedy Report (Kennedy, 1997) had raised the question of the wider accountability of colleges to their local communities and in the first draft the new model left open which community bodies were to be represented on governing bodies. In the consultation process FEFC was successful in persuading the DfEE to write into the regulations that the community bodies were to be identified by the corporations themselves, but was not successful in arguing that a governing body should retain a veto over nominations made by community bodies. Surprisingly, it was also not successful in inserting a requirement that colleges should hold annual meetings where their past record and future plans could be commented on by the public.

The new constitution also brings back representation from local authorities, a category of membership banished by the previous regulations. This was by far the most controversial proposal. Although it was supported by 137 of the 239 respondents to the consultation exercise, 61 rejected it outright, 46 supported it only if the governing body could veto the nomination put forward and 24 believed that it would only be acceptable if there was cross representation on local authority committees. FEFC supported the latter proposal unsuccessfully and also urged without success that all nominations should be subject to vetting by a governing body search committee so that individuals should be appointed on merit rather than, in effect, as the local authorities' representatives. FEFC was anxious that local authorities should not pay their members expenses for attending college meetings.

A third change was the removal of mandatory representation from Training and Enterprise Councils (TECs). The TECs were created by the previous government and, in 1992, the TEC/FE partnership was seen as providing a crucial underpinning to the linkages of colleges and the local skills base. The TECs' position was further strengthened by being required to approve colleges' strategic plans. The TEC representative was counted as one of the thirteen 'independent' members and so, as a quasi-permanent member, could play a very influential role on the governing body. In practice TECs seem to have nominated their own staff rather than their members, and their impact on the running of colleges has been much less than was intended. The DfEE consultation paper initially suggested that the TEC representative should be included as one of the seven business members, but this prompted the strongest adverse reaction in the whole consultation process, with 82 respondents being against continued TEC representation and only 35 supporting it. The majority view was supported by the FEFC and the DfEE withdrew the proposal.

The changes in internal college representation, though minor, also reflected the perception after the Kennedy (1997) report, that the previous employer-led approach to governing further education had not been effective in winning the hearts and minds of college staff and students to the enterprise, and the new constitution gives the governing body freedom to increase internal college representation if it wishes to. The decision to make the principal *ex officio* a member of the corporation rather than leaving the decision to the particular individual, as in the previous constitution, simply reflects the practice of the sector and the requirements for accountability as they have emerged over the period.

These changes are by no means as radical as might have been implied by the claim in the DfEE consultation document that governing body arrangements were 'ripe for reform'. Although the shift is not enormous, it is clear that the balance has been tilted away from a primarily business-driven to a more community-orientated governance structure. The consultation exercise showed that the sector's concerns were much more the fear that colleges might be returned to some kind of local control and that the commitment to corporate independence might be weakened, rather than that over the past five years the sector had been driven by the business members' interests. The reinsertion of local authority representation was treated with exceptional suspicion. These reactions should be seen not just as a reflection of the colleges' wish not to return to the *status quo ante*, but also as a vindication of the way the FEFC has carried out its responsibilities and the extent to which colleges have become self-confident in their powers of self-government.

Internal Governance and Management

We have no way of knowing how significant these constitutional amendments will prove to be in practice, but it is unlikely that they will be felt as much in the colleges themselves as the changes in internal governance and management that have taken place over the period. These changes have been introduced, not for philosophical or ideological reasons, but in response to the various breakdowns and examples of malpractice referred to at the beginning of this chapter. From one point of view they represent a growing set of procedural safeguards and internal controls which can stifle the entrepreneurialism and competitiveness which colleges were encouraged to demonstrate; from another they offer the best – if not under current legislation the only – guarantee that FEFC and the National Audit Office have that colleges will not abuse the legal independence that they received under the 1992 Act. Considerable impetus for these changes was provided by two reports commissioned in 1994 by the FEFC on behalf of the DfEE, the first into St Philip's College (Cairns, 1994) and the second into the affairs of Derby Tertiary College, Wilmorton (Shattock, 1994). St Philip's was a Roman Catholic sixth-form college and many of the findings were particular to the circumstances of the college, but the report threw up one problem which had more general significance: that of a governing body in effect usurping the management of a college from its principal. The Wilmorton inquiry, however, raised issues which cast a long shadow over the whole of the sector's governance arrangements. The report identified, as set out in Figure 8.1, a series of governance failures, many of which individually could probably have been found in many colleges, but which here occurred in the one institution.

Figure 8.1 Extracts from the Wilmorton Report

The Governing Body did not provide adequate 'oversight of the College's activities' (Articles of Government 3(1)(a)), or observe the principles for the proper conduct of public business and the pursuit of value for money laid down in *The Proper Conduct of Public Business (Public Accounts Committee, HMSO 1994)*. It failed:

(a) to observe due procedures for the management of governing body business including observing the legal requirements for maintaining a quorum;

(b) to make available minutes of Governors meetings and other papers, including committee reports, to members of the College;

(c) to act in accordance with natural justice in respect to the removal of one of its members;

(d) to take appropriate steps to obtain the effective and efficient use of resources;

(e) to take a positive role in strategic planning and the development of quality in College programmes;

(f) to approach the management restructuring of the College with due regard to the longer term needs of the institution and to observe appropriate procedural safeguards in the selection of staff for the new structure;

(g) to establish an Academic Board until January 1994 (when it did so it imposed the Vice-Chairman of the Governors onto its membership);

(h) to establish effective audit machinery;

(i) to ensure that the Principal was fully accountable to the Governing Body.

In addition it improperly paid remuneration to nine of its members, including differentiated remuneration to its Chairman and Vice-Chairman.

The Principal did not carry out appropriately his responsibilities 'for the operation, direction and management of the institution and the leadership of its staff' (Articles of Government 3(2)(b)). In particular:

(a) appropriate steps were not taken to recruit an effective senior management team in personnel, the management of buildings and in general management, including the provision of a Clerk to the Governing Body and to College committees who was able to provide independent advice to the Governing Body;

(b) the Principal did not give leadership in the strategic planning process required by the Further Education Funding Council (FEFC);

(c) the College's Financial Regulations were regularly breached in respect to procedures to assess expenditure on new projects, levels of authorization of expenditure and lack of tendering;

(d) there was inadequate financial control of capital projects;

(e) the Principal did not ensure that the Governing Body was adequately briefed on the content of circulars and directives from the FEFC.

The report recommended:

(a) That the Secretary of State use her powers within the Further and Higher Education Act 1992 to remove all the members of the present Governing Body and appoint a new Governing Body with an entirely new membership. This membership should include representation from the major private sector employers in Derby.

(d) That the new Governing Body should seek to establish a new post of Clerk to the Governing Body and Secretary to the Academic Board. The post should be combined with other central managerial responsibilities and be filled after public national advertisement.

(f) That the FEFC should take steps to disseminate the lessons of the failures of governance and management at Derby College, Wilmorton, to colleges in the FEFC sector.

In its final chapter the report stated of the Governing Body that:

It failed the basic tests of acting in the public interest: it organized its own business in an unprofessional manner and unconstitutionally, it was inequitable in its treatment of individuals, it took no cognizance of circulars and requirements from the FEFC and it took no interest in the College's strategic plan. As is evident from Chapter 5 in respect to property management and financial control, from Chapter 6 in respect to relations with the IT industry and the declaration of interest

> by its Chairman, from Chapter 7 in respect to its handling of the management restructuring of the College, and from Chapter 18 in respect to quality issues, the Governing Body failed to exercise proper oversight of the College's activities, failed to take appropriate steps to obtain the effective and efficient use of resources and failed to curb the impetuosity of the Principal.

The recommendations were accepted and implemented by the Secretary of State and the FEFC. In February 1995 the NAO issued a report *Managing to be Independent: Management and Financial Control at Colleges in the Further Education Sector* which – while much concerned with budget creation and management, financial control and audit arrangements – also addressed governance. Leaning heavily on the Wilmorton and St Philip's cases it devoted a quarter of the report to commenting on governance matters concluding that:

governing bodies should ensure that their contribution continues to be effective by:

- considering making formal arrangements to plan their future membership;
- establishing and articulating a clear understanding of their role in relation to that of the college principal;
- drawing up a register of business interests as a means of demonstrating to the public that such interests have not influenced their decisions;
- ensuring that their committee structures enable business to be transacted effectively and efficiently, and that the roles and terms of reference for each committee are clearly defined and distinct from each other and from the full governing body;
- requiring the principal to ensure they are provided with adequate briefing and financial information to enable them to carry out their role;
- ensuring that the person appointed as clerk to the governing body has sufficient time to devote to the role and receives appropriate training.

Clerk to the Governors

A year later the FEFC, together with the college representative bodies, issued a report entitled *Governance and Management of Further Education Colleges* (AfC *et al.*, 1996). It was significant that in twenty-five out of fifty-seven of the action points, the clerk to the governors was mentioned as having responsibility. In the meantime, the FEFC had issued *A Guide for Clerks* (FEFC, 1996) which also laid stress on the importance of the role of the clerk to the governors. In addition to emphasizing the need for governing body business to be conducted under due process, the clerk's role was interpreted as 'if necessary intervening when he or she feels that the governing body is acting inappropriately or even beyond its powers. The assumption is that the clerk's advice will generally be respected and accepted if it is correct.' The report goes on to deal with what steps should be followed if the clerk's advice was not taken and suggested that either the clerk or the chairman and the principal should seek advice from the FEFC. Tacitly, the clerk was being invited to become a 'whistle blower', a position later confirmed in the FEFC's response to the DfEE's consultation paper (FEFC, 1998d).

In the new DfEE regulations, provisions are made which entrench the appointment of a clerk as being a matter for the governing body, rather than for the principal, and which require the clerk's presence at any meeting of the governing body or its committees except when the clerk's own remuneration is being considered. All this represents a considerable upgrading of the status of the post of clerk to the governing body. Historically, the post was given to a fairly low level local authority functionary who had the duties of sending out the agenda and the papers for a meeting (which were normally provided by the principal's office) and of writing the minutes. It was not unknown for the principal's secretary to act as clerk. Under the new arrangements a clerk is much more than a minute writer; they are the chief advisers to the governing body on all matters of procedure, capable of acting in this capacity independently of the principal.

There is clearly a danger that too much weight will be placed on a clerk's shoulders. Many clerks currently serving in further education were transferred from local authority to college employment with no expectation of the present changes. To attract competent individuals, able to command respect at governing body level, salary levels have to be made commensurate to the responsibilities involved. In most colleges this means creating a post analogous to that of a registrar in a pre-1992 university, a much larger and more mature institution, where there is an established career structure and where the secretary to the university governing body also carries major administrative responsibilities in the university and has the seniority and salary to match them. But college circumstances differ, and in small colleges where the prospect of malpractice is often greater than in larger colleges, the role of the clerk may be difficult to upgrade in this way. This means that there is a big task for the sector in recruiting, training, supporting and professionalizing clerks so that they can sustain the responsibilities that they have now been given.

Audit

A second line of attack in improving internal management and governance has been in the area of audit. In Wilmorton, for example, the audit committee was chaired by the chairman of the governing body's own solicitor, whose legal firm also acted for the college. The other audit committee members were members of committees which had executive powers so that the membership could in no sense be described as having the requisite independence. The audit committee could itself decide whether it reported to the finance committee or the full governing body. The internal and the external auditors came from different branches of the same accountancy firm and neither had raised questions about the financial affairs of the college (Shattock, 1994). Six months after the Wilmorton Report, the NAO (1995) drew attention to weaknesses it had found in the operation of audit committees in the sector. The fact that in one of its guidance notes, issued over three years later, the FEFC (1998b) also cast doubt on the effectiveness of audit committees – saying that many colleges experienced difficulties in persuading members to attend them in spite of the fact that audit committees might be required 'on occasion to examine evidence that is critical of the college's governance, management and professional advisers' – suggests that this may be a continuing problem. In another of its guidance notes, on internal audit, the FEFC (1998c) stated that:

> The Council has not been able to place reliance upon the work of a significant proportion of internal audit service providers in [the first five] years. This has been mainly due to internal auditors not fully complying with the standards set out in the *Government Internal Audit Manual*. The inability to place reliance on this work strikes at the heart of the Council's 'arm's length' relationship to the internal audit of Colleges.

The weight which the FEFC (1998a) places on the audit function is demonstrated most clearly by its *Audit Code of Practice* (published in May 1998) which emphasizes the need for a 'rigorous framework of audit and internal controls' to assist governors to maintain the 'high standards of conduct' necessary to meet their public responsibilities. The various guidance notes, issued together with the code, require the internal auditors – normally drawn from an accountancy firm and not an internal appointment – 'to give an annual opinion, through the audit committee, on the adequacy and effectiveness of the colleges' system of internal control, and the extent to which they can rely on it'. Further, it laid responsibility on the audit committee to inform the principal and the chairman of the governing body immediately, for report to the full governing body, if it believed there was evidence of any fraud or impropriety. Yet in spite of these provisions some colleges, like the Wirral Metropolitan College (FEFC, 1999b), Bilston Community College (Melia, 1999) and Halton College (NAO, 1999) have run up huge deficits, while others like Hereward College (FEFC, 1995) have been involved in fraud and impropriety.

FEFC's Role

The FEFC's 'arm's length' relationship with colleges inevitably makes intervention difficult. Formally, the FEFC's role is regulatory not managerial. The 1992 Act established the Council as an agency to allocate resources to colleges, not to manage them. Because its powers of intervention can only technically be invoked after the terms of the financial memorandum (which provides the funding contract between FEFC and the colleges) can be shown to have been abused, it tends to find itself tackling the problems after they have been widely publicized rather than before. In evidence to the Select Committee on Education and Employment (1998) the minister, Lady Blackstone, made it clear that, although governing bodies were 'in a sense accountable to themselves', where there was evidence of mismanagement she would expect the FEFC to intervene and if it failed the DfEE itself would do so. By implication, and certainly the Select Committee read her evidence in this light, she was urging FEFC to be more interventionist.

Two different approaches are currently being tried by FEFC. The first has been applied at the Wirral Metropolitan College. Here the FEFC made a recommendation to the Secretary of State to exercise his powers under the 1992 Act to remove the governors, but allowed the governors to resign once they knew the recommendation was being made. The second has been at Bilston Community College where a damning inspectors' report has been followed up by the appointment of a special rescue team of senior educationalists who have been empowered to recommend closure or take-over by another college. In spite of this, the DfEE is thought to be not yet convinced that the FEFC is able to take strong enough action and plans are afoot to set up a new initiative aimed at proving that the government, in its own words, is going to be tough on failure.

The FEFC, with so many colleges to look after and a relatively small staff, would find it impossible to police the system in the way that local authorities were supposed (but too often failed) to do, even if it were given the necessary legal powers. It has therefore employed two other mechanisms. The first is to give encouragement to direct communication from the colleges either under an official procedure, as for example from a clerk to the governing body, or by an individual or whistle-blower. From its very early days, FEFC set up a complaints office, mostly inevitably utilized for study-related issues. Both the Select Committee in its report (1998) and the FEFC itself in its response to the DfEE's constitutional proposals (FEFC, 1998d) recommended the creation of a further education ombudsman – or an 'ombuds function', as the FEFC put it – 'to bring greater confidence to staff and students and [to] ensure some external scrutiny of certain complaints and grievances'. The DfEE did not accept the recommendation and the FEFC must therefore give consideration again as to how it handles such complaints, major and minor, which find their way to FEFC's offices. This will involve reconciling its restricted legal responsibilities and its 'arm's length' relationship with the need to respond effectively to complaints or warnings which, at one end of the spectrum, can indicate a major malfunctioning of a college but, at the other, be merely a libellous accusation from an aggrieved employee or student.

The second mechanism is to include a review of governance and management within the quality and standards inspection framework. That this can be an effective tool in extreme cases there is no doubt. At Hereward College (FEFC, 1995), for example, it was the award of a 'five' (the lowest grade) for governance and management, which prompted the resignation of the governing body. But an audit of governance and management carried out as part of what is primarily an academic inspection, while bureaucratically tidy, is not the most effective way of identifying serious problems. The quality movement, whether in further or higher education, tends to see things in terms of boxes which need ticks, crosses or numerical ratings. An assessment of governance needs more than this. Competent as the FEFC's internal auditors included in such an inspection team may be, they are unlikely to have had experience either as a governor or as a senior manager in a college. Processes which appear to satisfy formal procedural requirements may in practice be wholly unsatisfactory. It is interesting that in the Chief Inspector's Annual Report for 1997–8 he found that only 6 per cent of colleges had 'less than satisfactory' governance arrangements and he reserved two of his most serious criticisms for the fact that colleges over-estimated the quality of their governance in their self-assessments and that there were weaknesses in the training arrangements they made for governors. (The third serious criticism was in respect to governors' failure to pay sufficient attention to academic performance; FEFC, 1998e).

When one turns to some of the actual reports from the inspectorate where low marks were given for governance, a preponderance of the weaknesses seem to be in procedural issues, like unclear terms of reference, lack of standing orders, unsystematic induction training, ineffective clerking arrangements or failure to appraise senior officers. Nothing is said about bad decision-making, what staff think about the governing body or even what individual governors (as distinct from corporate self-assessment) think about their effectiveness. When governing bodies can pass resolutions simply to write them into the minutes to impress the inspector, as some certainly do, one has to be sceptical about what these reports really tell us.

There is undoubted merit in the FEFC reviewing college governance at the same time as a college's academic quality. The revelations about inadequate governance arrangements at Hereward College (FEFC, 1995), Dewsbury (FEFC, 1998f) or Matthew Boulton (FEFC, 1999a) have been timely. But that does not mean that such judgements are in general wholly to be trusted. They certainly cannot be relied upon to make a numerical assessment of the sector: to argue that 'governance is good or outstanding in 67 per cent of the colleges', as the Chief Inspector's report does, is to suggest a precision of judgement which is unrealistic and liable to lead to complacency.

The FEFC's approach to improving governance and to curbing impropriety has been to try to institutionalize transparency and openness, and to impose on professionals – audit firms and clerks to governors – a duty to report on key issues. Such an approach is certainly to be preferred to trying to exercise the kind of managerial controls that were the prerogative of the local authorities and has had the effect of greatly increasing lay governors' awareness of the job they are being asked to do. But too much emphasis on governor training, search committees and giving high scores at inspections for observing the letter rather than the substance of the job will be counter-productive. It will turn off active and committed governors who will find better outlets for their civic energies if they think they are being patronized by procedural bureaucracy. There is a danger of expecting too much from lay governors. This applies both to the time they can be expected to commit to a college, and to the extent of their understanding of the complex and now highly bureaucratic world of further education, its financial structures, quality frameworks and maze of qualifications.

Governance breakdowns, impropriety and malpractice do not come about primarily because the rules have not been followed, but because individuals see some advantage, personal or institutional, in actions which break them. A governing body which wilfully sought to operate outside the rules could be stopped by the principal and the clerk, if all else failed, taking the matter to the FEFC. For a governing body to control a principal determined to operate outside the rules is more difficult, not least because, as so many of the breakdowns have shown, the principal will tend to have a core of allies among the governors. But, in any case, where the principal is full-time, and has the college under his/her control, the power of unpaid and very part-time governors to exercise control is, in practice, limited.

What this points to, is giving further attention centrally to the career preparation of potential principals and governing body clerks. According to the magazine *Further Education Now!* (1998), a third of colleges have appointed new principals in the period 1996–7 to 1997–8, a turnover considerably higher than might have been expected from natural wastage. The job of principal can undoubtedly be stressful, and those able to cope will be those who are best prepared and who have the most professional approach.

Looking Forward

If we are thinking of the next five years, the evidence suggests that the FEFC and DfEE should resist further ratcheting up of governance rules and constitutional change, but concentrate more on improving the professional input to good governance through the career preparation of principals and other college senior officers. Governors will give generously of their time if they can take pride in their college's performance. But they are realistic enough to recognize that it is the principal and the staff to whom they must primarily look for the delivery of good performance. Governors are only rarely prepared to give the same amount of commitment when things are going badly. While they, as individuals, are liable for blame, they do not have the executive power to turn things round; it is easier in such circumstances to stay away or resign. The best governing body is that which supports a good principal, continues to ask probing questions, keeps a firm check on the executive without stifling it and can suggest new ways of approaching difficult problems by drawing on its members' own professional experience. In all this, conducting college business according to best practice procedures is important and necessary, but it is not the essential substance of college governance.

References

AfC, ACM, ACVIC, APC, APVIC, CEF, FEFC, SFCEF and SHA (1996) *Governance and Management of Further Education Colleges*, Coventry: FEFC.

Cairns, J.C. (1994) *St Philip's Roman Catholic Sixth Form College: Report of an Enquiry into the Governance and Management of the College*, Coventry: FEFC.

DfEE (1998a) *The Learning Age: A Renaissance for a New Britain*, Cmnd 3790, London: The Stationery Office.

DfEE (1998b) *Accountability in Further Education: A Consultation Paper*, London: DfEE.

DfEE (1998c) *Accountability in Further Education: Results of the Consultation*, London: DfEE.

Education and Employment Committee (1998) Sixth Report, *Further Education*, vol. 1, *Report and Proceedings*, 264-I, London: The Stationery Office.

FEFC (1995) *Inspection Report: Hereward College of Further Education*, 128/95, Coventry: FEFC.

FEFC (1996) *College Governance: A Guide for Clerks*, London: The Stationery Office.

FEFC (1998a) *Audit Code of Practice*, Coventry: FEFC.

FEFC (1998b) *Audit Code of Practice: Supplement A, Guidance Note on the College Audit Committee*, Coventry: FEFC.

FEFC (1998c) *Audit Code of Practice: Supplement D, Guidance Note on Areas Common to the College Internal Audit Service and External Auditor*, Coventry: FEFC.

FEFC (1998d) *Accountability in Further Education: Response from the Further Education Funding Council*, Coventry: FEFC.

FEFC (1998e) Chief Inspector's Annual Report, *Quality and Standards in Further Education in England 1997–98*, Coventry: FEFC.

FEFC (1998f) *Inspection Report: Dewsbury*, 22/98, Coventry: FEFC.

FEFC (1998g) *Inspection Report: West Cumbria College*, 103/98, Coventry: FEFC.

FEFC (1999a) *Inspection Report: Matthew Boulton College of Further and Higher Education*, 18/99, Coventry: FEFC.

FEFC (1999b) *Inspection Report: Wirral Metropolitan College*, 69/99, Coventry: FEFC.

Further Education Now! (1998) 'FE's vanishing principals', 49 (November).

Kennedy, H. (1997) *Learning Works: Widening Participation in Further Education*, Coventry: FEFC.

Melia, T. (1999) *Bilston Community College: Report on an Enquiry into its Future*, Coventry: FEFC.

NAO (1995) Report by the Comptroller and Auditor General, *Managing to be Independent: Management and Financial Control at Colleges in the Further Education Sector*, HC Session 1994/95 (8 February).

NAO (1999) Report by the Comptroller and Auditor General, *Investigation of Alleged Irregularities at Halton College*, HC 357 1998/99 (15 April).

Newby, H. (1998) *Review of Complaints against St Austell College*, London: DfEE.

Shattock, M. (1994) *Derby College, Wilmorton: Report of an Enquiry into the Governance and Management of the College*, Coventry: FEFC.

9 The Changing Campus

George Edwards

Since gaining their independence, the fabric of college campuses has changed in response to successive property policy priorities. Initial emphasis was on bringing buildings up to a good standard by addressing health and safety and legislative issues. This was followed by a drive towards improvement in the quality and fitness for purpose of buildings and facilities, accompanied by an increasing reliance on college internal resources, asset sales and borrowing (and private finance) to fund these capital schemes. More recently, the emphasis has changed to meet the new government's more socially inclusive priorities for the delivery of education.

Responsibility for the State of Buildings

Prior to incorporation, the local authorities had the major responsibility for ensuring the compliance of further education buildings with the relevant thirteen acts of parliament and their associated regulations and regulatory authorities. There was an implied limited immunity from prosecution. Schools and colleges, for example, were thought to be partially exempt from the 1971 Fire Precautions Act by virtue of the legal powers of the then Department of Education and Science, because schools and colleges could appeal to the ministry against any closure ruling by the Fire Officer. Local authorities also seemed to enjoy a quasi-Crown immunity, because if a local authority were sued for negligence, its defence might be that it had insufficient funds due to government-imposed cuts in local expenditure, hence (it might be argued) it was the Crown which should be sued. In addition to being responsible for the operation of the fire service, the local authority was also responsible for the planning consents under the 1920 Town and Country Planning Act for enforcing building control regulations. This meant that local authorities had the capability to give themselves deemed planning consent for further education college developments.

The situation was dramatically changed by the 1992 Further and Higher Education Act. Previous immunities were not explicitly carried forward. There no longer appeared to be exemption from any relevant building legislation, so it was necessary to demonstrate that best efforts were being made by the Further

Education Funding Council (FEFC) and by the colleges themselves to comply within the shortest possible time.

Some colleges felt the full force of these changes immediately after incorporation. The campus at Woodberry Down, in Hackney Community College, was closed as electrically dangerous within days of college incorporation. Another college building found to be structurally dangerous had to be temporarily shored up by the local authority. There were scores of such problems across the country. Hence there was an urgent need for an authoritative survey of the physical condition of the colleges.

The Hunter Surveys

The embryonic FEFC, established in September 1992 in anticipation of incorporation, considered as one of its first tasks how best to deal with the property inheritance of further education colleges. It was assumed that the state of repair and maintenance of buildings in sector colleges could be expected to be no better than those in the polytechnics sector (which had earlier been removed from the ambit of local authorities) and initial estimates of the possible costs of recovery of the estate were made on that basis. Anecdotal evidence, however, suggested that the condition of the further education estate might be much worse, as there appeared to have been minimal or token maintenance for a number of years. Colleges were also asked (in their responses to Circular 92/03 – FEFC, 1992a) to advise the Council of any prohibitions, works orders or warnings which had been issued by the regulatory authorities (for example, the Fire Officer and the Health and Safety Executive) for any buildings likely to come under college ownership.

The FEFC decided to commission from Hunter and Partners[1] a limited sample condition survey of some forty-four colleges – just under 10 per cent of the total – to check the validity of these estimates. The results of the sample survey demonstrated that the college buildings were indeed in a much worse state than those in the polytechnics sector had been. The cost of recovery of the buildings appeared to be about half as much again as it had been in those for which the Polytechnics and Colleges Funding Council had assumed responsibility, and for the most urgent categories of work there was an overcost of about 70 per cent.

Two potential problems emerged: first, the scale of the recovery costs in relation to likely sector capital funds and, second, the urgency of some key health and safety problems in a few colleges. The sample survey showed that so much work needed to be done to remedy the legal defects of buildings that the top priority had to be split into 'immediately urgent' and 'less immediately urgent' categories.[2] Premises included in the new first category had often been put under notice[3] for the remedy of deficiencies by such regulatory authorities as the Fire Officer or the Health and Safety Executive. The initial survey results are shown in Table 9.1.

The survey was conducted to the standards laid down by the Buildings Cost Information Service (a subsidiary of the Royal Institute of Chartered

Table 9.1 *Initial results of the Hunter surveys*

	Priority 1(a)	*Priority 1(b)*	*Priority 2*	*Priority 3*	*Total*
Works identified	£135,907,264	£223,221,435	£276,583,777	£202,271,451	£837,983,927
Less: non-eligible buildings	£5,463,064	£7,357,103	£8,897,716		£21,717,883
Less: disputed buildings	£3,444,736	£5,589,429	£14,216,455		£23,250,620
Net Hunter need	£126,999,464	£210,274,903	£253,469,606	£202,271,451	£793,015,424

Source: *The Hunter and Partners Surveys of Further Education Colleges,* April 1993 (see Note 1).

Surveyors). The elements of each building (the foundations, walls, windows and roofs) and the associated services (electrical, mechanical and plumbing) were inspected by a surveyor and an engineer. Each building in the college was separately assessed and detailed back-up notes were available to support the judgements. The results were overseen by a team in London who had the task of ensuring consistency of approach. These results were shared with colleges at the first annual conference with all college principals. While the methodology and quality of the condition survey were on occasions questioned, the findings were never seriously faulted.

It was, however, initially less than complete. Some local authorities would not let the surveyors into disputed buildings which colleges were expecting to occupy, because the local authority took the view that these buildings were still in its possession. The Education Assets Board was mandated to settle such disputes, but inevitably this took some time. Once these disputes had been settled, the buildings were surveyed, and the completed Hunter results are shown in Table 9.2.

It is important to remember that the Hunter survey was primarily a visual survey and neither the surveyors nor the engineers were permitted to cut into the fabric of a building to assess (say) the extent of dry rot or to measure the degree of failure of the electrical systems. They were, however, encouraged to take into account the responses of colleges to Circular 92/03 (FEFC, 1992a)

Table 9.2 *Final results of the Hunter surveys*

	Priority 1(a)	*Priority 1(b)*	*Priority 2*	*Priority 3*	*Total*
Works identified	£137,547,635	£230,882,866	£279,101,381	£204,087,040	£851,618,922
Less: non-eligible disputed and vired	£17,960,088	£22,862,045	£24,853,208		£65,675,341
Add: vired	£8,651,698	£11,013,059			
Net Hunter need	£128,239,245	£219,033,880	£254,248,173	£204,087,040	£785,943,581

Source: *The Hunter and Partners Surveys of Further Education Colleges,* April 1993 (see Note 1).

which had invited colleges to report on the known failures of legislative compliance in their buildings, including the verbal cautions and written warnings from the regulatory authorities, the works orders and closures relating to the buildings they expected to inherit, and the relevant acts of legislation and regulatory provisions. These identified failures in legal compliance were made known to the surveyors to be taken into account.

Colleges often went beyond this review, commissioning their own more thorough (intrusive) surveys. The usual challenge to the quality of the condition survey would allege that the fuller survey had shown that a building was more defective than had been reported. This could well have been true, but it was not usually possible to accept the new information since the condition of all colleges would have had to be reassessed on an intrusive basis to achieve like-with-like comparisons. Moreover, the funds available for remedying college buildings were hardly sufficient to deal with the problems identified in the visual survey.

A set of temporary quick fixes had to be developed to ensure immediate compliance with health and safety considerations while plans were put in place to deal with the underlying problems. These were:

- unsafe buildings or parts of buildings were taken out of use;
- circuit-interrupt fuseboxes were installed where wiring was dangerous;
- the areas below a roof with loose slates were made safer by fixing slate-catching fences around guttering;
- asbestos was resealed in locations where it had to be ultimately sealed thoroughly or removed.

The FEFC set aside a capital contribution of £67 million in the financial year 1993–4 (equal to £80 million in the sixteen-month period from incorporation on 1 April 1993 up to 31 July 1994) and each college was required to contribute 1.3 per cent of its income towards the solution of the topmost priority problems. These funds were distributed to colleges through a cash grant to all sector colleges of £40,000 in 1993–4, which was paid regardless of the level of Priority 1(a) needs (see Note 2). Colleges were required to apply for the cost of works beyond that level. This operated via a claims system which required proof of relevant expenditure. A tracking system was put in place to record the works which had been claimed and to produce regular quarterly updates. Progress in implementing this minor works programme was initially slow and advance payments equal to half of the Hunter 1(a) allocations owed to colleges were made in 1993–4 to accelerate the works. All of the most urgent problems were tackled during the first sixteen months.

Allocation of funds during the next two academic years – running at £100 million per year – also made sufficient money available to deal with all Hunter 1(b) problems (as defined in Note 2). A cash grant of £50,000 was made during both years to all colleges. Advance payments equal to half the cost of a specific planned list of works were also made to sector colleges during 1994–5. The Council did not require these health and safety works to be carried out in every case. Some buildings, where the cost of recovery was over £400 per square metre, were better demolished than repaired, for it was usually cheaper to replace these buildings than to bring them back to an acceptable condition (FEFC, 1993a). The running costs of old buildings was about £50 per square metre, while that of new buildings is about half the amount. Potential savings of £25 per square metre were therefore available if an old building was replaced. These savings could repay a loan of £250 per square metre, and adding this to the recovery costs of £400 per square metre, gave £650 per square metre, which was the all-in construction cost for classroom buildings in 1993–4.

There was no need to repair all the floorspace in the majority of colleges, for many colleges had more than was needed. Some colleges, such as Hugh Baird College in Bootle and the City of Liverpool Community College, prepared plans for the diversion of Hunter funds from buildings which were beyond economic repair into the construction of smaller, better and more fit-for-purpose facilities. These funds are listed as 'vired' in Table 9.2. Colleges were also encouraged to save Hunter funds wherever possible by bundling lists of works into larger projects and taking advantage of the consequent economies of scale. The funds saved could either be cascaded to the next priority of works (FEFC, 1993a) or, with the consent of the Council, be reapplied (or vired) to other allowable lists of building works. This procedure was widely used and there were 859 agreed virements by December 1998.

The objective was to attain, wherever possible, the best value for money in the expenditure of public funds. The average cost of recovery of buildings in the sector was about £38 per square metre to ensure legal compliance and about £60 per square metre to fix all problems in categories 1(a), 1(b) and 2 (as set out in Note 2). One-third of buildings had no significant problems, so the real cost of recovery was about 50 per cent higher in those buildings where problems existed. The overall costs of recovery of the sector were about £850 million if Priority 3 was included, which was less than a fifth of the £4.4 billion written-down replacement cost of the estate. There were also issues arising from the inheritance of the ministry's capital programme. All local authorities had been asked in Circular 92/17 (FEFC, 1992b) to identify major educational works which were either in progress or on which commitments had been made. In several cases – in Hackney and in Nottingham, for example – the commitment to a capital programme had been made by the ministry to the college, but not yet agreed with contractors. In these circumstances, and in the light of the substantial Hunter funding which was also available, the Council encouraged colleges to revisit their plans on a more radical basis.

Accommodation Strategies

The Hunter surveys had shown that many college buildings were not ideal for education. About 20 per cent of college buildings, about 10 per cent of the total area of the sector, were temporary constructions. Many of these buildings had not been adequately maintained and were on sufferance with the planning authorities as they were regarded as time-expired in terms of both planning consents and their suitability for educational use. Advice on accommodation strategies was offered in *A Good Practice Guide* (FEFC, 1996) which indicated how a college's estate might be transformed, over a three-year planning period, into a more fit-for-purpose resource for further education. In particular each college was asked to:

- assess the present condition and suitability for purpose of each building and site;
- examine the workplace utilization in buildings by conducting a representative survey and, from this, assess their need for floorspace;
- carefully examine options available to the college;
- prepare financial appraisals of the options to the standards of the Treasury's (1980) 'Green Book';
- set out a preferred strategy, with associated funding sources for identified investments, and a timescale for its implementation.

As might have been expected, many colleges struggled to produce adequate accommodation strategies, despite some help from consultants. Some strategies were based upon the acquisition of property without any proof of need. Others set out the options, but did not plump for one. Still others set out strategies which depended upon uncertain, sometimes very large, external funding. The major failing in most strategies was the lack of a credible linkage to the strategic and academic plans of the college – usually because there was no rigorous mapping from needs to facilities. They were helped by Circular 97/37 (FEFC, 1997) which gave guidance on the use of floorspace. After discussions with the FEFC, many accommodation strategies developed into working documents which were sufficient to make progress between the college and the Funding Council on property issues.

All accommodation strategies were required to be fully consistent with the strategic plans and financial forecasts of a college. Property assets were only the physical plant required to deliver the educational provision which was the mission of each college. If the educational mission of the college was not fully reflected in the accommodation strategy, that was unacceptable. Similarly, if an accommodation strategy was not demonstrably affordable, using funds which might reasonably become available, it could not be agreed. These fundamental principles were reflected in the concurrence procedures for projects within the Council. Each project had to be signed off by the regional director, the regional finance director and by the property adviser. The regional director had to certify the project as educationally sensible in terms of the needs analysis and educational provision of a college; the regional finance director had to certify that it was affordable and a sound project which would not prejudice the survival of the college; and the property adviser had to certify that it was acceptable value for money and an improvement in the property assets of, and acceptable space use in, the college. Each of these signatories had their specific criteria for consent to a project.

As the policy emphasis changed, so did the nature of projects. During the first three years of the sector, additional buildings were usually justified by growth or the replacement of very substandard teaching facilities. In later years, rationalization and downsizing was more often the reason. With the spread of student-centred learning, over half of all proposed projects after 1 April 1996 involved an increase in the floorspace of learning resource centres, often by adapting under-utilized assembly halls. About four-fifths of projects involved the sale or removal of buildings which no longer met their purpose.

The Private Finance Initiative (PFI)

The theory of the Private Finance Initiative was that the private sector was better equipped to design, build, finance and operate new buildings for colleges, charging a single annual lease payment to cover all the costs (leaving the colleges to get on with their core business, the provision of education). Furthermore, it was expected that if facilities managers were part of the project team, buildings would have lower lifetime running costs through built-in better design. The theory had considerable plausibility, but the practice fell some way short of these high expectations. Facilities managers were not usually in a lead position in project teams and bids often ignored the affordability of the project to the college. Despite considerable efforts by colleges, results of PFI project testing continued to be disappointing. This was unfortunate because the capital funds of the Council had been more than halved in the financial year 1996–7, in the confident expectation that private funds would step in to meet the shortfall.

Capital Project Loan Support Scheme

In November 1996, in line with the then government's expectations of the PFI, the FEFC was advised of a sharp cut in its capital funds from £126 million to £59 million. It had to come up with a scheme for making a little go a long way and it devised a system of capital project support. This had two parts. The first was that each college was entitled to a notional capital contribution, a proportion of capital project funds which varied inversely with the average level of funding (ALF) (see Chapter 4, p. 47). A college at or below the lowest tenth percentile of the ALF distribution could receive 75 per cent of the allowable capital costs of a project, but a college at the other end of the spectrum, with an ALF at or beyond the ninetieth percentile, would only receive 10 per cent. It was argued that colleges with high average levels of funding had the greatest ability to make savings and fund capital projects, while colleges with below-average levels of funding would be more dependent on FEFC funding of capital projects. These capital contributions could not be paid as grants, for the Council did not have the funds to pay for such a policy, but instead paid a contribution based on the interest rate of a fifteen-year loan.[4]

Property Improvements

During the period 1993–8, there was a change in the pattern of college property development. The early years were largely focused upon the recovery of college estates and in ensuring compliance with health and safety legislation. For the first two years, there was no FEFC funding for capital projects, so colleges had to find the money for any essential development from their own resources.[5] As the sector matured, the Hunter funding tapered off and limited funds became available to support projects. This development is illustrated in Table 9.3.

By December 1998, the colleges had committed over half a billion pounds (£503.7 million) to 287 major projects agreed by the Council and notional loan support of £236.2 million (involving first year payments of £25.7 million) was made available. At the time of writing £262.7 million of these projects had been completed and were being partly paid for by the Council, while 113 projects costing £240.8 million were still under construction. These will involve a Council contribution of £116 million when completed. About 60 per cent of the projects were funded by loans, but asset sales of about £100 million (20 per cent of the capital cost) paved the way for half a billion pounds worth of new major projects. In addition to these projects which were partly Council supported, colleges sought consent for 149 independently funded projects with a total value of £185 million. The total notified investment in property by colleges since incorporation has been £689 million for 436 projects.[7]

Most of these projects had been effectively financed by a reduction in the floorspace of the college estate and an improvement in its quality. New teaching buildings cost, on average, about £750 per square metre. The cost of repaying debt was about 10 per cent, so a college would need to save £75 per square metre of new build. Table 9.4 illustrates the required trade-off ratio between floorspace disposal and new build as required to fully fund a new build project by floorspace reductions.

Table 9.3 *Minor works (Hunter) funds and capital projects advised[1] to the Council (£ million)*

	Hunter Funding	College Capital Projects		Association Capital	
		new	*retrospective*	*funding*	*support[2]*
1993–4	65.7				
1994–5	72.7				
1995–6	58.5	49.6	81.3	58.2	4.1
1996–7	31.7	131.5	49.1	83.0	9.8
1997–8	27.0	54.6	33.0	42.8	5.4
1998–9(Jan)	14.0	84.7	19.8	52.2	6.4

Source: *Unpublished data from FEFC.*
Notes:
1 *See Note 6.*
2 *In the first year after completion.*

Table 9.4 *Capital project funding in FE colleges*

Running cost (£ per m²) of existing estate	Running cost (£ per m²) of new build	Ratio of disposal to new build	Savings per m² of new build
60	25	5:3	75
50	25	2:1	75
45	25	2.2:1	75
40	25	2.5:1	75
35	25	2.9:1	75
30	25	3.3:1	75
25	25	4:1	75

Thus supposing a college had 20,000 square metres of floorspace and needed only three-quarters of that. With average running costs of floorspace at £50 per square metre for the most expensive 50 per cent of the estate, the college could consider closing 10,000 square metres of floorspace and making gross savings of £500,000 per annum. If the college were to build 5,000 square metres at £750 per metre, the cost would be £3.75 million. As new buildings would have a running cost of about £25 per square metre, the running costs would be about £125,000 per year. The resultant annual net savings of £375,000 would be enough to repay a loan of £3.75 million. This does not take account of the fact that the new buildings could attract FEFC capital project support, and there might also be a sales receipt from the sale of assets.

The main property issue for a college over-provided with space has been how to use the same annual revenue costs in a more imaginative way. Given the reality of convergence of payments to colleges, the managers and governors of colleges have had to face many hard choices. If too much was being paid for an old, unfit-for-purpose, over-sized estate, then correspondingly less was available for teaching. If a college had substantial excess space, then new capital projects were always potentially affordable, costing no more than the existing level of revenue commitments to property. Furthermore, property savings were only part of the picture. More effective methods of teaching often doubled or trebled property savings, as rationalization created the opportunity to use centralized resources more efficiently. Capital projects usually improved college facilities for staff and students, college finances, and property running costs and space utilization.

Since incorporation, colleges have reduced their net floorspace by over a million square metres. Much of this reduction has been due to the removal of temporary buildings in the sector. About 300,000 square metres of poor floorspace have been taken out spontaneously, but the disposal of 700,000 square metres has been directly associated with projects. Actual disposal or demolition of the gross internal area of floorspace has accounted for about 1.3 million square metres, because colleges have built new about 600,000 square metres. A further million square metres of pre-existing buildings have been refurbished since incorporation. The net recorded area of the FEFC sector fell from 9.5 million square metres on incorporation to its current level of 8.2

million square metres through the process of improving the quality and reducing the width and cost of the colleges' estate.[8] Over a fifth of the colleges' estate has been rebuilt or upgraded in a major way through the innovative activity of college managers and governors. There are very few colleges which have not seen some improvement in the college campus since incorporation. Most colleges, however, are still at an intermediate point in their accommodation strategy, with part of the estate upgraded but with much still to be done. In just a few cases the entire estate has been rendered fit for purpose.

A Changing Agenda

The Blair government changed the focus of further education. There was increased emphasis on cooperation, collaboration and partnership, and less upon competition and duplication of provision. In property terms, colleges were encouraged to bring forward revisions of their accommodation strategies. The FEFC's projects criteria were changed to give more emphasis to floorspace rationalization. The government's inclusiveness agenda meant that colleges had to give greater priority to complying with the 1992 Disability and Discrimination Act. They have had to improve accessibility, including full access for all wheelchair-bound students and improved facilities for the sensory impaired, through the modification of buildings wherever this was necessary.

The implications of the new government's agenda are still being considered by colleges and the Council through a consultation on capital project support (FEFC, 1999). Some likely outcomes are clear already, however. The tempo of college property development is expected to accelerate in response to higher levels of funding. The Council is thinking in terms of raising its grant to perhaps 30 per cent of eligible project costs during the three years after consent has been given. Colleges have reported that, in response to the proposed higher capital funding, they would expect to bring forward about half a billion pounds worth of new capital projects during the next three years. This implies an activity level about 65 per cent higher than the historic average of about £100 million a year. College asset sales are also on a sharply rising trend. The increased capability of colleges to invest without reference to the Council is likely to produce new developments of about £250 million over the next three years. Together, these trends suggest that spending on college buildings could amount to £750 million over the next three years.

Conclusions

College managers and governors have greatly improved college campuses and educational facilities for students. There has been visible and measurable progress. Yet while much has been achieved, much remains to be done. The principals of colleges are signalling that they have embraced the present government's agenda of widening participation. As part of that response, the college campus, already much better than it was at incorporation, is forecast to change as much over the next three years as it did in the previous six.

Notes

1 The Hunter Surveys were not published, but copies have been lodged in the House of Commons Library, as well as the FEFC Archive.
2 Four levels of urgency were recognized:

Priority 1(a) Items of urgent work relating to breaches of legislation which should be undertaken as soon as possible, and certainly within one year of the date of the survey. These included works relating to the heath and safety of occupants, fire regulations and environmental health requirements, particularly when premises had been condemned under notice for the remedy of deficiencies.

Priority 1(b) Items of urgent repair which should be carried out within one year of the date of the survey. These items of work related to less serious breaches of legislation, urgent repairs and works to the listed parts of buildings.

Priority 2 Items of work to be undertaken within two years of the date of the survey to maintain the use of the building, including works to the structure or fabric of the building and general water-, wind- and weather-tightness. Such works should not be delayed, as failure to remedy within the two-year period may lead to further and expensive consequential damage to the interior of the building.

Priority 3 All items of work identified to be undertaken within five years of the date of the survey in order to maintain the condition of the building.

Some buildings (such as student or other residences, or commercial buildings) were not eligible to be funded because the rents or income raised were due to cover the repair costs.

3 The regulatory authorities (for example, the Fire Officer, the Health and Safety Executive) have powers to recommend improvements in building services (for example, in fire exits or electrical wiring) and if these recommendations are not taken seriously such authorities can enforce a compulsory improvement order, listing works which must be done within (say) 90 or 180 days.

4 The FEFC could pay 12.59 per cent of the notional capital contribution in the first year, reducing to 90 per cent of the first year's contribution in year 2, 81 per cent in year 3, and so on. The 12.59 per cent contribution was the calculated annual repayment rate of a fifteen-year loan at 9.25 per cent. When the bank rate subsequently fell, this rate was reduced in July 1998 to 11.86 per cent, which was the repayment rate of a fifteen-year loan at 8.25 per cent.

5 Possible sources included asset sales, from reserves, bank loans, Hunter virement and, in some cases, European Regional Development Funds (ERDF).

6 Under the terms of the first (May 1993) financial memorandum, projects in excess of £100,000 had to be advised to the Council for consultation or consent (paragraph 25 of Circular 93/23 refers to this – FEFC, 1993b). Under paragraph 24 of the revised financial memorandum (Circular 98/30 – FEFC, 1998) each college now required Council consent for projects exceeding 5 per cent of their income or £1 million, whichever is larger.

7 Projects below £100,000 did not need to be notified under the financial memorandum in force from incorporation until July 1997, and projects below 5 per cent of college turnover or £1 million (whichever was smaller) did not need the consent of the Council under the revised financial memorandum in force from 1 August 1997.

8 The net reduction in the college estate is actually only a million square metres because ineligible buildings not used for teaching (residential, farm, equestrian and horticultural) account for about 300,000 square metres.

References

FEFC (1992a) *Health and Safety Questionnaire*, Circular 92/03, Coventry: FEFC.

FEFC (1992b) *Capital Funding*, Circular 92/17, Coventry: FEFC.

FEFC (1993a) *Allocation of Minor Works Funds*, Circular 93/15, Coventry: FEFC.

FEFC (1993b) *Model Financial Memorandum*, Circular 93/23, Coventry: FEFC.

FEFC (1996) *Estate Management in Further Education Colleges: A Good Practice Guide*, London: HMSO.

FEFC (1997) *Guidance on Floor Space Management*, Circular 97/37, Coventry: FEFC.

FEFC (1998) *The Financial Memorandum*, Circular 98/30, Coventry: FEFC.

FEFC (1999) *Capital Project Support Consultation on Possible New Arrangements and Other Property-Related Matters*, Circular 99/06, Coventry: FEFC.

The Treasury (1980) *Economic Appraisal in the Public Sector*, London: HMSO.

10 Partnerships with the Community

Julian Gravatt and Ruth Silver

Schools are compulsory. Universities are selective. Colleges are the adaptive layer in the education system. Shock waves from the worlds of work, politics or the family often rebound off school walls or ivory towers, but frequently permeate further education. Colleges teach new recruits in their first week at work and recruit redundant workers on their first day on the dole. Colleges fill the gaps left by secondary schools. They offer chances to those on school-linked programmes and second chances to school leavers.

Universities recruit students from the colleges, both sixth-formers and mature students, and work through the colleges to extend their reach. Civil servants think they understand colleges, but rarely grasp the scale of the inter-action between them and government. Colleges reach beyond education and employment, to encompass the environment, transport, regeneration, trade and industry, crime and punishment, social security and health. Colleges employ hundreds, educate thousands and are generally the largest public-sector organi-zation in their locality after the district hospital and the town or county hall. College students often defy the neat patterns of policy-makers: they study part-time in their teens when they are expected to be studying full-time and they sometimes want to study full-time as adults when it is reckoned they should be studying part-time.

The hallmark of further education is its diversity. As a open system with permeable boundaries in a complex society, intended to be work-related, it has continually adapted. Courses open and close, qualifications start and finish, students join and leave to be replaced by others with different interests and goals. Colleges attempting to stand still tend to find themselves drifting back-wards. To survive, a college has to learn quickly how to tell the difference between a fashion and a forecast.

Work-relatedness is an important characteristic of further education, but it is not the defining one. Colleges are more than trade schools or professional proving grounds. Their identity and their purpose is rooted in the areas and communities which they serve. They were established by local authorities, not chambers of commerce. Community focus is also a fact of geography. Further education students tend to study where they live rather than live where they study, as university students often do. A further education college is generally chosen because it is nearest. Unlike schools, however, colleges do not have a captive population because there is always an alternative to attending. Colleges need to work inside their local communities, not just respond to them. They also need to build bridges with other organizations, as well as open doors to them. 'Community' and 'partnership' are two of the most powerful words in the current further education lexicon.

Community

Colleges are community organizations, are often the largest local building and have the potential to create a community focus which might otherwise be missing. Colleges have the ability to do more than offer qualifications and should aim to meet the needs of their communities in part by helping to organize them. Even the most active college may have difficulty doing this by itself – one reason for forming effective local partnerships. But colleges in seeking to serve their communities must beware of merely meeting the needs of well-organized groups – for example, local religious groups or residents' associations. These groups have a significant contribution in community formation – they generally have open membership and they organize individuals and families around shared concerns. Dealing only with organizations that have established themselves runs the risk of missing out the vulnerable who do not know how to use the system.

Several decades of change have called into question the very concept of community. It is difficult to sustain the concept of community based on place when so many neighbours are strangers to each other, and it is difficult to find communities in the workplace in a time of systematic economic change. The most visible communities are often those formed for specific purposes (for example, in opposition to a school closure) or around a shared activity (support of a football team), but these are communities that often fade as quickly as they appear. The strongest bonds are probably those of family and friends – these days a difficult foundation on which to build large networks.

Local versus National

It is only since 1992 that it has made sense to talk of a *national* further education sector with its own structure, its own leaders, its own lobbies and its own language. The pace of change since 1992 has been fast. Within a couple of years, the Funding Council and colleges have developed new funding, finance and quality-assurance systems; have opened new student markets and modes of attendance; and have introduced new contracts for most staff. The creation of a national system attuned to government agendas has contributed to a nostalgic version of the past in which the college was at the heart of its local community and uniquely responsive to its concerns.

But the reality was often rather different. For every college in close touch with its community, there were perhaps five that were controlled by cosy closed networks. The college principal with a well-connected manager or two, and perhaps the union branch official, would in effect run the college through informal contacts with key councillors and local authority officers. Decisions to change something – or more often not to change it – might just as easily be made in a local pub as in the college or County Hall. Those colleges could be said to be characterized by an almost masonic conservatism. Heads of department enjoyed great autonomy over such matters as timetabling and promotions. The beneficiaries of the further education system at this time were the staff, the employers and the students *in that order*. If the community came into view at all, it was in a separate department of the college or, more often, in a separate part of the local authority – its adult education service.

This comfortable world came to an end with the establishment of the Further Education Funding Council (FEFC) with a remit to fund, regulate and improve further education. The FEFC's reorganization started with finance, property and payroll systems in 1992–3. It moved on to personnel and student administration in 1994. It has extended into quality assurance in the years since. In all cases, the FEFC has consulted with colleges about its objectives, has introduced new data-collection systems, and has introduced new rewards and penalties. Colleges that do not return data do not get paid. For example, the FEFC withholds money from colleges which do not return financial forecasts, accommodation strategies and student data returns. Colleges have had therefore to organize themselves so as to be more openly accountable.

The FEFC took the view that the purpose of the colleges was to meet student needs. It made this explicit in various ways, but most significantly in its approaches to funding and quality assurance. From the very beginning, the FEFC's funding policy has been to respect individual student choice and to fund colleges that successfully respond to those choices. Colleges that recruit and retain students gain more money; colleges that don't, don't. The views of third parties in this process have been secondary. Colleges have been encouraged to pay attention to the needs of employers and Training and Enterprise Councils (TECs), but these views have made no difference to the level of FEFC funding. Making student choice the key principle has won widespread support and it has helped focus colleges' attention on their most important people – their students.

The FEFC underlined its student-focus in the way it handled strategic planning. It made it clear that it was a funding, not a planning, council and left colleges to write their own plans. The old local authority rules came to be replaced by four new ones:

1 Colleges could claim growth funding (the 'demand-led element'; see Chapter 4, p. 39) for any type of student from any part of the country. Growth funds were restricted to full-time students in 1993–4, but were extended to all types of student in 1994–5.
2 Colleges could claim funding for fee remission for students wherever recruited – a move forward from previous local authority policies that linked concessions to location.
3 Colleges could claim funding for courses from any section of the national tariff without needing prior approval to open courses.

4   Learning was not restricted to the college campus. If the student wouldn't come to college, then the college was encouraged to go to the student.

New Freedoms, New Communities

The new approach allowed colleges to write their own missions and identify their own communities. It took time for this freedom to sink in, but when it did colleges seized the new opportunities. Business-minded colleges took to marketing in a big way. Each August advertising campaigns hit the hoardings. The proverbial three buses that come along at once could easily be publicizing three different colleges.

In the new context, some colleges located their communities geographically and made new links with the people living immediately around them. But others moved beyond geography and defined their community in different and surprising ways. 'Community' came to mean, in these terms, social or religious groups, or the employees of large companies or networks of small employers, or nationally organized groups of volunteers – for example, the St John Ambulance Brigade or Red Cross volunteers. Even scuba divers became in these terms a 'community'.

There may have been an element of justification after the event in some of this. Colleges that are good at marketing their courses to diverse groups of students are often equally good at marketing their corporate image to the Funding Council. In such cases, they needed to persuade the authorities that their latest wheeze was a carefully considered part of their strategy to serve a defined community. However, in a climate of growing scepticism, obvious funding contrivances have rarely lasted beyond a couple of audit visits or funding changes. The point remains that incorporation has led to the crossing of old geographical boundaries. Table 10.1 shows the proportions of students on courses franchised outside the college's region.

There are no comparable published figures for in-house provision offered by colleges to out-of-region students. This has always existed in colleges offering specialist courses to a wide catchment area, but nothing on the scale of the franchising boom. Franchising grew from almost zero in 1993–4 to a peak in 1996–7, which was the last year of the demand-led element and unrestricted growth. Since then, franchising has fallen back and colleges have been encour-

Table 10.1 *Franchising outside region (in thousands)*

Year	Total funded by FEFC	Total on franchised courses	Franchised outside college's region
1994–5	2,600	130 (5%)	n/a
1995–6	3,050	492 (16%)	167 (5%)
1996–7	3,549	740 (21%)	232 (7%)
1997–8	3,707	687 (19%)	169 (5%)

Source: *FEFC, 1998a, 1998c.*

aged by government and by the FEFC to concentrate more on 'local priorities'. The FEFC confirmed this policy by establishing a Local Priorities Group in 1998 to agree the ground-rules. This has changed the emphasis somewhat, but the national outlook will remain. Many colleges with large franchises have already altered their approach by bringing the courses in-house and by employing staff directly all over the country. The new University for Industry and on-line learning are likely to give added impetus to the growth of out-of-region provision.

A Business-Like Approach

The responsiveness of colleges to student and community needs has been among the aspects of provision to be inspected. In the first cycle (1994–8), the grades given were consistently higher on average than for other cross-college areas, with in 1996–7, for example, 91 per cent of colleges being rated 'outstanding' or 'good' (FEFC, 1997). This positive verdict is contrary to the generally negative perception of colleges as unaccountable businesses.

Adverse comments about accountability sometimes come from local people and organizations excluded by the new arrangements – for example, staff or councillors who are no longer on governing bodies. But it would be wrong to see this is as being the only basis for their criticisms. At the same time as colleges were becoming more responsive to student demand, they were also taking a more business-like approach to course provision. Colleges are at root in a mass-production business, where one member of staff (the lecturer) serves twenty or so customers (the students) simultaneously. The costs to an individual customer (the student) and to the public purse can only be minimized by organizing the customers into groups above a certain size. In this it is like the travel industry. The marginal income earned from each extra person recruited to an existing group exceeds the marginal costs. In order to cover fixed costs, there is a constant financial incentive to concentrate on popular areas to maximize returns. Linking funding to individual students increases the marginal income for extra students and makes more popular courses perform even better financially than unpopular ones.

Incorporation happened at the same time as strict public expenditure control which has placed demands on colleges to do more for less and to use their assets more efficiently. As a result colleges have been under financial pressure to do at least four things.

1   Reduce the number of small groups by merging them or closing the entire course.
2   Develop and expand courses which are popular or financially rewarding.
3   Move courses out of under-used buildings so that these can be vacated and sold to release money for investment in the other sites.
4   Develop new forms of delivery to move away from the mass-production economics of the course; most innovation has been in the area of IT workshops, on-line learning and employer-franchising but has not, as yet,

changed the way in which the majority of college-based courses are delivered.

Few colleges make decisions solely on financial grounds, but the need to generate income cannot be ignored. A large minority of colleges have run regular deficits, while many more have only avoided them by tight cost-control. Individual colleges have therefore taken decisions to close marginal courses and to close outlying buildings. Local protests which link these closures to accountability, such as the protests in Wirral, have often missed the point about the overall financial context. Inner London provides a very good example of the impact of the policies described by George Edwards in the preceding chapter. By 1997 the twelve colleges had reduced the number of buildings that they use from over eighty to sixty-eight, and there are plans to rationalize to forty by the year 2001. Contraction here has probably had to go further than elsewhere because of past neglect but, nevertheless, it is a reasonable estimate that more than a hundred colleges have withdrawn from some of their buildings in the past five years. Faced with choices between responsiveness to national policies implemented by the Funding Council and responsiveness to particular local communities, colleges have followed the national lead and aimed to satisfy the maximum number of students that they can afford to while balancing their budgets.

Responding to the Community

The attention given in further education to meeting community needs comes at a time when it is increasingly difficult to pin communities down. Communities of work and place have been destroyed by relentless economic change. Coal mining is a conspicuous example, but the change has been pervasive. The large businesses and trade unions that used to take a lead in local communities have been undermined, leaving large gaps. These have been only partially filled by the local public sector or new employers. Communities have fragmented and diversified, leaving an increasing role for colleges in meeting the needs of the disadvantaged – people at various ages without work or qualifications.

Incorporation, the approach of the FEFC and the stance of Conservative governments gave colleges a measure of freedom. Community needs had to be met but, so long as students were being recruited, retained and qualified, colleges could work out how best to do it themselves. There was encouragement to identify and meet the needs of local employers, but this was not translated into any change in funding approaches. The present Labour government has taken a more determined approach to this issue, which has been reflected in a number of its decisions including:

- the allocation of money for widening participation;
- more emphasis on communities in its various regeneration bids, including a New Deal for Communities;
- proposals to increase the accountability of colleges to their communities.

The freedom given at the outset to colleges to define their communities and to respond to their needs has permitted a great deal of flexibility which was lacking before incorporation. This has allowed colleges to develop in new ways and with new structures to meet community needs, without having to seek prior permission to do so. The element knitting these different approaches together is often partnership – the multi-purpose solution to public service problems.

Partnership

Partnership is an umbrella term for a great variety of arrangements, but in the broad sense partnerships are attractive to government because:

* they bring local organizations together to deliver shared goals;
* they are a way of bridging the public and private sector, and of harnessing private sector investment to deliver public goals;
* they can be formed – and dissolved – quickly;
* they make it possible to deliver new programmes without the costs of setting up new organizations or of restructuring existing ones.

Figure 10.1 *Partnerships to deliver education and training*

Form of partnership	Other partner(s)	Typical purpose
HE franchise	University	Higher education courses in colleges
FE franchise	Training providers Employers Community groups	Further education course in new locations
Adult education	LEAs Adult Education Service Schools	Adult education
Sixth-form consortium	Secondary schools	Courses for 16–18-year-olds in schools and colleges
School links	LEAs Schools	Provision for disaffected 14–15-year-olds outside school
Youth or adult training	TECs	Training provision for 16–18-year-olds or unemployed adults
European education, training and youth programmes	Colleges in EU	Education exchanges and cooperation

The concept of 'partnership' has developed rapidly since the early 1990s as an alternative to pure market-based approaches to the public sector. These market-based approaches were developed by Conservative governments in the 1980s and included deregulation, privatization of services, compulsory competitive tendering and public sector internal markets. Alternatives based on partnership already existed but they grew quickly in the early 1990s. Michael Heseltine's Department of Environment, for example, allocated large sums of money to City Challenge which depended on partnerships of local authorities and local businesses. The model of inviting competitive bids from 'partnerships' has spread to other parts of government, particularly since the election of a Labour government keen to try out new initiatives. The present government has also seen partnership as a way of moderating the excesses of public service competition and of developing new approaches in social services, crime prevention and job creation.

Further education's involvement in numerous different public services means that colleges contribute to a variety of partnerships in a variety of roles. Figure 10.1 attempts to summarize the range of partnerships by the intended beneficiaries and Figure 10.2 by particular provision and projects. The lists are by no means exhaustive and may not do justice to the scale or complexity of some

Figure 10.2 *Partnerships to coordinate provision or projects*

Form of partnership	Other partners	Typical purpose
New Deal	Employment service, TECs, employers	Coordination of training provision for unemployed 18–24-year-olds
Single Regeneration Budget	LEAs, TECs, developers, housing associations	Training provision as part of regeneration programme
Collaboration fund	Other FE colleges and institutions	Cooperation between FEFC-funded institutions
Wider collaboration fund	Universities, employers	Cooperation between organizations engaged in education and training
Widening participation	Other colleges, LEAs	Cooperation between local organizations to widen participation
Strategic partnership (Circular 98/23)	LEAs, TECs, other colleges	Cooperation, focusing on 16–19 provision and achievement
TEC-led programmes	TECs, training providers	Cooperative training
Education action zones	LEAs, schools, businesses	Cooperation to improve school and pupil performance

partnerships, particularly those involving regeneration. There has, for example, been a bidding round of the Single Regeneration Budget (DETR, 1999) each year since it was initiated under the Conservative government in 1995–6, and each one may involve as many as three projects in a local authority area, depending on the extent of local deprivation. The lists also do not mention the numerous *ad hoc* alliances formed by colleges to promote their interests, including college-specific lobbying groups and local groups set up to achieve specific objectives. At the last count, Lewisham College was a member of twelve such partnerships in addition to thirty-four of the types listed in the figures.

Successful Partnerships

Partnerships are now so common in further education that you can almost guarantee that at any time of the day at least one member of staff will be engaged in communication with one of the college's partners. The late 1990s has become an era of compulsory collaboration in which colleges have had to form partnerships to secure funding. The aim may have been to stem competition and to maximize the value of local efforts, but there is a risk that imposition dampens the spirit that makes the best partnerships work. Figure 10.3 gives an analysis of the elements that have contributed to successful partnerships at Lewisham College.

The partnerships that have worked at Lewisham College and, we suspect, at other colleges are those that have evolved from shared aims, desires or intentions, which have become a *shared purpose* to achieve a particular end, for example, local improvements or curriculum innovation. Partnerships that are *conscious* acts of cooperation between two organizations make it possible for staff at the front-line of delivery to understand the purpose of the joint working. *Voluntary* action to achieve these aims, *respecting differences*, makes it possible for colleges to commit themselves from the governors and principal downwards. Organizations are collections of people – they move in directions that make sense to the majority and it is for those with influence to accept or resist.

Figure 10.3 *Successful partnerships*

Work	Don't work
Shared purpose	Forced geographically
Conscious acceptance	No trust
Voluntary	No guarantees
Respect difference	Own agendas
Shared values	Forced into frameworks
Outward-looking	Resist change
Allowed to evolve	Over-control by external audit

Shared values are also important and a reason why some of the most effective college partnerships link colleges that are at a considerable distance from one another. Organizational partnerships need to be *outward looking* to be effective because otherwise the cooperation has no purpose – meetings, visits and cooperation need to be focused outside the organizations involved, not simply navel-gazing. Finally, the relationship needs to be *allowed to evolve*. The regeneration partnerships that work best are those which have developed through several rounds of bidding and programmes to establish what is effective and what is not.

Partnerships which don't tend to work are those that are *forced geographically*. Neighbouring colleges that wish to cooperate will do so; those that have differences will not act harmoniously even if pressured to do so because it looks convenient on a map. Some partnerships have *no trust* – something colleges in south London discovered when South Thames Training and Enterprise Council was forced into receivership in December 1994 (Nash, 1995). This left four colleges unsecured creditors for £2 million of completed work, because a public body had been mismanaged and the government was not prepared to underwrite it. *Lack of guarantees* has bedevilled many franchising partnerships in further education because colleges have been unable to anticipate the twists and turns of funding guidance and have left partners high and dry when new regulations come out. Partnerships have also failed when one organization has its *own agendas* which preclude exchange and support. Colleges frequently find this when they try partnerships with local councils or universities that will not accept alternative interpretations of need or priority.

Partnerships that are *forced into frameworks* also often founder on the differences between organizations that are not always apparent on paper. Frameworks cause a particular problem where they demand exclusivity, for example, an insistence that a college with an extended catchment area work with a single TEC or local council, or the requirement for single contracts, for example, with a university.

Partnerships constructed as a way of *resisting reorganization* also frequently fail because of the unspoken agenda that prevents full cooperation. This is a regular problem with partnerships for the sixteen- to eighteen-year-old age group which link many secondary schools and colleges in the delivery of A-levels and GNVQs on a local basis. It is likely to be an issue with the Local Learning Partnerships set up in 1999, when they come to consider issues like student support.

The final enemy of effective partnership is *over-control by external audit*, a recurrent and growing problem in the public sector, where increasing demand for public accountability has overlapped with the drive for efficiency to give public sector auditors tremendous power, without having to justify their expense. Audit and partnerships make uneasy bedfellows when an insistence on implementing audit regimes results in a partnership becoming subject to two different audits.

Lifelong Learning Partnerships

Partnerships moved to a new stage in 1999, with the establishment of Lifelong Learning Partnerships in all parts of England for post-16 education and training. There is a political imperative for the DfEE to have in place structures to anticipate the demands created by the Regional Development Agencies. There are dangers that this will result in the partnerships being set up quickly, without full account being taken of the current organizational and geographical complexities of current provision.

The speed with which Lifelong Learning Partnerships are being implemented is in contrast to the long period of planning that has preceded them. The FEFC has been working at a national level to develop 'local strategic partnerships'. This work started with a much publicized rapprochement with the Local Government Association (LGA) in October 1997 and has developed since then to include the TECs and to produce a wide-ranging set of proposals (FEFC, 1998a). The Circular states:

> There is no intention to impose frameworks or new layers of bureaucracy. However it is increasingly important that there should be local partnerships in place in all areas of the country and that, whatever other functions they might serve, all partnerships demonstrate a number of common features.

Among the common features identified are:

- defined geographical areas determined nationally;
- national protocols on who should be involved, sharing of information, standardization of procedures and rules on appointment to governing bodies.

All of these proposals secured majority support in the consultation, and the government has developed and extended the ideas and taken them forward as Lifelong Learning Partnerships. Following an announcement by the Secretary of State, the Department (DfEE, 1999) has circulated its Lifelong Learning Partnerships Remit. This makes clear that what is envisaged are partnerships which will be responsible for coordinating local action in learning provision for adults and workforce development, as well as provision for sixteen- to nineteen-year-olds. The intention is that local partnerships should seek approval of the Government Offices and there should have been nationwide coverage by September 1999. The government has earmarked £2 million for monitoring and evaluation of the new student support arrangement through them. They may also assume responsibilities for advancing local mergers, for assisting the allocation of regeneration money, for approving council and college plans, and for organizing local University for Industry (UfI) hubs.

The committee room activity around partnership looks very much an alternative to making difficult organizational changes (for example, the sort of tertiary reorganizations that local authorities managed before 1992). One outcome will be more sharing of information at a local level, but this would not be so necessary if there was more action on data collection at a national level. The main obstacles to data sharing are different systems within the DfEE – a situation exacerbated by New Deal systems.

However, it is likely that the very existence of the partnerships will give them a role. We were here ten years ago at the birth of Training and Enterprise Councils. TECs were created mainly to enable employers to cooperate in identifying local skills needs, but within two years found themselves managed mainly by transferred civil servants running million-pound unemployment training programmes. TECs were also hamstrung from the very beginning by inadequate thought given to geographical issues, which resulted in many areas being too small to carry through their remit effectively.

The design work on strategic partnerships is reminiscent of what happened with the TECs and it is conceivable that, like TECs, they will become a dumping ground. One of their first responsibilities could well be the administration of 16–18 maintenance grants and an assortment of special funds passed on from elsewhere (for example, widening participation funding). It will only take a small sum of public money routed through the partnerships for the whole panoply of public audit and funding controls to follow.

An Alternative: Co-construction

Our argument, from experience, is that further education needs to tread carefully in the matter of partnerships. Partnerships help organizations achieve objectives and add value to their activities, but they are not a panacea for all public sector problems. Too many partnerships established too hastily with too many overlapping aims just add to the confusion and complexity that gets in the way of education and training. It cannot be healthy for either democracy or efficiency to have so many agencies involved with no one in charge apart from the overview taken by ministers at the DfEE. It cannot be beneficial for accountability to make colleges responsible for their actions, but then to force them into compulsory collaboration as an alternative to quango rationalization.

Perhaps there is no choice but to do things in this way, in which case colleges need to take what opportunities they can to use partnerships constructively for the benefit of their students and their wider community. A college which aims to be a learning organization will open itself to partnerships and see itself as an open system with porous boundaries. Rather than take a narrow commercial approach in which every decision and relationship is judged on financial grounds, the college needs to start with its objectives, then work out how these can be financed.

Given that colleges are public organizations established to meet community needs, and given the fragmentation and ineffectiveness of many community organizations, perhaps an early objective for any college would be to help construct its local and regional community. Colleges are communities themselves of students, staff and stakeholders. Through effective partnerships, colleges can work with other organizations to build and strengthen their wider community. We call this 'co-construction'.

Partnerships with the Community

Further education is nothing without its students. Its students are little without their families and communities, which define their experience, education and identity. Further education meets community needs through a network of long-established community-based institutions called colleges, which organize students into yet more communities – the course groups, tutor groups and social groups that define its existence. Individual programmes and on-line learning are already changing those groups, but all the evidence is that the most effective learning is shared. On-line learning creates new ways of sharing (e-mail rather than personal contact), but it does not change the fundamentals.

The relationship between colleges and communities has sometimes been misjudged. This happens where colleges narrowly serve limited communities (the white male apprentices of the 1960s) and has often led to excluded communities setting up alternative organizations – with or without local government help. The failures of colleges to serve the needs of employers and employees has similarly resulted in a growth of private providers. Colleges have now risen to this challenge and most people in further education recognize the importance of community involvement. There may be arguments over which community and how to define it, but the importance of the task is not in question.

Communities can be said to start at home. Colleges are themselves communities of students, staff and stakeholders. They are one of the largest local communities in most areas. In order to meet the external challenge of meeting community needs, colleges have to take on the internal challenge of building and strengthening their own internal relationships. This is not easy. Colleges are collections of disparate groups covering vast ranges of age, class and ethnicity. Most students are non-residential and part-time. Nevertheless, the challenge is there and it is one that colleges must take up if they are aiming to make the difference that justifies their existence and their future.

Lewisham College expresses its approach to this in its mission to be 'More than a College', offering 'More than a Qualification'. Our aim is that those studying with us shall be more than students. This is why we involve so many of them in the organization of college life – whether as sub-contractors or as 'study buddies'. Many colleges do similar things, but may not necessarily articulate it in the way we do. The challenge for further education at the turn of the millennium is for all colleges to express their community role, both internal and external, so as to justify their existence both now and in the future.

References

DETR (1999) *DETR Annual Report 1999, The Government's Expenditure Plans 1999–2000 to 2001–02*, Cmnd 4204, London; The Stationery Office.

DfEE (1999) *Secretary of State's Letter to Chief Education Officers, College Principals, TEC Chief Executives, Careers Service Chief Executives and Attached Partnership Remit*, 6 January.

FEFC (1997) Chief Inspector's Annual Report, *Quality and Standards in Further Education in England 1996–97*, Coventry: FEFC.

FEFC (1998a) *Strategic Plans, Including Financial Forecasts, 1997–98 to 1999–2000*, Circular 98/06, Coventry: FEFC.

FEFC (1998b) *Standards, Accountability and Cost-Effectiveness: A New Partnership in Post-16 Education and Training*, Circular 98/23, Coventry: FEFC.

FEFC (1998c) Report from the Inspectorate, *Collaborative Provision: National Survey Report*, Coventry: FEFC.

Nash, I. (1995) 'Inquiry plea after TEC goes bust', *Times Educational Supplement*, 3 February.

11 Widening Participation

Annette Zera and Tom Jupp

The widening participation debate provides the opportunity for further education to create a new brand, a new identity, a new direction and purpose – one
that everyone can understand. Colleges have been challenged by the Kennedy
report (1997) to think again about their fundamental purpose and reassess
'what is further education for?' It is no longer good enough to say that further
education isn't school and it isn't university. Similarly, making much of the rich
diversity and multiplicity of the range of provision from sixth-form to agricul-
tural colleges won't wash either. Both statements are undeniable, but neither
amounts to a definition of purpose and, in the words of Isaiah, 'without a
vision people will perish'.

It is interesting to speculate on the reasons why the sector apparently lacks
identity and confidence in the public and political arena. Perhaps it simply
reflects the lack of confidence felt by so many of our students. A more likely
explanation, however, is the general reluctance to claim precedence for one
purpose above all others. The college sector is cautious when it comes to
making ideological statements, and perhaps with good reason. Helena Kennedy
was derided when she suggested that students in further education were disadvantaged compared to their peers in higher education and that the priorities
needed to be rebalanced. London colleges won no friends in the rest of the
country when they pleaded they had higher than average operating costs as a
result of high prices in the Capital and the large volume of students at or below
Level 2 on the qualifications framework (see Chapter 5). But perhaps it is the
obfuscation of the term 'widening participation' that says most about the lack
of clarity and purpose. We don't literally mean 'widening participation', which
could be met equally by putting on Level 3 Golf Studies or setting up franchises with Eton. We mean something more precise: targeting people who have
had the least benefit from the education system. It is a reflection of the sector's
need to please all the people all the time that we find it impossible to be direct
about our priorities.

In our view, the defining mission of further education is to raise the national
level of success at Level 3 (the equivalent of passing two A-levels) to include
people who have previously failed to succeed at Level 2. It is our contention
that these people, who have had the least benefit from the education system,

provide the central purpose and focus for the sector. While we believe there needs to be an entitlement to education and training to at least Level 3, most people, in fact, fail to reach Level 2. Pearce and Hillman (1998) report that if someone even partially succeeds at Level 2 they are more likely to progress to Level 3 and beyond. There is therefore a strong case, in our view, for defining the sector's mission as getting people to and through Level 2. This could be embraced by all colleges leading, as it would, to much greater success at Level 3 for all.

Who is Excluded?

One of the current truisms is that society and the economy needs as many people as possible to be qualified to degree level. Consequently considerable attention has been paid to expanding numbers in higher education. However, lower down the education hierarchy – despite a huge and acknowledged waste of potential (AC and OFSTED, 1993) – less focus has been placed on progression and extending participation. This is where we find the evidence of the mass failure of the British education system. It is at Levels 1 and 2 that the majority of people in this country 'get stuck'. The introduction of GCSEs should have ended the division between O-levels and the rest which excluded many from the education ladder at an early stage. However O-levels have been replaced by the benchmark of four or five GCSE grade A*–Cs and there remains a majority of people for whom this is still the critical barrier. It is therefore at the entry stages that there are serious problems of non-participation, retention and underachievement.

For our purposes, lack of a Level 2 qualification defines educational exclusion with all its social and economic consequences. We believe the following overlapping groups are disproportionately represented in this category. They should therefore comprise the main targets for widening access:

- people with a background of failure in the school system, which includes the majority of school leavers in inner-city areas;
- adults with no formal qualifications;
- people with learning difficulties;
- adults who are unemployed or in caring roles;
- adults in manual occupations;
- men and women living in poor housing;
- people with difficult family circumstances, including the experience of being in care;
- particular ethnic groups, such as white working-class men, and men and women from Bangladeshi and African-Caribbean communities;
- non-aspirational young women;
- people in prison.

Making Connections

Academic ability and social class are well recognized as the main determinants of educational participation (Steedman and Green, 1996). Those from higher socio-economic groups tend to be plugged into constructive learning from birth and rightly demand an educational system which meets social and economic expectations. There is a direct alignment between their personal aspirations and the benefits of the education system. People from the middle to high socio-economic groups living in the inner cities go to great lengths to maintain connections by choosing to buy education or homes in the catchment areas of good schools. These opportunities are obviously not available to all. To genuinely widen access therefore, we need to create as a birthright a good start in life through education.

Those who have failed at school have an even greater need to be reconnected to the education system in a positive way. They may have to be lured, encouraged, enticed into something that promises not to repeat their first dismal experiences of failure. It is unlikely, however, that people who fail pre-16 will have the connections and resources to take them back to college or into a job with a good training scheme off their own bat – they need someone to come and find them.

So how do we go about finding and then encouraging people who have failed? How do we persuade them it is worth trying again? How do we get past the adage, so well expressed in *Learning Works* (Kennedy, 1997), that 'if at first you don't succeed, you don't succeed'? Further education marketing people recognize that word-of-mouth and personal connections are the key influences that can attract excluded students. In the past, door-to-door selling to working-class people was powerful in building movements (the Labour party) and empires (life insurance). The mass expansion of adult basic education in London under the Inner London Education Authority in the 1970s was due, in part, to a coordinated network of community educators pounding the streets in search of customers.

Outreach work is still just about alive in some community education settings, where tutors work the housing estates, knock on doors and talk to people about the possibilities. Perhaps for the future we can devise a mix of something more sophisticated, but equally personal, to make the connections. We need to engage the active involvement of an army of well-briefed outreach workers (health visitors, social workers, probation officers, youth workers, school teachers, personnel officers and others) to explain that it's worth keeping connected. The University for Industry pilots in cold-calling and setting up learning centres in shopping centres provide a more sophisticated approach. Storylines in soaps and dedicated media campaigns have a part to play. One of the most successful media campaigns of all, *On the Move*, gave hundreds of thousands of adult literacy students the courage to pick up the phone and get help. Whatever the marketing approach taken to getting the message across, it will need to be reinforced by consistent personal contact and enduring support if students are to succeed.

It's hard to be an adult student with domestic commitments, financial responsibilities and competing pressures. Similarly, it is tough to be young and streetwise, yet lacking basic skills. Previously excluded students need encouragement and, unlike those from more affluent households, are less likely to have easy access to supportive role models. They need people with time to talk after the lesson, time to listen, time to encourage, time to help with organizing the work, time to discuss aspirations. The most appropriate people, but regrettably rarely with the time, are teachers.

Over the last five years, the college managements' discussions with teaching unions have focused almost exclusively on the quantity of time that teachers spend teaching students and have scarcely discussed the quality. The role of teachers obviously varies greatly depending on who and what is being taught. Teachers faced with the job of inspiring people who have previously failed to reach Level 2 have among the most demanding of jobs. Students who have failed in the past need someone to be there for them. These are the most unreliable group of students, the people least likely to attend consistently, the people most likely not to deliver their coursework on time, the people most likely just to leave with no explanation. They need to be rung at home when they don't come to college. They need someone to stay behind after class and sort out their personal difficulties with, for example, the Benefits Agency.

Who is going to care enough to keep them connected? In many cases it is the teachers. The same teachers who, over the past fifteen years or so, have been hugely burdened with administrative loads which waste their time. The same teachers who have been constantly reminded that they are not to be trusted. We need to reinvent the values of teaching and reassert the professionalism of teachers. Nowhere is this more true than for those working with students in Basic Education (FEFC's Programme Area 10) who tend to have the worst employment conditions of all teachers. The majority are employed on a part-time basis and often on low rates of pay, and this despite teaching arguably the most challenging students.

Teachers are, of course, not the only people who can help and support students. For example, at City College, Birmingham, everyone contributes: all staff spend time as mentors or helpers working with college students or children in the local community. In City and Islington College, mentors from local communities are having an impact on raising students' motivation and self-esteem. Everyone needs someone to be interested in them and, if a student doesn't have that, it needs to be provided or the student may fail. Informed interest in what the student is engaged in, which so many of us take for granted, is an inescapable component in raising expectations, aspirations and achievement.

The essential contribution of parenting and home support for children is now widely recognized, but support for young people and adults is just as important, particularly if they have never had it. And this is likely to be true for many of our priority students. If we are serious about building a mass movement in further education with the majority progressing beyond the second level of the Qualifications Framework, then we have to provide this extra dimension. And the support roles cannot be provided on a voluntary basis or all fall to teachers. We need advice and guidance staff, learning assistants, perhaps an army of mentors. People giving support not only to provide encouragement but to understand what is involved in learning and in the course and qualification that a particular student is attempting to achieve. So we need to organize and train a new cadre of support workers, and to some extent this is already happening. At the same time we also need to reassert the values of the teaching profession and encourage new entrants, from diverse educational backgrounds, to be the inspiring teachers of tomorrow.

Over 40 per cent of those entering post-16 education on the first two rungs of the Qualifications Framework fail to complete or fail to gain a qualification within the standard timescale (FEFC, 1998a). Their failure is usually a second attempt at this level and a repeat of the failure from earlier years. All too often second attempts, far from inspiring, motivating and encouraging people to aim high, end up as even more discouraging. Too many people spend a term, a year or even longer, and gain no or low results. This is a waste of people's lives, public money and our skills potential. And at the heart of this problem is not, as many would have us believe, poor teaching or poor management, but our poor qualification system.

Qualifications

Unfortunately, qualifications have for some time been a major arena for the exercise of power and prejudice in contemporary politics. Politicians who have been served well by A-levels seemed disinclined to abandon them. Meanwhile, there are endless discussions on post-16 content and process, and inevitably we return again and again to the need for a credit framework – an issue that just seems too difficult for either politicians or educationalists.

The reform of post-16 qualifications has been the subject of debate for at least the past fifteen years (see Chapter 5). There is now an urgent need to bring some order to the bewildering and chaotic world of qualifications. Only the most exclusive sacred cows (A-levels and degrees) are understood at all, while the huge collection of arcane acronyms that label the majority of qualifications are an inaccessible mystery to most people. The lack of understanding of the worth and content of different qualifications contributes to their lack of value in the eyes of everyone – students, teachers, employers, university admissions staff. At the very least, a system that allowed students to accumulate and transfer credits would make some sense of some 17,000 existing qualifications (FEFC, 1997b) by mapping and including their value within an overall structure (one of the failed ambitions of the NVQ system).

It is now widely accepted (not quite, but almost, by that bastion of the educational establishment: the university vice-chancellors) that our current arrangements are not fit for their purpose. There is growing belief among practitioners that an over-arching credit framework that would break down achievements into modules that could then be accumulated, will eventually be introduced. There is no lack of ideas of how to devise an alternative: they will be able to draw on models ranging from the International Baccalaureate to more modest rearrangements of the deck chairs which is how we see the recommendations of the Dearing Review (1996). Tony Henry, Principal of City College, Birmingham, is leading a group of colleges with a vision of a 'signature qualification' (Mager, 1999) for which all learning credits are a step towards an Associate Degree, a title redolent of educational status and personal dignity. Why shouldn't everyone have a slice of this cake, even if they might never achieve the whole? One of the successes of further education is that it has demonstrated that it is possible to devise a creative alternative qualification for adult returners, access-to-higher-education students, so why not for everyone?

Access courses were pioneered in the 1970s as an alternative to heavily knowledge based GCE A-levels. They were designed specifically to widen participation in further education and access to higher education. The accreditation arrangements place emphasis on the design of appropriate curricula and so are powerful tools of curriculum and staff development. Course design and accreditation is modelled on the old Council-for-National Academic-Awards (CNAA) model of course approval, with internal and external moderation through the National Open College Network (NOCN). The FEFC recently acknowledged the NOCN as one of the four main vocational awarding bodies.

The growth of NOCN qualifications at all levels reflects the needs identified by colleges to produce their own qualifications in order to provide a more appropriate alternative for students. It is, after all, what universities have always done in devising and awarding their own degrees and it seems odd that colleges, with their considerable buying power and infrastructure of quality control, don't combine together more to exploit the same freedoms. At the moment the sector acquiesces to an annual list of eligibility – Schedule 2 – from the FEFC (e.g. FEFC, 1999) and pays millions of pounds to examining boards for the privilege of buying qualifications that are often not fit for the purpose. This is particularly an issue for students on the first two rungs where they need general education skills. The focus on appropriate and rigorous curriculum design at this level has been sadly swamped by the development of bureaucratic assessment-based GNVQ. There are now diminishing numbers of students following GNVQ Levels 1 and 2 (Joint Council of National Vocational Awarding Bodies, 1998) perhaps because these pseudo-vocational courses are poorly constructed, repetitive in content, boring and frequently use culturally biased tests for accreditation. These standard qualifications are not what is needed to capture the interest and enthusiasm of the disaffected in learning.

Programmes should be devised which stimulate and tackle the malaise of poor motivation, that are progressive and recognize small steps towards a larger goal. And the goal needs to be ambitious, explicit, recognizable – not a muddle-headed and inappropriate application of the words 'vocational' or 'academic'. Would it not be sensible to accept that the essential principles on the first levels of the Framework are, without exception, those of general education? We could then pay more attention to what motivates people to learn, what method and what content is most effective, and when and where people want to learn. Increasing motivation through offering choices is the one very welcome innovation that has come with the government's New Deal programme (DfEE, 1997).

'New Deal' introduces a dimension of choice for clients (or should we call them 'conscripts') who are invited to make a decision about which route to follow. All routes are intended to end in the same place (with a job), but it is recognized that how you get there needs to relate to individual interests and ambitions. Instead of just focusing on training for qualifications, a likely recipe for failure, people are being asked to opt for one of four approaches (all of which include training): a job, work in the voluntary sector, studying in education, or joining an environmental task force.

This notion of motivating people through offering a choice could be extended to everyone studying up to Level 3 (and perhaps beyond). Everyone still working towards Level 1 or 2 qualifications could be offered a choice of learning styles through the development of a 'threshold programme'. This would be a general preparation offered in a variety of contexts using a variety of processes. The choices could include IT-focused programmes, work programmes, active learning programmes, an outward-bound programme and community projects. There is enormous potential for options if, as would be the case, there were a very large cohort of participants. The central difference between this approach and the current Level 1 and 2 routes is the focus on matching interest to learning experience and thus increasing motivation. The 'threshold programme' would include core skills and a successful outcome would have equivalence to other Level 1 and 2 qualifications in the overall framework. The key feature of any new programme must be the allocation of time. Research from the USA (Sticht, 1999) tells us that people who have failed in the past take longer to get there next time round. It's not a message anyone, anywhere, wants to hear because we all want a quick fix to intractable problems. And, of course, more time means more money and possibly a really fundamental review of the funding methodology.

Funding

The current FEFC funding methodology is far from transparent; indeed the values that underpin it are implicit and hidden. Nowhere in the impenetrable annual publications on 'How to Apply for Funding' (for example, FEFC, 1994) or the 'Review of the Funding Tariff' (for example, FEFC, 1997a) is it stated that the funding tariff favours people who can learn fast, stay on course and gain a qualification in record time, but this nevertheless is the case. The people whom the funding methodology favours are those who have succeeded educationally in the past, those who are studying for Level 3 qualifications – the very-likely-to-be-successful-in-the-shortest-time students. Absolutely not the students we define here as the priority for the sector.

The characteristics of these learners are precisely those least attractive to funding under the current arrangements and, there are no two ways about it, radically raising student numbers and achievement at Levels 1 and 2 is going to be difficult. This is the weakest area of full-time further education provision. Level 1 and 2 students are frequently people who cannot learn fast, who don't attend consistently, who start and stop and start again, and who do not achieve the qualification in the prescribed time. At present less than 60 per cent of students at Levels 1 and 2 ever achieve their qualification aims (FEFC, 1998a). If these students are to be prioritized, then (unless there is a substantial injection of additional funds into the sector) there will have to be new winners and new losers. The funding regime will need to change and resources will need to be moved away from work at Level 3 and above.

What must be avoided are the scams caused by the simple expansionist (demand-led) models of the past. Then the FEFC sought to drive up numbers but funding was hijacked by artificial boosts of students franchised from existing external provision into the sector. The sheer complexity of the funding formula invites abuse, as well as demanding an extraordinarily costly administration simply to count units. While we would like to recommend a major overhaul of the system (see Roger McClure, Chapter 4, for an alternative view), we will content ourselves with suggesting some straightforward changes that follow the recommendations of the Kennedy Committee (1997):

- identify students for additional funding through their post codes and provide an additional 5 per cent per student;
- enhance funding by 10 per cent for all Level 1 and 2 students on long courses;
- establish a special 'achievement fund' for raising achievement for Level 1 and 2 students – that is, an uncapped fund which pays 15 per cent instead of 10 per cent for achievement at this level.

The upshot of these changes would be that a successful long-term Level 1 or 2 student carries up to a 20 per cent premium. This would not be excessive: it recognizes these are the students with the greatest disadvantage and the ones with whom colleges currently have the weakest track record. There needs to be a steady and maintained growth in funding at Levels 1 and 2 for at least five years to attract the extra investment and specialist staff required. This would encourage college commitment to staff and curriculum development as well as the provision of additional learning hours, additional learning support, learning assistants and the sustenance of mentoring and enrichment schemes of the types described earlier.

Finally, we would like to argue for an end to the financial disadvantage experienced by people studying in further education. If you can't find the bus fare, the money for lunch or to get access to a PC, it is obvious that getting to the end of the course and gaining the qualification will be significantly more difficult than if these problems do not arise. Ours is a bizarre country that provides a subsidy for those with the highest incomes and most educational experience (the majority of those in higher education), but denies it to many on the lowest incomes who cannot get a grant or even a cheap loan to enable them to study (Herbert and Callender, 1997). When Helena Kennedy had the audacity to suggest that this most sacrosanct of all mainstream education traditions be changed, and we stop subsidizing the rich at the expense of the poor, the vice-chancellors poured down scorn from on high. But perhaps her time has come – certainly the recommendations of the Lane Report on Student Support (DfEE, 1998a) go some way to providing a minimum entitlement for those students most in need. The implementation of a national strategy for student support would make a considerable difference to widening participation but, like so many of the issues discussed in this chapter, it will need national leadership backed by local commitment.

Planning to Widen Participation

What many politicians seem to forget when planning for change is the sheer size and potential power of the sector, and that it is only the concerted efforts of colleges that could deliver the ambitious social inclusion agenda. Further education is a £3 billion sector with more young people over sixteen attending every day than all the sixth-forms in schools put together (DfEE, 1998c; FEFC, 1998b). Colleges are long-term institutions and could be used as agents of change to dramatic effect. However, time and again relatively small projects and budgets are devised to attack mainstream problems. There is a proliferation of initiatives, many directed to remedying failure at Levels 1 and 2. The fact that colleges have not been chosen to date is an implicit criticism of how further education has been seen by politicians, the civil service and the public. The TECs would not have been given significant control of training provision if the colleges had been perceived as serving needs adequately. Would the Employment Service, with no experience whatsoever of education and training for the unemployed, have been chosen over FEFC to manage the New Deal programme if politicians believed in what colleges can do? This lack of conviction and credibility of the sector has to be overcome if its potential weight is to be used to tackle education and training needs, and social exclusion, coherently and effectively.

Lack of leadership is one of the most striking features of post-incorporation further education. Ask the question 'Who's in charge of post-16 education here?' in any part of the country and you won't get a straight answer. The sector has no identifiable spokesperson. The responsible body for the sector, the FEFC, has assumed a coy back-seat role, insisting that they are merely a funding body with no responsibility for planning or leadership. This sit-on-your-hands-and-leave-it-to-the-market ethos has had a cost and is neither straightforward nor honest. And it is the most vulnerable students who have paid the price for market failure, unregulated competition and lack of planning.

It has always been disingenuous of the FEFC to disclaim responsibility for planning. The FEFC funding methodology, their listing of acceptable qualifications, their inspection and audit processes are not neutral tools. As we have described earlier, the funding tariff has an immediate impact upon the kinds of people colleges seek to enrol. FEFC, in determining that their main priority for the sector was to converge resource allocation and to achieve a national funding level for all colleges across the country, implicitly made the decision to prioritize the more affluent. While no one would argue against equity of funding for the same kind of people doing the same kind of things, whether in Salford or in Solihull, most people recognize that some people in some places cost more to teach than others. As Helena Kennedy has now convincingly argued, excluded students cost more to find, more to teach and more to retain. The power of FEFC's funding methodology, inspection and audit processes needs to be used to steer and support the country's educational priorities, of which widening participation is now a key feature.

Lack of explicit leadership nationally has been mirrored by lack of coordination and collaboration at a local level. Over the last five years, the competitive ethos has taken root in the sector and it is going to be hard to weed out some of its more negative consequences. The main loss in the exchange of the straitjacket of local authority control for the battery of central regulation was the loss of any strategic oversight. This is manifest in the duplication of provision, for example in London, where twenty-eight colleges now teach Art Foundation courses when previously four sufficed. No one worries whether there will be the jobs and higher education places for the students emerging. Similarly, within one local authority known to us, A-level groups are tiny because seven schools with sixth-forms and two colleges compete for the small cohort of eligible students. There is no evidence that leaving planning to the market works in favour of excluded students. Far from it. There has until recently been no incentive to make the determined investment necessary to successfully attract and retain Level 1 and 2 students, and the pressures of competition and convergence may well have pushed some colleges in the opposite direction.

Things are changing however. The New Deal (DfEE, 1997), the Kennedy (1997) report, the Lane report (DfEE, 1998a) and the work of the Social Exclusion Unit (DfEE, 1998b) all focus attention on regional and subregional planning and concerted local action. At the moment there is considerable uncertainty about how the new regional planning processes will impact upon the relatively independent nature of incorporated colleges. While colleges are happy to talk rationalization and collaboration, it will prove much more difficult to convince them to give up their autonomy, or to stop doing some things to do others, without serious financial levers or changing the rules that govern colleges. Nevertheless, when all is said and done, the prospects now look brighter for those hoping to widen participation than at any stage in recent memory.

Conclusion

People excluded from education and training do not need anything fundamentally different to achieve than those who currently benefit from the system. However, while affluent people tend to have education opportunities built into their life experience, like wardrobes in the bedroom, those on lower incomes may well not. If we are serious about including people with a history of educational failure, people for whom English is a second language, ethnic minority groups, then we have to reproduce for them some of the things that the middle classes take for granted. Sooner or later we will have to recognize the lack of a convincing strategy to combat educational failure. Sooner or later the country will have to make changes to the sacrosanct mainstream so that the norms for one group become the opportunities for all. A vision for the future of further education which prioritizes the achievement of Level 1 and 2 students will contribute to a more confident sector, which will in turn win more public recognition for its contribution to the success of the nation. Achieving at Level 2 opens access to Level 3. Ultimately we believe that the positive action measures outlined in this chapter will benefit everyone.

References

AC and OFSTED (1993) *Unfinished Business*, London: Audit Commission.

Dearing, R. (1996) *Review of Qualifications for 16–19 Year Olds*, London: School Curriculum and Assessment Authority.

DfEE (1997) 'Blunkett's call to the nation to join his crusade for jobs', *DfEE News*, 178/97 (3 July).

DfEE (1998a) *New Arrangements to Support Students in Further Education and Post-16s in Schools*, 26 November, London: DfEE.

DfEE (1998b) *United Kingdom Employment Action Plan: Combating Social Exclusion*, London: DfEE.

DfEE (1998c) *Statistics of Education: Schools in England 1998*, London: The Stationery Office.

FEFC (1994) *How to Apply for Recurrent Funding 1995–96*, Coventry: FEFC.

FEFC (1997a) *Funding Methodology: Convergence of Average Levels of Funding and Review of the Tariff for 1998–99*, Circular 97/38, Coventry: FEFC.

FEFC (1997b) Chief Inspector's Annual Report, *Quality and Standards in Further Education in England 1996–97*, Coventry: FEFC.

FEFC (1998a) *Benchmarking Data 1995–96 and 1996–97: Retention and Achievement Rates in Further Education Colleges in England*, Coventry: FEFC.

FEFC (1998b) 'Student numbers at colleges in the further education sector and external institutions 1997–98', *Statistical First Release*, 22 December, Coventry: FEFC.

FEFC (1999) *Schedule 2*, Circular 99/10, Coventry: FEFC.

Herbert, A. and Callender, C. (1997) *The Funding Lottery*, London: Policy Studies Institute.

Joint Council of National Vocational Awarding Bodies (1998) 'GNVQ completion rates up', *Press Release*, 5 November.

Kennedy, H. (1997) *Learning Works: Widening Participation in Further Education*, Coventry: FEFC.

Mager, C. (1999) *A Signature Qualification: The College Diploma*, Working Document, London: FEDA.

Moser, C. (1999) *A Fresh Start: Improving Literacy and Numeracy*, Report of the Working Group, London: DfEE.

Pearce, N. and Hillman, J. (1998) *Wasted Youth: Raising Achievement and Tackling Social Exclusion*, London: Institute of Public Policy Research.

Steedman, H. and Green, A. (1996) Report to the FEFC, *Widening Participation in Further Education and Training: A Survey of the Issue*, London: Centre for Economic Performance, London School of Economics.

Sticht, T. (1999) *Oral Evidence*, in Moser, 1999.

12 The Web of Interaction with Employers

Patrick Coldstream

Until 1996 I was the founding Director of the Council for Industry and Higher Education. The Council is a body of some forty leaders of large companies, universities and colleges. Its job has been to mark out common ground between academic and business people, and be a joint 'strategic' voice to government, education and employers. Although, as its name implies it was originally grounded in higher education, as it has systematically considered the interrelationships between education and employment, it has come to realize that it had defined itself too narrowly (Smithers and Robinson, 1993). Accordingly, while retaining its established acronym, it has widened and strengthened its membership to include, among others, further education college principals. Choosing carefully from the education lexicon, it now takes as its remit 'post-18 education'.

The Employers' Perspective

Before Sir Ron (now Lord) Dearing's committee (1997) was thought of, the last Conservative Education and Employment Secretary, Gillian Shephard, decided to review 'the aims and purposes of higher education'. She invited academics, industrialists and others to contribute. In replying, the CIHE (1995) implicitly widened the question's terms of reference. 'Post-18 education', it said, would need to become 'comprehensive'. Such education must come to cater for the large majority; it would challenge educators to develop quite new styles of learning to make the best of ordinary people's talent.

Pondering the 'aims and purposes' for Gillian Shephard, the Council proposed the special qualities that ought to be expected of an educated future workforce:

> The UK has belatedly achieved the position where the roles we traditionally think of as 'professional' jobs, including (for example) nursing, are now generally filled by holders of degrees or higher diplomas. A new challenge, however, is already urgent. The more thoughtful employers (not just in industry and commerce either) are now expecting to extend the idea of 'professionalism' with appropriate variation *throughout their workforces*

[my emphasis]. They look for employees not only at the top, but in almost all roles, to be educated to reflect critically on what they do, change it to meet new circumstances, and to take personal responsibility for continually improving method or product.

The thought is compressed but radical. The task of employers is not, of course, to dictate the educators' agenda, but to offer a considered view of the likely demands of the future working world on human intellectual capability. Most people, CIHE considers, will need minds schooled not to efficient routine but to constant critical reflection on the work in hand. Moreover, those minds will see the reflective outcome as a cue for practical innovation. Those capacities for reflection-generating-innovation will equip people to take personal responsibility for progress, for continually improving things. Such educated people have much more than a range of 'vocational skills'; they have learnt to stand back and question their own practice even while actually engaged in it. Their education has managed to give them both the tradition of good practice associated with vocational learning and, above all, the habit of dispassionate critical thinking, which is among the classic marks of the college-trained mind. The well-schooled intellect is turned outside the discipline onto the practical challenges of work.

Applied Education

This sort of educated person, who (the Council is proposing) should be everyman and everywoman in future, will spring largely from a type of education still in its early stages. 'Everyperson' will be neither attracted nor well-equipped by courses that are 'over-theoretical' (too 'academic'), on the one hand, or, on the other, narrowly focused on yesterday's competence ('merely vocational'). Much imaginative effort is needed, the Council suggested, to develop new forms of learning, not to replace but to complement the older ones. To convince students of the worthwhileness of rigorous study, they would generally need to be organized around areas of the working world's concerns and ways of doing things. Those new forms of learning are what the Council has tried to group under the title of 'applied education'.

The range of educational opportunities needs radical widening, in the CIHE's (1995) view, towards:

> broad, general education which is rooted in the applied rather than the pure; its approach to theory will typically derive from practical engagement with objects, operations and projects. Students will learn to draw appropriately on a mixture of disciplines with their banks of accessible information to help them define and solve problems.

'Applied' education for most of the workforce is a huge undertaking, though it can build on the tradition of the Technical and Vocational Education Initiative (TVEI), of the General National Vocational Qualification (GNVQ) and Enterprise in Higher Education (EHE). 'Comprehensive' post-18 education cannot be contained within universities and university colleges. This is particularly so when many of the 'new', ex-polytechnic, universities have recently seemed keener to fly an academic flag than to build up their 'applied' inheritance. That is why the Council called their plea to Gillian Shephard, *A Wider Spectrum of Opportunities*. It is also why they plainly look to the colleges of further education to give something of a lead:

> To offer the full range of post-18 places we envisage, the local colleges of further education will need to play a special and properly acknowledged part. We should not be surprised if over the next decade the colleges come to match their Scottish counterparts in taking as many as one student in four for some part of their courses.

The Dearing Committee (1997) never succeeded in pushing its terms of reference beyond 'higher' education so as to cover a future full spectrum of post-18 opportunities. In recommending that higher education be allowed by the government to expand again, however, it did suggest that the bulk of growth should take place in the further education colleges and most of it in higher national diplomas and the like. The government itself seems to have been less cautious. Within a few months of coming into office, Tony Blair, the Prime Minister, had promised an additional half million students a year. More recently, a Select Committee of the House of Commons (Education and Employment Committee, 1998) has reported that it expects that more than 85 per cent of that extra half million new students, some 430,000, will come to the colleges. Lady Kennedy's Committee for the Further Education Funding Council (Kennedy, 1997) looked to the colleges for 'wider access', which meant not just more students but more from less advantaged backgrounds.

Universal Post-18 Opportunity

The ideal for post-18 education, then, has moved beyond the expansion of university education, successfully prosecuted by recent Tory governments, in the direction of near-universality of post-18 opportunity as employers begin to aim for fully reflective and innovative workforces. In the approach towards universality lies the special summons to the further education colleges, for they are the only education institutions open, as they have always been open, to virtually everyone. The colleges have always had the knack of attracting working people to higher education. Research at Anglia Polytechnic University (cited in CIHE, 1995) showed clearly that more 'first generation' students would venture on courses, if they were offered in familiar surroundings close to home and also, for many of them, clearly related to local work opportunities. It is, of course, a new generation of students, taught to be critically reflective, innovative and responsible, who will be the natural 'lifelong' learners for the future. Their changing work will highlight for them new areas of their own ignorance and profitable avenues for enlarging the stock of knowledge. 'Applied education' is about questioning, not ready-made answers. The applied learner ought to be the lifelong learner because of their quality of curiosity, scepticism and constructive dissatisfaction.

If the lifelong learner too is 'everyman' or 'everywoman', the colleges can make them their customer. Distance-learning notwithstanding, adult students will need to debate, compare experience, build confidence and, indeed, become each other's teachers and encouragers. For most, and for most of the time, that needs to happen close to home and to work. That 'localness' is the colleges' forte, their 'unique selling proposition'. It is that particular style of teaching, convenience of access, openness, vocational tradition, unsnobbishness and general engagement with the everyday world that justify giving the colleges a bigger place. To quote the CIHE (1995) again:

> Employers and their staff will be customers of the Colleges for re-skilling and professional updating. Colleges are dispersed throughout the UK and *only they* [my emphasis] are close enough at hand to most employers for the large-scale provision of education opportunities to the whole of their workforces. High levels of 'lifelong learning' ought to provide a big market for them.

I am saying, then, that for people to flourish, contribute and grow in the world of competition and complexity, we have to set course towards near-universality for post-18 education, 'appliedness' and 'lifelongness'. Those ideals cannot be realized, except with the wholehearted participation of the further education colleges. It can be done only if the colleges can do much of it. If not, 'education, education, education' will not have turned out to be the priority we hoped.

'Lifelong learning', of course, implies that many of the colleges' future student body will be people in work. To bring them towards the colleges means persuading both them and their employers. 'Applied learning', the habit of critical reflection on work in hand, means using the doings of the workplace, its materials, processes, organization and decisions as the raw materials of study. To choose the best courses to offer and to follow, colleges and students need an understanding of the shape of their surrounding economies. Only that can help them weigh up what sort of understanding and skills seem likely to have a useful contribution to make. To attract the working student, to use work to learn with, and to plan the right courses to offer for the developing economy – all three demand that colleges make employers their allies.

Partnership

Whether the further education colleges can meet these high expectations we have for them depends on how far they can learn to interweave their people, teachers and students, and their programmes, into the economic life around them. How can they encourage employers to become their intimates? That has been a central question for the CIHE. As the enormous role for the sector grew clear, in 1996 it commissioned (in association with the FEFC and the DfEE) a research investigation by the Institute for Employment Studies (IES) at the University of Sussex on the then 'present state of the partnership' between further education colleges and employers (Rawlinson and Connor, 1996). The outcomes help us to understand what will in future help or hinder maximum fruitful interaction between the two.

Information was canvassed by interview and discussion to build up an understanding of present practice among colleges and employers, and of the motives and energies underlying it. The researchers held discussions with about a hundred staff and twenty groups of students in nineteen colleges, as well as seventy-five employers across the range of sizes, and representatives of five Training and Enterprise Councils. The participants were clustered in six regions, chosen as having contrasting economic and social characteristics.

The outcomes were encouraging: 'fruitful interaction' between employers and colleges is widespread and ready to be intensified. 'There is an encouraging hum of dialogue and joint activity', Rawlinson and Connor suggested, 'between staff of colleges and employing companies'. Many departments in all colleges visited were in webs of varied activities with a wide range of employers. Dialogue was already a habit. A large college might have connections, though not all of great intensity, with several thousand companies of all sizes. 'The college sector as a whole', remark the authors, 'has a connection with small and medium enterprises that looks unrivalled. There is a great deal of college/employer interaction in all areas, and clearly many beneficial outcomes.'

From the evidence and the earlier study by Smithers and Robinson (1993), we can conclude that colleges look to employers to play at least five distinct roles:

- as customers;
- as places of learning (primarily through a range of placements for students);
- as subcontractors for learning 'franchised' by colleges;
- as advisers;
- as joint planners in the regional or local economy.

On the employers' side approaches may be made to:

- commission from colleges, education or training for their (the employers') staff;
- help educate and train their own staff, and accredit the training (often through National Vocational Qualifications) to standards laid down by the college and with money from the FEFC, channelled through the college;
- offer the workplace and its activities as the context for students' learning (work experience, work-shadowing, projects and exercises);
- advise colleges or individual departments through boards and committees or informally;

- join colleges (and other bodies including TECs, Business Links and schools/industry partnerships) in predicting the shape of employment to come and in local sharing of responsibilities.

Employees as Students

Until the beginning of the 1990s, many companies sent staff in large numbers to college once a week. Rawlinson and Connor (1996) found that most of the colleges' long-standing connections with employers had grown from that 'day-release' tradition. Those connections have often been the main or only channels by which teaching staff could keep abreast of current industrial realities. But recently companies have abandoned old-style apprenticeships and with them their commitment to train people for a lifetime job. Correspondingly, the flow of day-release students to colleges has shrunk. The colleges visited in the IES study reported a fast-diminishing flow of students from the engineering industry and almost none from construction; numbers were increasing, but still comparatively small, in more fashionable sectors, like commerce, finance and healthcare.

'Day-release' had been in its way a starting-point for the limited learning apprentices might be expected to undertake during a craftsman's working life – normally with that single employer. It represented the educational leaven in an apprentice-course largely devoted to skills training. Day-release students have traditionally attended classes specified and planned by colleges as part of their own standard programmes. Recruits from several or many employers have typically followed the same courses in the same classroom. But to try to rebuild numbers, colleges have striven to respond to individual employers' particular orders for special courses run exclusively for employers' own staff.

The standard and the tailor-made, however, do not run easily alongside each other. The rigidities of a repetitive and regular daily timetable have made for efficiency in college arrangements. Employers, on the other hand, not always quick in foreseeing their needs and able to blame it on the vagaries of the marketplace, expect rapid responses when they enquire after bespoke training. Colleges, keen to win customers for fee-paying new business and to appear 'responsive', can be tempted to be reallocate teachers, energy, management effort, space and equipment at the expense of their routine staple work.

In a report which it entitled, *Colleges and Companies: Sharing Great Expectations*, the CIHE (1996) saw that conflict as the sure sign of an organization creaking to accommodate change it was not designed for:

> Typical college organization is still designed essentially for older purposes. The new work is often felt within colleges to carry a special prestige; it attracts fees supposed at least to cover its cost. The relative glamour of 'consultancy' can seem to staff and managers to contrast with the continuing ordinariness of the everyday college timetable.

Diversion of resources to employer-led work, according to Rawlinson and

Connor (1996), caused 'some disquiet in some colleges, as the relatively small revenue generated [is] seen by staff who [are] not involved in it as disproportionate to the resources devoted to it'. Here is a real dilemma. One apparent solution has been to seek extra public money from the FEFC and funnel it directly to employers as subsidy for training they themselves would largely carry out. The college would oversee the process, undertake assessment and endorse the award of national qualifications. This 'franchise' has seemed to enterprising colleges a real means towards a working partnership with employers (as indeed with private training organizations eager for new business and a range of community organizations as well). It has also been lucrative. Sometimes colleges can show a profit on a franchising deal, as well as using it to demonstrate cost efficiency on which their own level of future public funding partly depends.

In the mid-1990s 'franchising' was the largest source of new students for the colleges' books. In only two years from 1994–5 to 1996–7 the proportion of those students paid for by the Funding Council who were enrolled on franchised courses rose from 5 per cent to 21 per cent (FEFC, 1998; see also Table 10.1, p. 118), though nearly 60 per cent of them were recruited by only twenty colleges. Those may prove to be peak figures. Funding Council money is being cut to meet criticisms that public funds were used to subsidize work employers would otherwise have paid for themselves. Colleges will be expected to show a close and effective oversight and take proper responsibility for the quality of training.

Nonetheless, abuses and the occasional financial killing notwithstanding, 'franchising' has marked a path for education out of the college buildings and away from the standard timetable into the workplace and towards a curriculum partly related to actual work in hand. Much of the training has reached people who might otherwise have been neglected – franchised work is often given to get employees on to the lowest rungs of qualification ladders. Such bespoke education reflects a desirable part-shift in influence from 'producer' (college) to 'customer' (employer). One might see in it the recognition by businesses and educators of the real nature of the partnership: a shared responsibility for enabling employees to learn to make the best of their working lives.

But perhaps it is a change that reaches far. The CIHE (1996) was already warning of how great a shift in their own direction and management colleges would be confronted with.

> Inevitably, the new work for employers sits uneasily with the relative rigidities and daily timetable which have traditionally made for efficiency in regular college arrangements [not to speak, I would add, of a quiet life for less dynamic staff]. *The strains are set to intensify* [my emphasis] as colleges and employers persuade each other (as they must) to embark on longer-term and large-scale education, personal development of workforces.

Though the balance of funding for franchising and its rules must change and evolve, a big market certainly awaits colleges able to offer first-class work-related teaching with some public subsidy.

In recent years, many industrial managements have recognized similar strains in their own businesses, as they have tried to approach new markets with organizations built (and staff trained) to cater to traditional ones. To release energy for innovation becomes essential, but means big choices of priorities. Those choices make debates about 'mission statements' very far from formalities. One's 'mission', after all, means one's *raison d'être*. Colleges will find that the constraints of timetabling and systems designed for (as it were) standard mass-production, conflict quite sharply with the freedoms they need to cater for on behalf of the individual employers and employees who are now beginning to present themselves. Colleges have a tradition of debate about the 'flexible college' (a term of art within the sector), organized to be accessible to a wide variety of people with different needs and conflicting demands on that time. It has parallels in industry's conversion to 'flexible manufacturing'. The key is rapid response to varying markets. The task for college governors, who of course include many businesspeople, is to urge their institution towards clarity of purpose and organization to match. For that colleges need to understand their local employers much more closely.

Workplace Learning

The colleges' central educational challenge is to continue developing a first-class mode of applied education, that is neither academic nor vocational in quite the traditional sense. That means students, college lecturers and employers themselves will need to learn how to use the real-time context of working life as the raw material of learning. The first reason for colleges and employers to interact is to share responsibility for turning workers into learners, as I have discussed. The second dialogue needed between the two is about the nature and value of work-related applied education. Work placements, 'live projects' and so on are fundamental, not supplementary to it. Up-to-date plant and equipment are of its essence. Where real life is not available to study, carefully designed simulation and case studies have to suffice.

Research has shown that students, lecturers and employers share a strong conviction that college students not yet employed learn much of great value from first-hand experience of workplaces during their courses. Students believe their placements help them choose a career and learn the 'key skills' to which employers constantly refer (Rawlinson and Connor, 1996). Those aiming for universities say that the experience helps them with entrance interviews; others believe it helps their job-seeking. College staff and employers agree with them. They have in recent years been arranging more placements. Companies have claimed that their 'company profile and image' improve from their engaging in this kind of community activity. Perhaps even more important, college staff report that contact made with companies keeps them up to date with employer thinking and with job prospects in their field.

Work placements, moreover, get employers and lecturers working beyond the demands of mere commercial imperatives. The CIHE (1996), quite a hard-bitten group, has been moved to comment:

We do not doubt our researchers' conviction that employers and teachers devote energy and time to students' work experience, work-shadowing, project activities and the rest, beyond any returns they themselves or their organizations directly can expect from it. This is an area where many employers display a largely altruistic sympathy with teachers' professional concern for students. The fifteen years drive for education/business partnership has certainly helped.

The enthusiasm of individual lecturers is a marvellous asset for a learning society, but it needs to be matched by a clear commitment from those who manage them, make college policy, set priorities and allocate staff time and resources. Students learn best from work placements if they (the students) are thoughtfully matched with the opportunities employers can offer; good results usually reflect painstaking preparation, careful mentors and diligent monitors. Yet Rawlinson and Connor (1996) reported that most college managements had yet to make any formal provision for managing work experience properly:

> Very few [staff] had a time allowance for this work but, if they did, the caseload was viewed as being too large. Administrative support was considered inadequate in almost all colleges. Examples included operating out of shared staff rooms with limited access to telephones to make arrangements, no one to take calls while [staff] were teaching, and problems getting documents typed and copied.

If the colleges are to embrace applied learning, college managements must face the consequences of redefining the jobs of their teachers and deploying space and back-up resources accordingly. Applied learning means persuading employers to allow educators and their students to study their (employers') methods and processes. Lecturers have a new and potentially absorbing research role in exploring what might serve as effective projects and modes of enlarging students' understanding of the world. The employer–educator interaction is crucial, not marginal, to the ideal of lifelong learning. Research speaks highly of students' work experience and of the powerful good will surrounding it. There often is a sense of real partnership and community feeling. As lecturers on occupationally related programmes come to see work activities as part of the essential subject matter of teaching, demand on employers should increase. Yet when demand even for placements is beginning to outrun supply, how easily may employers come to see colleges as unprofessional in relying as heavily as they have done on staff good will and extra extracurricular effort?

Understanding Employment Prospects

As colleges gain access to employees as students and to the workplace as the raw material for learning, they will grow in their ability to guide their clients in their choice of study. They need to. There has been a strong temptation, and one not easily resisted, for colleges to offer courses which are popular so as build their numbers and to take less interest in whether they match what the labour market may be expected to want. Financial incentives to colleges to recruit exacerbate that. It implies that many students choose the 'wrong' things to study, through not understanding the likely demands of the working world they hope to enter. In so far as students see college education as a preparation for working, they need that education to give them both a broad grounding (on which to build continued learning) and the chance to learn to do something useful, usually by acquiring some readily marketable skills.

Formal qualifications, therefore, ought to attest to the combination of a good grounding with useful skills. The students' choice of an occupational area for the broad grounding (for a GNVQ, for example) ought to reflect an informed medium-term view of the development of a local/regional/national economy. Sensible choice of an immediately marketable skill is a different matter and must imply an understanding of likely present employment openings. Regional forums will be useful – and the proposed Regional Development Agencies (DETR, 1997) are probably those – where representative business- and college people can come to a shared view of the economies they and the students are part of. Within the colleges themselves, staff need to pool their week-by-week knowledge of local employers' needs and prospects and so advise students on which skills seem to be of most immediate use.

To achieve the range of interaction with employers outlined in this chapter, the colleges will need to give a lead. For many years their senior spokespeople have urged them to be 'responsive' to local needs (rather than being caught in a traditional spread of curricula traditionally offered and taught). But now 'responsiveness' cannot be enough. To promote good learning is the sectors' *raison d'être*, whereas it is only one of many concerns for employers, employees and TECs. We ought to look to the colleges to take the initiative towards employers around the three essential objects we have discussed, namely:

- expanding the market for applied education;
- improving the application of applied education;
- discerning the most useful directions for applied education.

In the mid-1990s inspectors for the Funding Council (FEFC, 1996) reported that most colleges had a very limited view of marketing as a matter of a little more than 'selling' their existing products. The most thoughtful colleges, though, were beginning to see marketing as actively exploring their surrounding economies in order to develop the sort of demand (that is, create the clients) they as colleges were best placed to serve. The CIHE (1996) addressed this issue also:

> We hope that much up-to-date marketing thinking will come to underpin and energize colleges' strategic planning. It would depend on assembling within colleges comprehensive data on all their relations with the client and employer world and on an evaluation of them and their usefulness to the

college's mission and its financial viability. That information would be the foundation for managing the whole spread of a college's interaction with its working environment, that is to say its potential client and employer base.

Active and imaginative marketing by educators is the real engine of lifelong learning.

References

CIHE (1995) *A Wider Spectrum of Opportunities*, London: CIHE.

CIHE (1996) *Colleges and Companies: Sharing Great Expectations*, London: CIHE.

Dearing, R. (1997) *Higher Education in the Learning Society*, The National Committee of Inquiry into Higher Education, London: HMSO.

DETR (1997) *Building Partnerships for Prosperity, Sustainable Growth, Competitiveness and Employment in the English Regions*, Cmnd 3814, London: Stationery Office.

Education and Employment Committee (1998) Sixth Report, *Further Education*, vol. 1, *Report and Proceedings*, 264-I, London: The Stationery Office.

FEFC (1996) *College Responsiveness*, Coventry: FEFC.

FEFC (1998) Report from the Inspectorate, *Collaborative Provision: National Survey Report*, Coventry: FEFC.

Kennedy, H. (1997) *Learning Works: Widening Participation in Further Education*, Coventry: FEFC.

Rawlinson, S. and Connor, H. (1996) *Developing Responsiveness: College/Employer Interaction*, Report 300, Institute of Employment Studies, Brighton: University of Sussex.

Smithers, A. and Robinson, P. (1993) *Further Education in the Market Place*, London: CIHE.

13 Franchising

Guardino Rospigliosi

Franchising[1] is an arrangement 'where a college makes an agreement with another organization to deliver on behalf of the college provision funded by the [Further Education] Funding Council. The college retains the responsibility for the transfer of funds to the franchised organization' (FEFC, 1994). Its essence is the transfer of funds out of the college sector to another organization. Franchising does not include distance teaching, where a college instructs people off its main premises by providing textual or electronic teaching materials backed by tuition (for example by a marking service or telephonic or video links); it does not include outreach work, whereby college staff go into locations not owned by the college to teach there. However, the practice of franchising has sometimes been defended (by Kennedy, 1997, for example, and in a letter to me by Baroness Blackstone, Minister of State for Higher Education) as including outreach and distance teaching.

It is the argument of this chapter that franchising does not represent, as do distance teaching and outreach work, an extension into the community of further education's delivery of its core mission, but rather offers, in place of the progression into higher levels and widening of intellectual horizons, an *ersatz* activity that displaces the beneficial experience of mainstream further education. This chapter also develops the case put before the Commons Select Committee by the Plymouth Further Education Corporation (1998) that the funding difficulties of further education have largely arisen from the franchising of college work to non-college providers. It is suggested that in a context where funds for mainstream college work have had to be capped, the hard choice has to be made to restrict franchising in the interests of mainstream provision.

A declared aim of the 1992 Further and Higher Education Act was to increase participation and attainment. Between 1992–3 and 1993–4 there was a rapid growth in student enrolments from 2,391,000 to 2,462,000 (FEFC, 1995); a growth of nearly 3 per cent. Since 1984, this rate of increase had previously been exceeded only once. The full-time enrolments grew from 610,000 to 667,000, an impressive 9 per cent, although this figure may have been over-stated by a redefinition of the boundaries between full-time and part-time students. (The FEFC had successfully lobbied for a more helpful definition of the sixteen-hour rule, making it easier for people to continue to receive unemployment benefits while studying.)

But then the basis of counting students was changed, making comparisons more difficult. The traditional unit, the full-time equivalent (FTE), had measured student volume by relating it to the amount of teaching an individual student received. Roughly speaking, a student taught for six hours was reckoned to be the equivalent of half a student taught for twelve hours. The new Funding Council, following consultation with the sector (FEFC, 1992), introduced a funding mechanism whereby colleges were funded on the basis of 'learning units' (see Chapter 4). These were not directly related to the amount of teaching a student received, but were awarded in relation to enrolments, courses and qualifications. A student achieving an A-level in one year earned a college the same number of qualification units as someone taking twice as long. More seriously, the colleges were partly funded on the basis of the new National Vocational Qualifications (see Figures 13.1 and 13.2, for an example) which were, in effect, awarded by the colleges themselves. The value of the service provided by the college to the student was no longer gauged from the time the college spent teaching that student. It was measured by the student's achievement, usually without reference to prior attainment, and that achievement was assessed by the same organization that stood to gain 10 per cent more if students passed than if they failed.

The first effect of this change in funding mechanism, with its consequent effects on student record-keeping, was to show an apparent reduction in student numbers. The first statistics issued by the FEFC based on the Individualized Student Record showed enrolments in 1994–5 falling back from 2,462,000 to 2,425,000, with a drop in full-time students to 652,000 (FEFC, 1996). But the new arrangements also opened the way to franchising. Data issued by the Funding Council in 1998 (FEFC, 1998, and summarized in Table 10.1, p. 118) showed franchising to be the main driver in the strong growth of part-time enrolments between 1994–5 and 1996–7 (see also Figure 3.2, p. 29).

Franchising was an attractive option for colleges whose budgets depended on continually expanding student numbers. Private training organizations regularly approached principals offering to use up any funding units for which the colleges could not find mainstream students. Additionally, many private providers were willing to take a payment at the demand-led-element rate of about £6, whereas a college would be receiving at least twice that sum for the same unit. The private trainers were receiving £6 per unit of activity which they were already carrying out. The difference pocketed by the college was pure profit.

As franchising spread through the sector, apparent growth was dramatic. It soon exceeded the contingency funds set aside by government to pay for demand-led growth, destabilizing the finances of the sector. Several colleges with high levels of franchising became embroiled in scandals. Moreover, the National Audit Office (NAO, 1997) found that it was in principle impossible to verify whether training funded through franchised payments would have taken place anyway – whether, in other words, the extra spent on national further education was buying extra learning. A further source of concern was quality. A report from the inspectors (FEFC, 1997b) noted that franchised provision put greater demands on quality assurance systems than did mainstream provision, but they were less likely to be developed for – or applied to – it.

A serious re-examination of franchised provision and of its tendency to displace mainstream provision might have been expected. However, such a re-examination would have involved facing up to some unpalatable facts. Among those which have already come to light are that the word 'student' has been extended to include learners previously funded from other sources; that the qualifications structure has moved too far from the world of teaching and learning to provide auditable measures of educational activity; and that the responsiveness of colleges to employer needs has often degenerated into a post box, with a substantial commission being retained for passing on to companies for, in effect, their in-house training, funds voted to the further education sector.

Dead-Weight Funding

A central concern over franchised provision is that it might just be the relabelling of existing provision hitherto funded from the private purse or from other public sector funding sources. (Certainly the proportion of college income derived from non-FEFC sources declined as FEFC numbers, many of them franchised, grew – see Figure 3.1, p. 28). The NAO (1997) makes clear that it is, in principle, impossible to audit whether provision paid for through franchising is genuinely additional to activities that would already have taken place. In the context of capped growth these arrangements, far from providing additional opportunities for further education, have always risked duplicating – and now risk displacing – existing college provision.

It is sometimes argued that franchised provision is a valuable replacement for declining uptake by employers of day-release courses. My college, Plymouth College of Further Education, has eschewed franchising as part of its growth strategy. Its employer day-released numbers have risen consistently and it won a national Beacon Award for its employer partnerships. Elsewhere in the sector, however, employer-sponsored day-release numbers have fallen as franchised activities increased. It is therefore arguable that franchising with employers and other providers displaces the broad educational benefits of traditional day-release with provision of much less demonstrable value.

The case of the Tesco national franchise is a good illustration (Nash, 1995a, 1995b). Most of the 'students' on this franchise at Halton College (which has recently come under further scrutiny – NAO, 1999) are understood to have been signed up for the NVQ Level 1 in Distributive Trades. In order to understand how little this involves beyond what would normally be required, we need to examine the details. The requirements specify that candidates must do five compulsory units and take one out of a menu of optional units.

From the listings of Figures 13.1 and 13.2, it is obvious that any employer will require *all* those employed in shelf-stacking to exhibit the so-called competencies relating to the health and safety of the workplace, to security, to personal hygiene and to maintaining relationships. Others of the units are more

Figure 13.1 *NVQ Level 1 Distributive Trades: Compulsory units*

Unit 1: Maintain Stock to Specified Levels
Confirm requirements for replenishing stock
Replenish stock to specified levels

Unit 2: Move Goods and Materials to Designated Locations
Confirm the requirements for moving goods and materials
Place specified goods and materials in designated locations

Unit 3: Contribute to Maintaining a Healthy and Safe Workplace
Implement procedures to deal with accidents and emergencies
Monitor and report risks
Lift and handle goods safely

Unit 4: Contribute to Maintaining the Security of the Workplace
Implement procedures to protect people, stock and premises
Implement procedures to deal with threats to security

Unit 5: Maintain Relationships in the Workplace
Cooperate with colleagues to achieve work objectives
Process routine information
Develop oneself in the job

---

specific to retail, but it is hard to imagine any supermarket employing people who could not refill shelves or move goods in and out of storage. The only justification for passing on further education funds to an employer must surely be that the employer is making available to employees training and education over and above what would have been provided in the normal course of the work. The presumption must be that the FEFC funds are not always purchasing additional learning.

Private Providers

Paying employers to do what they would have done anyway is only part of the problem. Over half (54 per cent) of franchising (Hall, 1997) is through private training providers. Most principals' in-trays are overflowing with letters from private trainers touting to take over funding units. They are able to provide training more cheaply than the colleges because their overheads are less. In particular, they generally offer little in the way of enrichment activities. Such support is important in sustaining the motivation for lifelong learning.

Students attending mainstream college provision, or taught by staff most of whose work is done in mainstream college delivery, are throughout their programmes in contact with learners and provision on a wider range of

Figure 13.2 *NVQ Level 1 Distributive Trades: Optional units*

Unit 1: Contribute to the Cleanliness and Hygiene of the Working
Environment
Clean work surfaces
Dispose of waste and litter
Maintain standards of personal hygiene

Unit 2: Maintain the Operational Effectiveness of Equipment
Clean equipment
Inspect and maintain equipment

Unit 3: Wrap and Pack Goods for Customers
Confirm packaging and presentation requirements
Package goods to meet customer requirements

Unit 4: Monitor and Maintain Sales Stock
Monitor levels of sales stock
Maintain sales stock to specified levels

Unit 5: Maintain the Condition and Appearance of Floral Products to
Optimize their Sales Value
*Condition, monitor and maintain the quality of in-coming fresh
materials*
*Monitor and nurture fresh floral materials and floristry products
to optimize their sales value*

---

programmes and at higher levels. *A priori* such students are likely to re-enrol on courses that extend their interests and make them more flexibly useful in the labour market, or to enrol on higher level programmes. Nearly a quarter of the students on the first year of programmes at Plymouth College of Further Education had previously been enrolled on other courses.

Level of Provision

The Kennedy (1997) report advocated a right to work towards Level 3 of the National Qualification Framework – the equivalent of two A-levels (see Chapter 5). But the great majority of franchised work is to Levels 2 and 1 or below (FEFC, 1997a, 1997b). There is plenty of research evidence (Robinson, 1997) to show that vocational qualifications stopping at Level 2 do not increase individuals' earnings or employability, or contribute significantly to an area's ability to create wealth. Where Level 2 is useful is as a stepping stone to higher levels of vocational qualification: the significant breakthrough comes at Level 3. The General

Household Survey 1992 (Thomas *et al.*, 1994) shows Level 3 gross weekly earnings (male) as £277, against Level 2 of £242, that is, a 13 per cent difference; it shows a vocational Level 2 unemployment rate of 15 per cent as against a Level 3 rate of 9 per cent. There is also evidence (Campbell, 1994) that achievement at Level 3 correlates with gross value added per person in employment.

Franchised provision tends to be mainly directed towards Levels 1 and 2 qualifications. Students on mainstream college programmes are much more likely to progress to higher levels than people whose training has been exclusively conducted in supermarket employment, or by low-level private providers.

Demand Led Element

The DfEE and its predecessors had a good record of planning and it was in this context that the Treasury felt there was not too much risk in offering an open-ended commitment to fund growth in excess of DfEE forecasts through the demand-led element formula (see Chapter 4). In 1996–7, the costs of the DLE were projected to exceed the DfEE's provision to the Funding Council by £84 million (Melville, 1997), arising from the unfunded units for the spring and summer terms. In that academic year, the FEFC funded 16,682,000 units of franchised work (FEFC, 1997a). Had these been funded at the low DLE rate of £6.50 per unit this franchised work would have represented a spend in the whole year of £108.43 million, of which the two-thirds to cover the spring and summer terms would have been £72 million, practically wiping out the overspend. In fact, a substantial part of this work was funded at the higher core rate, which varies according to each college's average level of funding.

It is therefore arguable that, without the funding of franchised work, the FEFC's call on additional funds would have been minimal, if indeed required at all. It is generally agreed that this unsuccessful call, and the resultant withdrawal of the uncapped DLE provision, had a significant effect on the financial position of the sector and has tended to destabilize the infrastructure.

Quality Assurance

Not only has the unforeseen rush to franchising had consequences for the funding of the colleges, but it also raises questions about quality assurance. The Chief Inspector's Annual Report for 1996–7 (FEFC, 1997b) states that 'there are no inherent weaknesses in franchising'. It recognizes that such provision can help colleges to provide courses for students who might not otherwise participate. But the Chief Inspector also cautions that:

> Much work remains to be done to ensure that quality assurance procedures are as rigorously applied to franchised provision as to that offered on college premises. Colleges need to improve the accuracy of the data they collect about franchised provision. They also need to pay more attention to evaluating the teaching and learning on franchised courses and to ensure that individual students on franchised courses receive the support they

need. The monitoring visits that colleges make to franchise partners as yet rarely include classroom observation by subject specialists.

The National Audit Office report on *The Further Education Funding Council for England* (NAO, 1997) echoes these risks, pointing in particular to the 'loss of control over course quality: the Funding Council's Inspectorate have identified a particular difficulty in achieving high quality in franchised provision which is remote from the college'.

Conclusion

In this chapter we have outlined concerns about franchised work and it is inevitably to some extent one-sided. Much work known as franchised provision has opened access to further education to groups who have traditionally been reluctant to participate. However, it is argued that some of the work that has achieved this sort of outcome is not franchising as usually defined but constitutes distance teaching or traditional outreach work. In any case, it is the position of this chapter that if there is to be rationing of learning units, it is mainstream provision that should be protected since mainstream provision has some difficulty in handling downward fluctuations in funding because of commitments to employment contracts and premises costs, either capital or leasehold. By definition, franchised provision does not bind colleges to either of these commitments, so that the significant curtailment or abolition of FEFC funding for franchised provision is preferable to the destabilizing of the mainstream college infrastructure.

To avoid being sensationalist, this chapter has deliberately not mentioned *causes célèbres* like the disappearing students in the Birmingham mosques (Nash, 1995a, 1995b) or the varied approaches the FEFC has taken to recreational diving courses (Crequer, 1997). But they have nevertheless happened. It seems inevitable that until the FEFC acts to substantially reduce the funding for or the proportion of franchised work, there will be other scandals leading to yet more appearances in *Private Eye*, as well as providing juicier pieces for the *Times Educational Supplement*. Rather, we have sought to set out our reservations about the funding of a significant quantity of franchised provision in the context of a capped further education budget.

Note

[1] I sometimes think franchising is the Monica Lewinsky of the Further Education sector. Its hollow claims to gargantuan growth have parallels in the Starr Report's thousands of pages of factitious turgidity. It illustrates important points of principle. It offers endless opportunities for scandalous anecdotes. It gives full scope to the exciting pastime of humbug. Franchising has been characterized by side-splitting redefinitions of further education more than rivalling the presidential interpretations of sexual abstinence. The debasement of political discourse in Washington finds parallels in the quality

standards reported of franchised provision. Franchising's incontinent appetites have the potential to discredit and destabilise a public service whose aim is to significantly combat the effects of poverty and social exclusion.

References

Campbell, M. (1994) *Education, Training and Economic Performance*, London: Policy Research Unit.

Crequer, N. (1997) 'Diving dilemma threatens to burst dual funding bubble', *Times Educational Supplement*, 11 July.

FEFC (1992) *Funding Learning*, Coventry: FEFC.

FEFC (1994) *How to Apply for Recurrent Funding 1995–96*, Coventry: FEFC.

FEFC (1995) 'Information on student enrolments during the 1993–94 college year and comparisons with 1992–93', *Statistics Bulletin*, 5, Coventry: FEFC.

FEFC (1996) 'Student numbers at colleges in the further education sector in England in 1994–95', *Press Release*, 23 January, Coventry: FEFC.

FEFC (1997a) *Annual Report 1996–97*, Coventry: FEFC.

FEFC (1997b) Chief Inspector's Annual Report, *Quality and Standards in Further Education in England 1996–97*, Coventry: FEFC.

FEFC (1998) *Strategic Plans, Including Financial Forecasts, 1997–98 to 1999–2000*, Circular 98/06, Coventry: FEFC.

Hall, G. (1997) Presentation to FEFC Annual Conference, 6 February.

Kennedy, H. (1997) *Learning Works: Widening Participation in Further Education*, Coventry: FEFC.

Melville, D. (1997) *Letter to College Principals from Chief Executive of FEFC*, 19 February.

Nash, I. (1995a) 'Dispute hits franchises', *Times Educational Supplement*, 7 April.

Nash, I. (1995b) 'Franchise courses in fraud inquiry', *Times Educational Supplement*, 7 July.

NAO (1997) *The Further Education Funding Council for England*, Report HC233, London: NAO.

NAO (1999) Report by the Comptroller and Auditor General, *Investigation of Alleged Irregularities at Halton College*, HC 357, 1998–9, 15 April.

Plymouth Further Education Corporation (1998) *Franchising in Further Education*, Memorandum from Plymouth College of Further Education, Appendix 44, in Education and Employment Committee (1998) *Further Education*, vol. 2, *Minutes of Evidence and Appendices*, 264-II, London: The Stationery Office.

Robinson, P. (1997) *The Myth of Parity of Esteem: Earnings and Qualifications*, London: Centre for Economic Performance, London School of Economics.

Thomas, M., Goddard, E., Hickman, M. and Hunter, P. (1994) *General Household Survey 1992*, London: HMSO.

14 Accountability and Audit

Jim Donaldson

In this chapter we turn to the accountability of the colleges for academic quality through quality assessment and inspection. The line of accountability runs in the opposite direction to the flow of funds. The large and diverse further education sector in England has a framework for financial and academic accountability which derives from the 1992 Further and Higher Education Act. This transferred to colleges and to the Further Education Funding Council (FEFC) a range of functions previously administered by local authorities. Public funding for the sector is voted by parliament through the Department for Education and Employment (DfEE) and allocated to colleges by the FEFC according to a method which is consistent across the country. Colleges are accountable to the FEFC for their use of public money and for the quality of the education they provide, and the FEFC itself is accountable to the DfEE and to parliament. As part of the process for ensuring the proper use of public funds, the FEFC has a financial memorandum with the DfEE and with each college setting out terms and conditions for funding. The FEFC also has a control framework which monitors colleges' accounts and financial forecasting, their individualized records of staff and students, their claims for funding, their strategic planning and the academic quality of their provision.

To meet its responsibilities under the Act for ensuring that there are satisfactory arrangements for assessing the quality of education and training in the sector, the FEFC has a quality assessment committee and an inspectorate. The committee advises the FEFC on the quality of education provided in the sector, receives assessment reports on the quality of the education and advises on any action that is needed, and agrees the inspectorate's work programme and monitors its performance. The committee reports annually to the FEFC on the overall quality of education in the sector. After consideration by the FEFC, the report is forwarded to the Secretary of State for Education and Employment. The inspectorate assesses the quality of provision and informs the work of the quality assessment committee. Its terms of reference are to:

- assess standards and trends across the sector and to advise the FEFC on the performance of the sector overall;

- identify and make more widely known good practice and promising developments in further education and to draw attention to weaknesses that require attention;
- provide advice and assistance to those with responsibilities for or in institutions of the sector, through its day-to-day contacts, its contributions to training and its publications;
- keep abreast of international developments in post-school education and training.

The independence of the committee and of the inspectorate are crucial elements in the FEFC's provision for the assessment of academic quality. The members of the committee are prominent people from the sector, such as principals of colleges, and directors and senior managers from commerce and industry. There is also a student representative member. The chairman of the committee, an industrialist, is not a member of the FEFC. Within the FEFC itself the inspectorate is independently organized and managed, at arm's length from the other directorates. The Chief Inspector gives advice to the FEFC directly and his independent position is acknowledged in the FEFC's management structure. Inspections are carried out by the FEFC's full-time inspectors, assisted by part-time inspectors who are not employees of the FEFC. Most of these are current or recent teachers and managers in the sector who contribute an important element of peer assessment to the process of inspection.

The First Framework for Quality Assessment

Continuity and consultation are key elements in the FEFC's approach to quality assessment. Shortly after the 1992 Act was passed, almost twelve months before colleges became self-governing corporations, the FEFC published Circular 92/02, *Preparing for Incorporation*, with an annex which gave details of the procedures and criteria then used by Her Majesty's Inspectors (HMI) in assessing academic quality in further and higher education (FEFC, 1992). The FEFC also convened a group of college representatives and others with an interest in the sector, chaired by the Chief Inspector, to consider how the assessment of achievement by colleges might be carried out in the future. The recommendations made by this group were published in April 1993 in Circular 93/11, *Assessing Achievement*, which invited comments on the proposals from all those with an interest in the assessment of provision in the new further education sector (FEFC, 1993a). The FEFC received 259 responses to the consultation document from 189 sector colleges and from independent further education colleges, from higher education, from TECs, from local authorities, from associations and organizations of various kinds, and from individuals. Over 95 per cent of the responses were supportive of the approach to quality assessment proposed. An analysis and summary of the responses was considered by FEFC and the consultative group, and various modifications and clarifications were introduced. With these amendments, FEFC accepted the new framework for self-assessment and inspections, which was published in September 1993 as Circular 93/28, *Assessing Achievement* (FEFC, 1993b).

This framework was used throughout the first four-year quality assessment cycle and has served as the foundation for later developments. *Assessing Achievement* accepted the definition of the three levels of quality assurance in further education recognized by the government White Paper which preceded the Act, *Education and Training for the 21st Century* (DES and DoE, 1991). The first level was quality control – the mechanisms within colleges for maintaining and enhancing the quality of provision, for which colleges are primarily responsible. The second level was the examinations and validations carried out by external awarding bodies, which are responsible for guaranteeing the standards of their qualifications. At this level, colleges were responsible for overseeing assessments and examinations, and for complying with the standards of the validating and examining bodies. It is at the third level of quality assurance – external assessment – that the active participation of the FEFC was required. To meet this responsibility, the FEFC proposed to rely on the use of performance indicators and on quality assessment based on inspection. In the framework for inspection published in *Assessing Achievement* (FEFC, 1993b), the FEFC aimed to develop a distinctive approach to quality and its assessment which recognized:

> that provision must not only be fit for its purpose, but should aim for high standards and excellence, should satisfy and involve the customer, should encourage continual improvement, and should enable the government to be assured that the large sums of money devoted to this sector of education are being well spent.

The framework took account both of the approaches to quality and its assurance adopted in business and industry, and of the different aims and objectives of a public service. The inspections carried out in the first four-year cycle followed the framework. College inspectors were appointed to build up an in-depth knowledge of the college and its local context, to act as a first point of reference for the college with the inspectorate, and to plan inspections in consultation with the college which reflected its pattern of provision. The college's own aims, objectives, targets and criteria for success set the context for inspections. The inspection process embraced the direct observation of the delivery of the curriculum, monitoring the college's performance against the commitments in the national charter for further education, and the college's own charter, and evaluating the college's strategy for monitoring and enhancing the quality of its own provision.

There were three types of inspection. College inspectors routinely monitored college activities and responses to earlier inspections. Feedback on the findings of these inspections were given to colleges, but not published. There were also assessments by inspectors concentrating on particular areas of the curriculum or on specific cross-college topics, which contributed to national survey reports. The main assessment activity was a team inspection leading to a published report on each college within the four-year cycle. In preparation for these published inspections, colleges were asked to prepare a brief self-assessment report based on the findings of their own quality assurance procedures, giving their own evaluation of the strengths and weaknesses of seven main aspects of their provision, as a basis for discussion with the inspection team. The seven main aspects were:

- responsiveness and range of provision;
- governance and management;
- student recruitment, guidance and support;
- teaching and the promotion of learning;
- students' achievements;
- quality assurance;
- resources.

Colleges were also asked to contribute to an introductory section of the report, on the college and its aims. The college nominee, a senior member of the college, who joined the inspection team and took part in all aspects of its work apart from grading.

In team inspections, the main sources of evidence were observation of arrangements for the enrolment and induction of students; observation of teaching and learning in classroom lessons, tutorials, seminars, practical sessions in workshops and laboratories, and other guided learning activities; and the scrutiny of students' work, including lesson notes, essays and written assignments, practical projects and portfolios, examination and test scripts, and other forms of assessed work. In addition, inspectors held discussions with individuals or groups with an interest in, or view on, the quality of the college's provision. These included college governors, managers, teachers, support staff, students and parents, representatives of the local TEC, local industry and community groups, staff from local schools and, where appropriate, from local authorities and higher education institutions. Inspectors also examined a wide range of documentary evidence covering college governance, management, curriculum development, quality assurance and self-assessment. Provision was graded using a five-point scale, with provision of the highest quality being denoted by '1'. Grades were recorded for each cross-college aspect of provision and for each of the major curriculum areas inspected.

The published reports followed a standard format, beginning with the college and its aims, then covering the seven main aspects and ending with a section on 'conclusions and issues'. This summarized the college's achievements and any weaknesses, and suggested priorities for action in order to maintain and enhance the quality of provision. Colleges were required to provide a written response outlining their plans for addressing any weaknesses identified in the report within four months of its publication and to incorporate their proposals in their strategic plans. College inspectors monitored the responses to the assessment reports and, where appropriate, offered advice on the implementation of any action taken in the light of the inspection findings. Where the inspectorate assessed a curriculum area as having weaknesses which outweighed the strengths (Grades 4 and 5), the FEFC made it a condition of funding that the institution should not increase student numbers in the area until the inspectorate was satisfied that the deficiencies had been remedied. The FEFC also limited some aspects of a college's growth when the inspectorate judged that a college's quality assurance arrangements had weaknesses which outweighed their strengths.

Guidance on Quality and Standards

In preparing colleges for the first round of inspections, the FEFC needed to give guidance not only on the general framework for inspections, but also on how quality and standards would be judged, and how they could be improved. To meet this need, the FEFC provided inspection guidelines in an appendix to Circular 93/28, *Assessing Achievement* (FEFC, 1993b). Like the framework for inspections described in the circular, the inspection guidelines in the appendix had been the subject of consultation and had received general approval. The guidelines gave further details of the issues to be addressed across the seven main aspects of the colleges' work. These were expressed as a set of positive features or strengths which inspectors might expect to encounter in a good college. The preamble to the guidelines makes it clear that they were not intended as a checklist and were not to be regarded as exhaustive or unchanging. The inspection process could be expected to identify strengths other than those listed and responsive colleges would adapt to changing circumstances. It was unrealistic to expect there to be a single method of delivering curricula which would ensure a high-quality educational experience for students. Quality depended on many interrelated factors and their interrelation could not be prescribed in advance. Quality assessment was to be a dynamic and flexible process involving a constant dialogue between the assessors and the assessed which would be sensitive to the diverse missions of different colleges.

As the guidelines list more than seventy possible good features across the seven main aspects of provision, they are too numerous for detailed discussion here. Many of them bear directly on the quality of the students' learning experience. Strengths in this area include impartial guidance which ensures that students embark on suitable programmes of study in which they are likely to succeed; effective monitoring of their attendance; and the provision of well-planned and managed programmes of study which challenge and extend students, and meet the different learning needs of individuals. Among examples of good practice in teaching and the promotion of learning are:

- the providing of clear information or instructions, at a pace which meets students' needs and abilities;
- establishing good relationships which promote the achievement of learning;
- checking regularly that learning has taken place;
- ensuring that students' interest is engaged and sustained;

- establishing a regular schedule for setting, marking and returning work within agreed deadlines;
- giving students good guidance on how to improve.

This set of possible positive features avoids undue prescription of teaching methods based on the assumption that particular methods are bound to succeed with all students at all times in all circumstances. Instead the guidelines indicate as a possible strength that staff 'choose a variety of teaching and learning approaches which are appropriate for the subject being studied and encourage students to work on their own or in groups'.

The possible strengths relating to students' achievements include some which can be judged, at least in part, on the basis of observation, such as students developing appropriate levels of knowledge and understanding of their subjects and acquiring relevant skills like the ability to carry out practical work competently and safely. Some of the possible strengths, however, require measurement and calculation as a basis for forming a judgement. Among these are:

- the monitoring of retention and destination rates, accompanied by investigation of the causes of unusually low rates, and action taken to remedy them;
- the achievement by students of programme targets for success rates in external examinations and other assessments and in added-value ratings;
- the use in quality assurance of reliable statistics of student performance.

These guidelines provided colleges and inspectors with specific, agreed and extensive guidance on possible strengths which needed to be considered in the assessment of quality without being over-prescriptive, narrowing the focus in advance or over-simplifying complex educational processes. No rules were given on how the different elements should work together, or on how much weight each should receive in the overall judgement. Assessments of strengths and weaknesses were to be made by taking full account of different contexts. The emphasis on strengths rather than weaknesses helped to concentrate attention on good practice. Those who wished could easily create a list of possible weaknesses by turning the strengths into their opposites. The avoidance of blueprints and checklists required quality assessors to be thoughtful and open-minded, and to use their best professional judgement.

The Impact of the First Quality Assessment Cycle

In the first four-year assessment cycle, all the sector colleges assessed their own provision, with the exception of those in the first year of the cycle which had insufficient time to assess themselves before inspection. All colleges were inspected by teams of full-time and part-time inspectors. Over 70,000 lessons involving some 750,000 students were inspected. Reports were published on 452 colleges, 89 independent establishments providing for students with learning difficulties and disabilities and twenty-seven external institutions. The programme of surveys led to the publication of thirty reports on the curriculum and other aspects of college provision, including good practice reports on the main curriculum areas and nine surveys of post-16 education and training in other countries. In each of the four academic years of the first cycle (FEFC, 1994, 1995, 1996b, 1997f) the Chief Inspector, as he has continued to do (FEFC, 1998e), prepared and published a report giving a comprehensive evaluative overview of the quality of further education in England. The quality assessment committee drew on the inspectorate's findings in its annual reports, which were published for 1995–6 (FEFC, 1997c) and 1996–7 (FEFC, 1998a). The committee also monitored the work of the inspectorate and published annual reports on its work.

Overall, this system of accountability through quality assessment provided extensive published evidence of quality and standards in the sector, and placed quality and standards high on the sector's agenda. All colleges knew that they would receive a comprehensive external inspection leading to a published report within four years, a much more frequent rate than that achieved before 1993. They were required to assess their own provision in the light of their own aims and objectives. The circulation of agreed guidelines on quality helped to stimulate thought and action conducive to the maintenance and enhancement of quality and standards. Part-time inspectors learned more about educational quality from the training they received, from seeing what was happening in other colleges and from practising the assessment of quality as members of inspection teams led by full-time inspectors. They returned to their colleges with enhanced skills, insights and experience which could benefit their own colleges' practice. The inspections themselves took into colleges a team of trained and experienced practitioners who could assess provision from the disinterested perspective of people who had not themselves worked in that particular college. The extensive publication of inspection findings in reports which were circulated to all colleges gave useful assessments of strengths and weaknesses in their contexts, with supporting evidence. Survey reports on curriculum areas, in particular, provided detailed examples of good and bad practice.

Although the findings of inspections were sometimes disappointing or unwelcome to colleges, there were very few appeals against the judgements made by inspectors. Fewer than 2 per cent of grades awarded were subject to appeal. As required, colleges prepared written plans for tackling weaknesses found by inspectors, and college inspectors monitored the progress made during their termly visits and, where appropriate, offered advice. In cases where a curriculum area had weaknesses which outweighed the strengths, most colleges worked hard to remedy their weaknesses and were keen to be re-inspected within one year of the original inspection. Some had deficiencies which took longer to remedy, but the required remedial action was usually taken. In sixty-two curriculum re-inspections in fifty-two sector colleges, the action taken by colleges warranted re-grading by inspectors, and removal of the funding restrictions imposed on unsatisfactory areas, in all but two cases.

The Strategy for the Second Quality Assessment Cycle

Towards the end of the third year of the first cycle, the quality assessment committee began to consider how quality assessment should be taken forward in the second four-year cycle. The process of self-assessment and inspection had shown itself to be both robust and effective in providing evidence on quality and standards, and in stimulating improvements. The evidence from inspections, though incomplete, indicated that colleges were generally highly responsive to the needs of their communities, that most teaching was at least satisfactory and often good, and that many students successfully completed their courses and achieved the qualifications they were aiming at. There were also signs that teaching was being better planned, that support for students had improved and the achievement of qualifications had increased. These improvements had been made during a period in which colleges had greatly increased their student numbers and had experienced a steady reduction in funding per full-time equivalent student (see Chapter 3). The reduction amounted to 21 per cent from 1993–4 to 1997–8, an efficiency gain well above those achieved in other sectors of education, and by the end of the cycle there were signs that colleges were beginning to find it difficult to maintain quality. There were also some continuing weaknesses. Some teaching was still unsatisfactory and significant numbers of students withdrew from their courses or did not obtain the qualifications for which they had enrolled. There were some continuing deficiencies in management and quality assurance. These weaknesses were not evenly distributed across the sector.

In this context, the FEFC developed a strategy for the next cycle which would build on the strengths of the system of accountability through self-assessment and inspection, acknowledge the strengths of the sector, and give greater emphasis to spreading good practice and helping colleges to improve. It would provide additional help to colleges in tackling weaknesses, particularly deficiencies in students' achievements. Plans would be prepared for a system of accreditation which in due course would formally acknowledge that an increasing number of colleges had established a good record in managing their affairs and providing services of a high standard. Together with a more flexible system of inspections, this would allow the inspectorate to concentrate more of its attention on colleges most in need of help and give increased emphasis to spreading good practice.

The Revised Arrangements for Self-Assessment and Inspection

The process of detailed planning began when the quality assessment committee appointed a consultative group of college representatives and others with an interest in the sector to consider how the assessment of quality might be carried out in the future. Its terms of reference were to review the framework for the inspection of colleges with the main aims of retaining many of the features of the current inspection framework, encouraging colleges to take more responsibility for their own quality assurance and placing more emphasis during inspections on curriculum areas, teaching and learning, students' achievements, and quality assurance. The group's proposals were published in June 1996 (FEFC, 1996a). The 251 responses received were considered in detail by the consultative group, the quality assessment committee and the FEFC, and strongly influenced the arrangements for future inspection published in March 1997 (FEFC, 1997a, 1997b).

In deciding the new framework, the FEFC was keen to build on those features of the existing framework seen by colleges to be successful. It recognized that most of the provision so far inspected was sound and that colleges had been quick to address weaknesses in their provision, as revealed by the action plans put in place after inspection and the re-inspection of curriculum areas graded 4 or 5. As the primary responsibility for quality rested with colleges and they had devoted considerable resources to the development of quality assurance systems, the new framework emphasized regular self-assessment as a key indicator of effective quality assurance, with inspection being the means of assessing whether colleges' self-assessments were rigorous and accurate. The main purposes of inspection would be to validate self-assessments, to encourage continuous improvement of the quality of provision and the raising of standards, to enable colleges to compare their performance with that of others offering similar provision, and to assist the dissemination of good practice throughout the sector and the identification of issues of national significance. Greater attention would be given to the curriculum, to teaching and learning, and to students' achievements. The main aspects for assessment were to be:

- teaching and learning;
- students' achievements;
- curriculum content, organization and management;
- support for students;
- resources;
- quality assurance;
- management;
- governance.

The latter two, treated under the same heading in the first round, were now to be dealt with under separate headings. There would be a more selective approach to inspecting programme areas and other aspects of college provision, and if colleges had received good inspection reports in the first cycle, and carried out self-assessment effectively, it was envisaged that fewer days than were common in the first cycle would be allocated to these colleges. To reduce the burden of inspection and audit on colleges, joint working by inspectors and auditors in the assessment of management and governance was proposed (FEFC, 1997d).

The framework was accompanied by a new set of guidelines on self-assessment and inspection developed from those previously in use, and expressed (as before) as a set of positive quality statements which were not exhaustive or prescriptive and were not intended to be used as a checklist. The guidelines took account of the recommendations made in the Dearing (1996) *Review of Qualifications for 16–19 Year Olds*, the Tomlinson (1996) Committee's report, *Inclusive Learning*, and the Kennedy (1997) Committee's report, *Learning Works*.

Additional guidance on self-assessment was given in Circular 97/13 (FEFC, 1997b), based on the principles that self-assessment provides the impetus for quality improvement and is most effective when it is structured, rigorous and continuous, and that both self-assessment and external inspection should focus on the same criteria, at the forefront of which are the quality of teaching and learning and students' achievements. The circular summarized the inspectorate's view of the self-assessments made by colleges in the first cycle and distinguished the qualities of those that were effective from those that were of limited use. The inspectorate found that the most effective self-assessment reports arose from a comprehensive self-assessment system and were clearly presented under the standard inspection headings. They were evaluative, identified strengths and weaknesses, and dealt even-handedly with weaknesses as well as strengths. They addressed adequately the key issues of teaching and the promotion of learning and students' achievements. Their judgements referred to robust evidence and data, including findings from classroom observations, and they included agreed plans for action with measurable targets, deadlines and nominated responsibilities. In contrast, the weaker reports tended to be purely descriptive, or dealt with the strengths of provision but not the weaknesses, were not supported by adequate evidence, and gave insufficient weight to teaching and the promotion of learning and to students' achievements. In some of these cases, the production of the self-assessment report had not been linked to the colleges' quality assurance procedures and few staff had contributed, so that the report did not represent a cross-college assessment of provision.

The guidance on self-assessment therefore emphasized that reports should be evaluative, comprehensive and concise, and written under the headings used in the inspection framework. They should be based on evidence which includes internal and appropriate national performance indicators, should address students' learning experiences, should evaluate and take full account of students' and other customers' views, and should be integral to strategic and operational planning and other quality assurance arrangements. Action plans to address identified weaknesses should be included.

The Framework for Accreditation

In its consultation, the FEFC (1996a) had sought the sector's views on introducing a system of accreditation for those colleges that could take responsibility for their own quality assessment and would receive less external inspection. Various possible criteria for selection were suggested. Nearly all those who responded to the invitation to give their views saw accreditation as a logical development for the sector, although a range of views was expressed about how accreditation should be implemented. To develop some plans, the quality assessment committee asked the Chief Inspector to chair a working group which put forward proposals for consideration in Circular 97/25 (FEFC, 1997e). These received support from the sector and, with revisions, were published in *Accrediting Colleges* (FEFC, 1998c). This framework acknowledged that an increasing number of colleges had established a good record in managing their affairs and in providing services of a high standard to their students and communities. The plans for accreditation recognized outstanding achievements demonstrated by colleges in meeting their responsibilities and also reflected a commitment to change the way the FEFC used its resources. More focused attention would be given to assisting those colleges experiencing operational or academic difficulties and to promoting good practice in all colleges. Funding would be allocated to promote the dissemination of good practice by accredited colleges.

The purpose of accreditation was to encourage all colleges to achieve high standards of performance and accountability, and to maintain these over time. Colleges would be expected to demonstrate to the FEFC that they had established comprehensive, effective and rigorously applied systems of management control and quality assurance covering all aspects of their work. It should be evident that all these worked together to raise the standard of all college operations. Colleges which achieved accreditation would be required to continue to demonstrate to the FEFC, other stakeholders and the public that they meet the standards required.

There were five criteria for accreditation:

- the existence in the college of formal and effective control, quality assurance and monitoring arrangements;
- regular and rigorous self-assessment, validated during the course of inspection;
- the setting and consistent achievement of appropriate targets for institutional performance;
- the demonstration that standards of students' achievements were being improved and/or maintained at a high level over a three-year period;
- effective action to address weaknesses and demonstrate the college's accountability.

Detailed requirements were given under each criterion. Those for students' achievements, for example, referred to appropriate performance levels to be derived from FEFC guidance on a range of benchmarks for student retention and achievements, taking into account factors such as the age of students, the type of college being attended, the level of study in relation to the national framework of qualifications and the degree of economic deprivation within a college's community. The first instalment of these benchmarking data, for 1995–6 and 1996–7, was published (FEFC, 1998d) with the explanation that the term 'benchmarking data' is used to imply a reference point for comparison and not a standard of best practice.

The Quality Improvement Strategy

In June 1998 the FEFC also published its *Quality Improvement Strategy* (FEFC, 1998b). In this consultation paper, the FEFC set out a strategy which continued development of the FEFC's role in promoting the improvement of quality within the sector, built on the work of the inspectorate, and offered help to colleges in meeting the standards required for accredited status. The strategy was intended to help colleges meet the challenge of raising standards through action to improve student retention and achievement, such as setting targets for retention and achievement, using benchmarks for retention and achievement, and developing of added-value measures and benchmarks. It was proposed that college inspectors should provide additional support to colleges, particularly to colleges in difficulties, and should increasingly focus its publications and presentations to colleges on the promotion of good practice. In addition, unsatisfactory cross-college provision should be re-inspected like curriculum areas. Funding arrangements are being developed to encourage and support improvements in quality, for example by the establishment of an 'achievement fund' to ensure recognition of colleges which significantly raised the level of their students' achievements, and to ensure that all colleges were provided with an incentive to do this without detriment to other aspects of their provision.

The Impact of the Revised System in 1997–8

Inspections carried out in 1997–8 confirmed that colleges had responded well to the new approach, with its main focus on the validation of self-assessments. All the colleges inspected prepared a self-assessment report on the quality of their provision prior to inspection. The great majority provided a useful basis for planning inspection activities. Those colleges which were inspected some months after their self-assessment report was produced were often able to demonstrate that action plans had been implemented and provision improved. Colleges were asked to grade their own provision as part of their self-assessments. Overall, about 65 per cent of grades awarded by colleges matched those awarded by inspectors. In 8 per cent of cases, inspectors concluded that colleges had underestimated the quality of their work. However, in 27 per cent inspectors considered colleges were over-generous in their grading. In general, where there was disagreement about curriculum grades, inspectors concluded that colleges most commonly did not take sufficient account of low student retention and achievement. With regard to cross-college provision, inspectors concluded that about one-third of colleges overstated the quality of their governance and one-quarter overstated the quality of their management. Quality assurance continued to be the weakest aspect of cross-college provision, with 55 per cent of colleges judged to have good or outstanding quality assurance. However, this compared favourably with an average of 38 per cent awarded Grades 1 and 2 over the four years 1993 to 1997. The inspection programme for 1997–8 included re-inspection of twenty-three curriculum areas in twenty colleges which had unsatisfactory provision. Of these, all but one showed satisfactory improvement in quality.

Conclusions

Since its inception in 1993, the FEFC's system of academic accountability through self-assessment and inspection has provided extensive published evidence on the quality and standards achieved in English further education. The system was designed, developed and operated in consultation with the sector, and has retained its confidence despite the unwelcome messages it has sometimes presented. Measures have been taken to remedy weaknesses and disseminate good practice. The system has developed flexibly and with continuity. As the primary responsibility for quality and its control rests with colleges, the FEFC has placed increasing emphasis on their self-assessments in its procedures for external assessment and inspection. The move towards a more differentiated system of inspection, and the proposals for increased emphasis on spreading good practice and helping colleges to improve, derived from needs identified by the system itself. It is too early to assess the impact of these developments on the sector, but they sharpen the focus of accountability to meet the needs of different colleges and learners, and emphasize the maintenance and improvement of quality and standards.

References

Dearing, R. (1996) *Review of Qualifications for 16–19 Year Olds*, London: School Curriculum and Assessment Authority.

DES and DoE (1991) *Education and Training for the 21st Century*, Cmnd 1536, London: HMSO.

FEFC (1992) *Preparing for Incorporation*, Circular 92/02, Coventry: FEFC.

FEFC (1993a) *Assessing Achievement* (consultation), Circular 93/11, Coventry: FEFC.

FEFC (1993b) *Assessing Achievement* (framework), Circular 93/28, Coventry; FEFC.

FEFC (1994) *Quality and Standards in Further Education in England: Chief Inspector's Annual Report 1993–94*, Coventry: FEFC.

FEFC (1995) *Quality and Standards in Further Education in England: Chief Inspector's Annual Report 1994–95*, Coventry: FEFC.

FEFC (1996a) *Review of the Further Education Funding Council's Inspection Framework*, Circular 96/12, Coventry: FEFC.

FEFC (1996b) *Quality and Standards in Further Education in England: Chief Inspector's Annual Report 1995–96*, Coventry: FEFC.

FEFC (1997a) *Validating Self-Assessment*, Circular 97/12, Coventry: FEFC.

FEFC (1997b) *Self-Assessment and Inspection*, Circular 97/13, Coventry: FEFC.

FEFC (1997c) *Report of the Quality Assessment Committee for 1995–6*, Circular 97/20, Coventry: FEFC.

FEFC (1997d) *Joint Working: Audit and Inspection*, Circular 97/22, Coventry: FEFC.

FEFC (1997e) *College Accreditation* (consultation), Circular 97/25, Coventry: FEFC.

FEFC (1997f) *Quality and Standards in Further Education in England 1996–97: Chief Inspector's Annual Report*, Coventry: FEFC.

FEFC (1998a) *Report of the Quality Assurance Committee for 1996–7*, Circular 98/13, Coventry: FEFC.

FEFC (1998b) *Quality Improvement Strategy*, Circular 98/21, Coventry: FEFC.

FEFC (1998c) *Accrediting Colleges*, Circular 98/22, Coventry: FEFC.

FEFC (1998d) *Retention and Achievement Rates in Further Education Colleges in England: Benchmarking Data 1995–6 and 1996–7*, Coventry: FEFC.

FEFC (1998e) *Quality and Standards in Further Education in England 1997–98: Chief Inspector's Annual Report*, Coventry: FEFC.

Kennedy, H. (1997) *Learning Works: Widening Participation in Further Education*, Coventry: FEFC.

Tomlinson, J. (1996) *Inclusive Learning: Report of the Learning Difficulties and/or Disabilities Committee*, London: The Stationery Office.

15 Research

Geoff Stanton

It is the conventional wisdom that further education is under-researched. It is not straightforward to determine how true this is, but a lot depends on how the terms 'further education' and 'research' are defined. By some definitions there is plenty going on. This chapter will look at what definitions best fit further education and the link that needs to exist with its developmental needs. The many-faceted nature of further education and the fact that it relates to many other parts of the educational system, society, industry and the labour market, all mean that relevant research is both dispersed and lacking in coherence.

The special nature of further education both means that research and development (R & D) are much needed and that FE R & D cannot usefully follow models designed for other contexts. Research into schools, largely funded by universities, has been criticized for following an agenda set by researchers and for being irrelevant to practice. Research into further education, largely funded by government agencies, could be criticized for following too closely an agenda set by policy-makers and not exposing itself to public evaluation. I will therefore explore an approach to R & D which avoids these extremes. In doing so I will draw upon the experience of the Further Education Unit (FEU), one of the predecessor bodies of the Further Education Development Agency (FEDA), in sponsoring college-based research and development, and consider what should be the links between this and the work of universities and the inspectorate.

Research on Further Education

As long ago as 1969, Cantor and Roberts were bemoaning 'the relative overall paucity of research into further education'. Almost thirty years later Johnson (1997) was still able to conclude that 'there is little enough research about FE'. These are perceptions shared by many staff in colleges. On the other hand, Cantor and Roberts went on to list numerous institutions which were beginning to take an interest in researching further education. They also quoted a survey which identified over 600 recently completed and current projects. Similarly, in 1997, Johnson found that 'colleges research themselves prodigiously'. He reports that of 150 colleges surveyed, 93 per cent undertook market research and 66 per cent were involved in research to improve institutional performance or quality. He goes on to suggest that 'it is likely that colleges conduct much more institutional research than universities'.

The sense of uncertainty is borne out by a recent report on research into vocational education and training (VET) in the UK. Brown and Keep (1998) quote well over 300 projects published in the 1990s, but conclude that 'the overall picture that emerges is one of extreme fragmentation, with research located in a multiplicity of institutional and disciplinary settings, and supported by funding from a very wide range of sources'. Now VET is not coterminous with further education, but Raffe (1996) has pointed out that much research that is in fact about or very relevant to the sector has a title which does not mention the words 'further education'. The issue therefore does not seem to be one of quantity but rather:

- fragmentation – identifying and synthesizing the work taking place;
- boundary definition – for example, how far can FE be equated with VET?;
- definitions of 'research' – for instance, does college-based work count?

To this I would add the fact that much 'generic' educational research, into topics such as tutorial work, numeracy, the development of citizenship and so on, is conducted as if the sector did not exist. This is despite its size and diversity, catering for more sixteen- to nineteen-year-olds than attend schools and more adults than attend universities.

College-Based Research and Development

One of the reasons for the extent of college-based R & D was the approach adopted by the FEU. In 1977, the Further Education Curriculum Review and Development Unit was founded. Funded by grant-in-aid from the then Department for Education and Science (DES) it was governed by an independent board appointed by the Secretary of State. Soon renamed the FEU, it had by 1987 commissioned or conducted over 400 'research projects', most in the second half of the first decade of its existence. Most were funded from FEU's own very slim resources – its R & D budget was only a few thousand pounds in its first year and still less than £500,000 per annum by 1987. A substantial minority of the projects were funded by the DES or the Manpower Services Commission (MSC) and managed on their behalf by FEU development officers.

These development officers occupied a space between academic researchers and college staff. They were usually recruited from colleges, were employed on fixed-term (three- to five-year) contracts and, although most went back to colleges (many are now vice-principals or principals), some became inspectors or joined universities. Through them, the FEU conducted projects itself, commissioned and managed projects for others, and converted the outcomes into publications aimed at practitioners in colleges. Depending on the material and the intended audience, the output could be in the form of research reports, briefing notes, guidelines on good practice, theoretical frameworks or even audio-tapes for playing in the car. The FEU's status as a non-departmental public body meant that it could draw upon material and findings from a number of sources in producing a report, if this made it more useful for its audience. After 1987, following criticism of some lack of focus in the unit's work (partly because of its very volume), the FEU also used its development officers to consult with the sector and others in order to determine priorities for R & D and to inform the unit's strategic plan which was published annually.

Typically, FEU's R & D was commissioned from staff in FE colleges rather than universities. For instance, in a typical year FEU worked with more than half of all colleges in England and Wales. This was partly because of the developmental dimension of the work, but it was also – it has to be admitted – a way of working cheaply. Colleges were only paid their marginal costs for releasing a member of staff and often gave hidden subsidies in the form of administrative support and so on. However, it was also because there was little expertise about FE amongst university researchers and untapped potential among college staff. In summary, this approach:

- linked research to development;
- aimed to produce outputs relevant to practitioners;
- was informed by the needs of FE colleges and by national developments.

It was therefore largely and proudly pragmatic, but it also included, according to FEU (1993a), a 'visionary and speculative aspect which helps its customers to see what the future may be like'. Indeed, some of its most influential publications were of this kind, such as those which offered models to show why experiential learning was effective (FEU, 1978) or advocated unit-based credit frameworks (FEU, 1993b). But even this theorizing was intended to benefit practitioners and policy-makers rather than being aimed at other researchers.

This approach had problems. For instance, when instituting one of its major programmes, of great relevance to further education, the Economic and Social Research Council (ESRC) found difficulty in designating FEU as a body fit to receive ESRC funding because its staff did not publish in refereed academic journals and did not have research degrees. (There was little problem, however, in funding people to conduct FE research who had never worked in the sector. I will discuss the implications of this later.) It was also possible for an FEFC review group (FEFC, 1993) to conclude that:

> research which is devoted to testing conceptual hypotheses or exploring the empirical findings of research activity, without necessarily any immediate concern with delivery, is not undertaken [by FEU]. At the same time, academic and research bodies have eschewed involvement in further education. Consequently there is a lack of research findings to inform the assumptions which policy-makers and implementers have to make.

This review group called this a lack of 'strategic research'. This term, and the above definition of it, could – in another place – be disputed. Nevertheless, there is force in this comment – which makes an interesting contrast to the criticism to which research into schools and schooling has been subjected.

Relationship to Research in Other Sectors

Recently there has been criticism of the apparent lack of relevance of educational research to the prime task of enhancing the quality of what goes on in schools and colleges. During 1998 two reviews were published, one commissioned by OFSTED (Tooley and Darby, 1998) and the other by the DfEE (Hillage *et al.*, 1998). However, what in many ways was a more powerful criticism, which was also less open to the suggestion of there being a political subplot, was published in 1996 by Professor Hargreaves of the University of Cambridge (previously an LEA inspector). Hargreaves drew attention to the fact that hardly any practising teachers even read educational research, let alone are influenced by it. He argued that claims that this was due to lack of dissemination were misplaced. Most research, he claimed, would not be relevant to a teacher's concerns even if disseminated. Researchers set their own agenda, as well as writing for each other. Also, peer evaluation allowed the perpetuation of questionable methodology.

Unfortunately, Hargreaves repeated the tendency of many educational writers and ignored the FE sector altogether. Had he applied his analysis to further education he could have produced an interesting comparative study. The FE tradition, if it can be graced by that name, is to link research much more closely with development. As we have seen, taking the work of the FEU as a case in point, priority was given to the production of practical guidelines, frameworks and the dissemination of good practice. Hundreds of publications have been produced by FEU and its successor body, the Further Education Development Agency (FEDA), over the past twenty years, almost all of them aimed at teachers, managers or policy-makers.[1] In fact, if criticism could be made of this it would be that too little theoretical analysis of its own assumptions was made or commissioned by FEU. University researchers were sometimes used, but usually only with the aim of underpinning the practical advice it was intended to produce.

Cantor and Roberts (1969) in their early review commented that 'while universities are well-equipped for research in general they contain relatively few staff members who have been through or are informed about further education'. This is somewhat less true today, but it will remain a tendency as long as the expected route to a career in research is an excellent first degree followed by three years working for a PhD. This produces problems for educational research in general, but it is exacerbated in the case of further education because in many cases university researchers will not even have experienced the sector as students, let alone as teachers.

In its response to the Hillage *et al.* (1998), the DfEE (1998b) indicated that it would be looking at the possibility of 'concentrating funding in 10–20 centres of research excellence rather than spreading it too thinly as occurs at present'. The Higher Education Funding Council (HEFC, 1998) has also stated that it wished to ensure that 'the lion's share of funds for research go to departments producing work of the highest quality, as assessed through the Research Assessment Exercise (RAE)'. In the RAE what is rewarded includes an appropriate publication record, which means articles in 'refereed' journals. A refereed journal sends potential articles to a group of fellow academics for comment before agreeing publication. Often, this does not guarantee FE expertise, nor is the sector involved in setting the research agenda. Work of international repute is required for the higher levels of funding, which tends to favour generic work in such areas as educational psychology rather than context-specific studies into the idiosyncratic English FE system. Other factors relevant to the RAE grading of a university department include the number of PhD students supported by it. Success at obtaining resources from elsewhere, and the production of research results in more accessible forms and locations, is taken into account, but is given less significance.

As far as research support is concerned, funding gained by a university from a research council tends to carry more prestige than does funding from, for example, direct beneficiaries such as a college or a group of colleges, or even the DfEE. Although research councils are beginning to give more emphasis to 'end users' than they did, they are also (as we have seen) proud of the fact that funding tends to go to places that are already recognized centres of research, which employ staff with a recognized track record – as conventionally defined. I would argue that this approach is problematic as far as research into education is concerned and with regard to research into further education there are additional difficulties. The traditional approach may be appropriate for subjects such as physics or history, where the key test for the rigour and depth of a piece of research is to have its results exposed to the scrutiny of one's peers in the research community. Who else can comment on a proof in mathematics or replicate a claimed experimental result in chemistry? Also, it may be no criticism of such work that there is no obvious application for it.

However, education is of course an essentially applied activity and Hargreaves (1996) argues that adopting an overly academic approach has been damaging. He compares the situation in the applied subject of education with that in the equally applied subject of medicine. His argument runs thus:

> A consultant in (say) surgery, and even more so a professor of surgery, would be a practising surgeon of outstanding achievement. If practising doctors, especially those in hospitals, stopped doing research and left it almost entirely to a special breed of people called 'medical researchers', who were mainly university academics without patients, then medical research would go the same way as educational research – a private, esoteric activity, seen as irrelevant by most practitioners.

Hargreaves' remedy for some of the problems, particularly the one of a lack of what he calls 'evidence-based' practice or policy-making, is to rejig the routes through which money reaches researchers. He defends the approach of the research councils, though in my view their record with regard to further education has until recently been weak. This approach has meant, for instance, that even when the ESRC instituted its current £2 million programme called *The Learning Society* (1995–9), which explicitly encouraged a FE focus and even involvement, its own rules meant that most of the institutions which qualified as appropriate locations for the research were not felt by the sector to be part of its community. In particular, it is the staff of the ex-polytechnics who are most likely to have relevant experience, but only one of these 'new' universities was involved in any of the thirteen projects which were funded.

Hargreaves (1996) proposed that more research should be funded by the Teacher Training Agency and/or OFSTED rather than via money distributed to universities from the funding councils. Once again, had he looked to further education he would have found that some parallels to this approach already existed, not all of them entirely reassuring.

FE Research Funded by Government Agencies

Once one escapes from the conventional definition of 'research' it becomes evident that there is a considerable volume of FE-related research which has been funded by government agencies such as the MSC, the National Council for Vocational Qualifications (NCVQ) and the FEFC. For example, after the 1984 White Paper (DoE and DES, 1984) about a quarter of the money available for what was then called 'Work-Related Non-Advanced Further Education' (WRNAFE) was transferred from the ministry, the DES, to the Employment Department's MSC. The MSC in turn set aside a percentage of this to use as a 'WRNAFE development fund'. This was perhaps the first – and so far only – time that a fixed percentage of expenditure on education was allocated to related R & D and it is perhaps not surprising that it was a part of government with a more business-oriented outlook that took this approach. After all, almost any other knowledge-based industry would set aside a percentage of turnover for R & D as a matter of course. It would see its future health and prosperity depending on it. This fund, which went through a succession of names over the next few years, amounted to £5 million per annum by 1987 and supported some 500 'research and development' projects (Training Commission, 1988). Since it was a *development fund*, as well as a research budget, much of the money went to the colleges themselves for specific projects, rather than to recognized research institutes.[2]

In addition to the WRNAFE development fund, the MSC funded research connected with programmes such as the Youth Training Scheme, Employment Training (for adults), Open Learning and the Standards Programme for Vocational Qualifications. In particular, MSC commissioned vast amounts of research and evaluation in connection with the Technical and Vocational Education Initiative (TVEI) aimed at fourteen- to nineteen-year-olds, and which eventually involved most colleges. In respect of TVEI, at least, the government was reasonably comfortable about listing and publishing such research (in contrast to some other programmes), but – as Pring (1997) has pointed out – when it came to implementing the national curriculum almost none of the lessons about curriculum design and the management of change were taken into account. In other words, government seemed not to be interested in evidence-based policies. This possibility is often ignored by those advocating 'strategic research'. It is, of course, inconceivable that in medicine the government would take it upon itself to design courses of treatment, let alone that it would impose such courses in apparent ignorance of previous experience. This is one place where Hargreaves' medical analogy begins to break down.

The advent of the national curriculum and NVQs (see Chapter 5) brought a period in which, because government 'owned' the initiatives, the evaluation of them became a highly political matter. The first Chief Executive of the National Curriculum Council (NCC), Duncan Graham, has written with David Tytler (1993) about the difficulties government placed in the way of NCC when it came to evaluating the National Curriculum, a fact which possibly contributed to the need for a fundamental review some years later. A similar pattern of events took place with regard to NVQs (Stanton, 1997). When, eventually, the 'Top 100' NVQs were reviewed by a committee chaired by Gordon Beaumont (1996), a research effort said to have cost more than £2 million underpinned this work – but this was not publicly recorded or analysed in the same way that an ESRC programme of the same magnitude would have been. In fact, it is clear that some of Beaumont's conclusions (for instance about employers' attitudes) were based on a methodology and a sample-size that would not have withstood academic scrutiny (Smithers, 1997).

Ecclestone (1998) has written about what she calls the 'GNVQ research industry', which she claims is an example of a situation in which 'officially commissioned research projects must adopt an overtly technical and uncritical approach to a problem, in the face of extremely tight time constraints and acute political sensitivities'. Some insiders (Oates, 1997, for example) have argued that some of these things are inevitable in the case of R & D funded by agencies such as NCVQ, given government schedules and political priorities. A consequence is that a cohort of university researchers and independent consultants develops which certainly *does* follow an agenda set by government or its agencies, because the work is done under contract. However, either because of what the contract says or because of the need to remain in favour with the funders, those involved may feel unable to voice any fundamental concerns. In my experience, agencies close to government also censor themselves. Some work which they would like to do remains uncommissioned because even to investigate some possibilities is thought to risk giving out 'unhelpful' political signals. Medical research rarely gets as political as this (except possibly in the case of BSE).

In other words, the price paid for relevance and the possibility of influence may be an inability to make research public or to query the agenda set. This in turn results in those researchers who are not part of the 'official' activities tending to adopt a rival and essentially dissenting perspective, often putting their own objectivity at risk in the process. So from the practitioner's point of view, neither camp is of much use. The official research does not want to hear about flawed assumptions, which may need to be corrected before an initiative can work, and the dissenting research does not want the initiative to work at all.

The Nature of Further Education

In the FE context, the distinctive interpretation of 'research', the link with development and the fragmentation of activity are not things which have just occurred by accident. To a large extent they relate to the nature of further education itself. According to Raffe (1996),

> the field of study which is 'FE' has weak external boundaries and multiple internal ones. On the one hand, most research which is relevant to FE is not specifically and exclusively about FE. On the other hand, FE research encompasses a variety of disciplines, methods, and even paradigms of enquiry.

Learners and Learning Programmes

The range of learners described earlier, and therefore the range of required learning programmes, is what makes research into further education difficult to confine within simple boundaries. Further education is becoming increasingly *inclusive*. Both schools and universities are much more *exclusive* in that they do not aim to cater for some of the population – on the grounds of their age, mode of study, level of attainment, area of study and so on. Although this may make it easier for research into schools and universities to be more focused and visible, the very diversity of further education means that it is – in principle – a particularly fruitful topic for research, because of the comparisons and contrasts that can be made. For example, only within further education are all types of qualification regimes implemented: from GCSEs to degrees, from Open College programmes to NVQs. Over half of all A-level students are in colleges, but so are most of those taking GNVQs (DfEE, 1998a).

More sixteen- to eighteen-year-old full-time students attend college than school, but three-quarters of college students are part-time and over nineteen (15 per cent are over sixty). Therefore, research into those attending is complex, both practically and conceptually. To take a conceptual example, some FE students might be best described as *clients* of the organization and, indeed, many colleges now have functions such as 'client services'. At its best, this means that colleges adapt to students' needs, rather than asking them to fit into the colleges' arrangements. However, some full-time students would rather think of themselves as *belonging* to a college, having influence through this membership rather than through their purchasing power. Both outlooks have to be catered for.

Boundaries and Definitions

What is covered by the term 'further education' will vary considerably depending on which of the following dimensions is thought to be the defining factor:

- colleges funded by FEFC;
- courses;
- qualifications;
- defined groups of learners.

The reason that this is not such an issue for schools or universities is that, for the most part, each of these dimensions matches the others. This means, for instance, that if the research is into the implementation of GCSEs or degrees then it is also research into schools and universities respectively. In the case of further education, as we have seen, these dimensions are not coterminous and there is great variation. Consider the following:

1 A-levels are not thought of as an FE qualification and yet this is the single most common qualification aim of full-time FE students. Does this mean that we classify research into A-levels as research into FE?
2 The vast majority of GNVQs are offered in FE, but GNVQs make up less than 10 per cent of what colleges do.
3 In fact, for many colleges higher education is a more significant part of their portfolio and the sector as a whole provides 13 per cent of the country's HE.
4 At the same time, most colleges make special provision for students with learning difficulties, including those who have previously attended special schools.
5 NVQs are seen as being primarily a workplace qualification and yet the majority of them are offered either in further education or with the involvement of colleges.

All this means that what counts as 'research into the FE curriculum' is problematic and requires a special understanding. Research into FE students is equally difficult to focus. More sixteen- to eighteen-year-olds now study in the sector than schools, but three-quarters of its students are over this age.

Many people now simply equate 'FE' with colleges funded by FEFC. However, it has to be remembered that the 'sector' thus defined has only existed since 1992 and about a quarter of it – the sixth-form colleges – were previously schools. Many of their staff still belong to school rather than FE unions. The thirty-one agriculture and horticulture colleges have not traditionally felt much in common with either group, nor have the nine colleges specializing in art and design. (Though some of this may change as mergers and collaborative arrangements spread.) It also has to be recognized that although English 'sector colleges' provide for 3.3 million students with FEFC funds, a further 1.3

million students are funded from other sources. These sources include TECs and individual companies, for whom vocational course are provided, and LEAs who often contract with colleges for the provision of recreational adult education in the locality.

As a counterpoint to this debate about where further education fits within the world of education, there are many who would emphasize the fact that a lot of colleges grew out of 'technical' institutions. Further education is here perceived to have much in common with the world of industrial training. Indeed, when talking with European colleagues, further education tends to be described as part of VET. Its schizophrenia is well demonstrated by research involving international comparisons: the comparative institutions visited in Europe are often trade schools involved in VET, working with local and national industries. By contrast, the comparative institutions visited in the USA tend to be community colleges, which provide associate degrees, often in liberal arts subjects, as a stepping stone to local universities.

Variations in level of work, subject matter and the student body – within a working week and from year to year – means that FE staff are more in need of R & D support than are school or university teachers, or industrial trainers. Colleges also have more direct interfaces with other educational and training organizations – such as schools, universities, Industry Training Organizations (ITOs) and TECs – and are more immediately affected by changes in the local economy. To take an actual example, the closing down of an electronics manufacturer and the arrival of a large 'call-centre' can affect what the local college does within weeks. The effect on local schools and universities will come much more slowly and indirectly, if at all.

Incorporation, Funding and Qualifications: A Threefold Experiment

If all this were not enough, colleges have, during the past decade, been involved in radical changes to their systems of governance, to their funding regimes and to the vocational qualifications which form a central part of their work. All these changes have been imposed on them and, in the case of funding and qualifications, the changes have been highly innovative. It might be said, with some justice, that the FE sector in England has been the subject of three very large-scale experiments. What is more, the innovations became linked, in that the funding regime of the FEFC was related to qualification aims and their achievement. Contrary to what is implied by those advocating 'strategic research', these and other policies were not introduced as a result of such research, nor did the policy-makers always show a willingness to be overt about 'the assumptions they had to make' (FEFC, 1993). Whether or not such an evidence-based and analytical approach to change is always feasible in education, the fact is that it is rare. This emphasizes the importance of on-going evaluation and development. However, no coherent programme of this kind was established, despite the magnitude of the experiments being conducted and the number of learners involved.

It could be argued that two organizations did exist which could undertake these functions: the inspectorate and the FEU. However, the first – despite many strengths – has some weaknesses when it comes to an R & D function and the second was disabled at the crucial time by being reorganized.

Inspection and Research

With the new Funding Council[3] came a new inspectorate and a new inspection regime. The inspectorate became a section within the FEFC, as opposed to being a free-standing organization like the previous HMIs. The FEFC inspectorate judged that most colleges managed to implement change without harming student achievement or the classroom performance of teachers. Indeed, they have found that both continue to improve and the operation of the funding regime has meant that colleges have also paid increasing attention to the initial guidance given to students at recruitment, and to optimizing student retention and achievement.

Hargreaves (1996) argued that medicine is more 'evidence-based' than education, because of weaknesses in educational research. But in medicine there is no real equivalent of the inspectorate. Can inspection be counted as a form of research? To what extent can inspection provide the required evidence? Inspection activities are much more extensive and comprehensive than most research projects, with more right of access to colleges and a greater capacity to collect data. In the case of the FEFC inspectorate, they and the FEFC are in the process of developing a range of instruments which they hope will enable them both to measure retention and achievement much more systematically than was possible before, and to produce benchmarking statistics so that the performance of similar colleges in similar circumstances can be compared. In recent years, colleges have also been struggling to implement the FEFC's Individualized Student Record, which contains detailed information about the starting point and achievements of each learner. Only an organization with the clout of the Funding Council could have ensured that colleges went through what everyone found a very strenuous exercise, though all agree that it should provide a most fruitful data-source in years to come. In addition, the inspectorate conduct cross-sectoral studies into such issues as the implementation of GNVQs and the use of technology to support learning, and also undertake comparative studies of further education in other countries (for example, Japan and Korea).

On the other hand, when compared to a research project, the inspectorate has a number of drawbacks. Inspectors are employed by the FEFC itself, which is obviously a party with a vested interest. Colleges and their staffs are bound to put on the best possible show during an inspection, because of the likely impact of a negative report on their own futures.[4] An independent university research team which guaranteed anonymity would be far more likely to pick up any negative messages or be pointed towards areas of concern. This is important if one believes that positive developments can only come once problems have been identified and admitted. Even so, the inspectorate has identified teaching quality and the level of student achievement as areas where further development is required. Too much is merely satisfactory, they say, and there is too much variability (FEFC, 1998).

This gives rise to the issue of development linked to, and arising out of, research and/or inspection, and who should be responsible for it. There is a strong argument that to make inspectors responsible for conducting develop-ment work – or even for proposing specific developments – is to create a conflict of interest. At some time in the future they will be required to inspect the results of their own proposals. It is not just that they might let their judge-ment be affected. It is also likely that those being inspected will conceal from them any problems, being aware of the source of the initiative.

The FEU: A Case Study

As we have seen, in further education a tailor-made organization had been created to promote and undertake development work. The FEU was founded in 1977 as an advice and intelligence body to 'review and develop' the FE curriculum and to promote good practice. It had begun in a very small way, with a director and two other professional staff, its creation stimulated by the need for new provision catering for that 40 per cent of young people who entered jobs without any structured education or training attached. It soon became involved in what became the much higher profile need to provide schemes for the suddenly much increased numbers of unemployed school leavers and for those who wished to stay on in education for a further year beyond the end of compulsory schooling.

By 1992, the FEU had grown to include twenty-five development officers, ten of whom were based in the English regions and in Wales. Also in 1992 it took on, at the request of the Secretary of State, the work and staff of another development agency, the Unit for the Development of Adult and Continuing Education (UDACE). Having started life as a curriculum R & D body, it is fair to say that FEU's interest in research derived from the need to produce effective support for practitioners (and therefore advice to policy-makers on their behalf) rather than from the intention to create a body of coherent and long-term research projects. Indeed, it did not have the funding to do this, even if this had been its role. However, in addition to producing much advice about good practice, it also 'theorized' about such things as learning in further educa-tion, the nature of the student's curriculum entitlement and the pre-vocational curriculum. On the basis of its activities, the FEU increasingly felt able to comment on and attempt to influence government policy, and despite the fact that the unit was funded by a grant-in-aid from the DES, it came to be seen as a body with considerable independence of view.

The need for independence was identified when the FEU was set up. A decade later, in 1987, and after the first review of the unit's future, the then Secretary of State, Kenneth Baker, reaffirmed the need for 'maintaining the independence appropriate to a body engaged in the professional tasks of curriculum review and development' (DES, 1987). There was also a recognition that ministers themselves needed information and advice on curriculum matters. When, in 1992, the FEFC was asked by the then Secretary of State to review the activities of the FEU, together with its sister body the Further Education Staff College, it was explicitly asked to comment on 'the significance or otherwise of the FEU's current independence for the effectiveness of its work' (Patten, 1992). In so far as the FEFC (1993) review group showed itself willing to consider this question at all, it tended to regard independence as a bad thing which gave 'a licence [to FEU] to choose for itself what to become involved in and whether or not to be helpful'. The review uncritically adopted a market-led approach to things, stating that:

> What did not seem to the group any longer to be appropriate is for the FEU itself to determine where it should be positioned without being subject to the discipline of satisfying customer requirements.

This does of course beg the crucial questions of who the customers of R & D are, and how they can express their requirements. It was implied that colleges were the customers, but it was also recognized that 'the requirements of the sector could not be left solely to the aggregation of the individual choices of colleges.' Therefore, the FEFC did not distribute the funding among the 400 or so colleges for them to use as they chose. Instead it 'top-sliced' their funding in order to fund the FEDA (FEU's successor), in effect making itself the customer. When it was also decided that it would make FEDA more 'market-oriented' if half this money was issued to FEDA via a series of FEFC contracts rather than in the form of a block grant, as previously, this just emphasized the FEFC's role and influence as customer. This is an example of what has become a classic problem with regard to educational research. On the one hand, researchers claim the right not only to be independent, but to be seen to be so. On the other, this leaves them open to the suggestion that their activities are, in reality or appearance, self-indulgent, inefficient and irrelevant.

A Way Forward?

The way forward could be to develop a model of R & D which involves colleges as partners, rather than simply being the object of research or even the customer. 'Pure research' should continue, but unless it is designed to have a practical application it should be seen and funded as a branch of whichever discipline (for example, sociology or psychology) it is using. Research commissioned by the government and its agencies will continue, but this should not be at the expense of R & D for the benefit of colleges and their students. The government needs to recognize that it will always be tempted to control and censor any research over which it has direct control and the politics of any given moment may make this inevitable. It should also recognize that it nevertheless benefits from fearless advice derived from independent research and that without it there is always the danger of designing an educational equivalent of the poll tax.

It therefore needs to fund an organization which is genuinely at 'arm's length' and which can run an FE-oriented version of the 'forum' which Hargreaves (1996) envisaged, at which the content of a R & D agenda for further education can be openly and regularly debated. The inspectorate should be influential participants in this forum. In order to inform the debate, those organizing the forum should have right of access to descriptions of research in relevant areas. In order to ensure that this happened, the requirement to provide information to the forum should be a normal part of any publicly funded research contract. The coordinating agency should not have the power to force interested parties to undertake any particular research, but should instead undertake advisory and 'brokerage' functions in order to encourage the fulfilment of the agreed agenda. The agency should, however, have sufficient funds of its own to commission or undertake research in order to fill any gaps that remained once these processes had been completed and in order to synthesize research findings into a form that is accessible to practitioners. This role could well be undertaken by FEDA, but only if it is funded to a level and in a way which means that it does not have to compete for contracts against those it is attempting to coordinate.

Much of the necessary R & D would be best undertaken by the colleges working in conjunction with universities. Most colleges already have some kind of R & D activity. Johnson's (1997) survey for FEDA also showed that almost 90 per cent of respondent colleges in principle support staff in pursuing higher degrees with some research content, though most of these would make the support conditional on the work advancing college objectives. Such R & D activity would therefore be an important form of continuing professional development for college staff, as well as contributing to the development of the sector. Universities like Greenwich, with its large school of post-compulsory education and training, have already experimented with MAs based on action research which would enable staff to gain a higher degree while simultaneously improving their own professional performance and that of their college. The involvement of universities in this way with colleges would avoid the dangers of college staff not taking a wide enough view, or of being uncritical of their own culture and assumptions, or of failing to take advantage of existing research findings or techniques. Conversely, the involvement of colleges would enhance and inform the experience and priorities of university researchers.

There would remain an important role for theoretical studies, particularly if these aimed to give practitioners useful insights, rather than just being produced for fellow theoreticians. As an example of this approach, an early FEU publication, *A Basis for Choice* (FEU, 1979), followed by another on 'vocational preparation' (FEU, 1987), offered a theoretical model of the curriculum which Pring (1995) has argued could still be called on in order to escape the aridity of some of the current debate about an 'academic/vocational divide'. The fact that there is 'nothing as practical as a good theory' is not new, but researchers into further education may have to make a case to the research councils and HEFC in order to get their work judged by its value to practitioners, as well as by its reputation among academics.

Pring (1995) has also pointed out that when FE teachers were centrally involved in R & D and set its agenda, the 'focus was upon what was worth learning and how people learn. This contrasts dramatically with the current concentration upon assessment and assessment models'. The latter always tends to be an obsession of governments, perhaps understandably, but they should not be the only ones determining priorities.

Summary and Conclusions

In preparing this paper I have come to question the common assumption that further education is under-researched.[5] On the other hand, there is evidence that the research effort lacks coherence and balance, and that research relevant to further education is widely dispersed. It is also the case that most people researching into the many issues which cross sectors, act as if further education does not exist – and this even applies to those writing about educational research itself. Therefore, research relevant to further education does need tracking and the results need synthesizing. FEDA could undertake this role,[6] but its funding mechanism would have to be adjusted accordingly, so that it could be seen by both researchers and colleges to be a disinterested party. Alternatively, some argue for a 'professional body' for FE staff (similar to that which exists for doctors) or an FE Institute for Teaching and Learning to undertake this and other roles.

The experience of FEU showed that an organization with the right status and role can also facilitate the exchange of personnel between research and practitioner communities in a way which benefits both. From its tradition of what might be called 'reflective pragmatism', further education is in a good position to develop models of R & D which are fit for its own purposes, which do not ape models developed for others and which may be of benefit to the rest of educational research. Models which fit the culture and functioning of further education will link research to development. It is noteworthy that much of industry also talks of R & D. It is in academia that the two are separated and given different statuses.

In terms of R & D aimed at enhancing quality and achievement in further education, the necessary action-research could be a joint activity between colleges and universities in a way that would enhance the morale and professionalism of FE staff and which would complement, with practical experience, the research expertise and critical approach of those in higher education.[7]

Notes

1 In 1992 alone FEU produced 30 new publications, had 250 in print, distributed 75,000 copies to colleges and responded to more than 9,000 requests for information.

2 Much of this funding is now distributed via local TECs which support a wide range of projects. While the WRNAFE fund had a poor record of producing influential publications, TEC projects are even more difficult to track down.

3 In England. In Wales, although there was also a new FE Funding Council, it continued to employ HMI on contract. In Scotland and Northern Ireland the

funding, governance and inspection arrangements remained unchanged for the time being.

4   On the other hand, the FEFC inspectorate had managed to avoid the high political profile generated by the schools' inspectorate, OFSTED. Nevertheless, a number of college principals and even more heads of department have gone quietly after a weak inspection grade. The contrast with OFSTED would, in itself, be well worth a comparative study.

5   Even the current NFER Register of Research shows as many projects under 'further education' as under 'secondary' or 'primary education'. There are more than twice as many listed under 'higher education', which may confirm suspicions about the self-regarding nature of researchers!

6   Which would link well with FENTO and also make links with those other related organizations, such as FERA, FERN and the recently formed BERA (SIG) (significantly this Special Interest Group has adopted the currently fashionable label of 'Lifelong Learning' – again raising the boundary issue).

7   Lewisham College already publishes what it calls 'praxis papers', written by its own staff.

References

Beaumont, G. (1996) Report to the DfEE, *Review of 100 NVQs and SVQs* (no publisher indicated).

Brown, A. and Keep, E. (1998) 'Review of VET research in the UK', paper presented to the European COST Conference, University of Newcastle.

Cantor, L. and Roberts, I. (1969) *Further Education in England and Wales*, London: Routledge & Kegan Paul.

DES (1987) *Secretary of State's Letter to the Chairman of the FEU*, 8 January.

DfEE (1998a) 'Participation in education and training by 16–18 year olds', *DfEE News*, 335/98, 30 June.

DfEE (1998b) 'Educational research needs greater focus', *DfEE News*, 406/98, 26 August.

DoE and DES (1984) *Training for Jobs*, Cmnd 9135, London: HMSO.

Ecclestone, K. (1998) 'Euston Road and the ivory towers: The impact of the GNVQ research industry', *Journal of Education Policy*, 13, pp. 679–97.

FEFC (1993) *Review of the Further Education Unit and the Staff College*, Coventry: FEFC.

FEFC (1998) Annual Report of the Inspectorate, *Quality and Standards in Further Education 1997/98*, Coventry: FEFC.

FEU (1978) *Experience, Reflection, Learning*, London: FEU.

FEU (1979) *A Basis for Choice*, London: HMSO.

FEU (1987) *Supporting Change: A Revision of Vocational Preparation*, London: FEU.

FEU (1993a) *Report Prepared for the FEFC Review Group*, London: FEU.

FEU (1993b) *A Basis for Credit*, London: FEU.

Graham, D. and Tytler, D. (1993) *A Lesson For Us All: The Making of the National Curriculum*, London: Routledge & Kegan Paul.

Hargreaves, D.H. (1996) *Teaching as a Research-Based Profession: Possibilities and Prospects*, Teacher Training Agency Annual Lecture (mimeo).

HEFC (1998) *Press Release*, 26 August.

Hillage, J., Pearson, R., Anderson, A. and Tamkin, P. (1998) *Excellence in Research on Schools*, Research Report RR74, London: DfEE.

Johnson, M. (1997) *Research in FE Colleges*, London: FEDA.

Oates, T. (1997) 'Interview on GNVQ research and policy-making', University of Sunderland, May, cited in Ecclestone, 1998.

Patten, J. (1992) *Letter to Chairman of FEFC*, 5 November 1992.

Pring, R. (1995) *Closing the Gap: Liberal Education and Vocational Preparation*, London: Hodder & Stoughton.

Pring, R. (1997) 'The curriculum perspective', in G. Stanton and W. Richardson, *Qualifications for the Future*, London: FEDA.

Raffe, D. (1996) 'FE at the interface: A strategic research agenda', in F. Coffield (ed.), *Strategic Research in Further Education*, Durham: University of Durham for the ESRC.

Smithers, A. (1997) 'A critique of NVQs and GNVQs', in S. Tomlinson, *Education 14–18: Critical Perspectives*, London: The Athlone Press.

Stanton, G. (1997) 'Patterns of development', in S. Tomlinson, *Education 14–18: Critical Perspectives*, London: The Athlone Press.

Tooley, J. and Darby, D. (1998) *Education Research: A Critique*, London: OFSTED.

Training Commission (1988) *Annual Report, 1987/88*, Sheffield: TC.

16 Colleges in the New Millennium

Alan Smithers and Pamela Robinson

The election of a Labour government in May 1997 transformed the education landscape – or at least its language. Elected on an agenda of 'education, education, education', it embarked, from the moment of taking office, on a whirl of initiatives and reforms. A White Paper, *Excellence in Schools* (DfEE, 1997a), was published after just sixty-seven days and this was rapidly followed by two more consultation documents with a bearing on further education, *The People's Lottery* (Department for Culture, Media and Sport, 1997) and *The Learning Age* (DfEE, 1998a). Two major bills were enacted, School Standards and Framework and Teaching and Higher Education, as well as an enabling bill to phase out assisted places in independent schools. A number of major reports were already published or envisaged – Dearing (1997) on higher education, Kennedy (1997) on widening participation, Fryer (1997) on lifelong learning, Tomlinson (1996) on inclusive learning, and Moser (1999) on adult literacy and numeracy. The previous government's spending plans were adhered to, with minor adjustments, for the first two years, but a Comprehensive Spending Review was undertaken to see what extra funding could be made available for education, among other things, and the results were published in July 1998 (DfEE, 1998e).

By November 1998, the government was in a position (in its own words) to 'paint the big picture'. In *Learning and Working Together for the Future*, the DfEE (1998f) revised its mission statement ('the Aim') which became 'to give everyone the chance, through education, training and work, to realize their full potential, and thus build an inclusive and fair society and a competitive economy'. That is, inclusiveness had become the watchword alongside prosperity. In support of the Aim, the DfEE also set itself three specific objectives:

1   To ensure that that all young people reach the age of sixteen with the skills, attitudes and personal qualities that will give them a secure foundation for lifelong learning, work and citizenship in a rapidly changing world.
2   To develop in everyone a commitment to lifelong learning, so as to enhance their lives, improve their employability in a rapidly changing labour market and create the skills that our economy and employers want.
3   To help people without a job into work.

The fledgling FE sector, already much changed since incorporation, could therefore expect to have to adapt still more . The second objective, which essentially recasts post-school education as lifelong learning, clearly has major implications for the colleges. But they will also be expected to play a part in promoting work-related learning for fourteen- to sixteen-year-olds (DfEE, 1997c) which is an element of Objective 1 and the New Deal programmes (DfEE, 1997b) which are central to Objective 3. The shape and survival of the colleges in the new millennium will depend on the nature of their response.

Changing Colleges

As local authority institutions, the FE colleges had taken on a wide variety of educational functions. Smithers and Robinson (1993) identified at least five: practical education, academic education, continuing education, catching-up, and learning for pleasure and personal development. The colleges were rooted in employment-related education, becoming 'the schools' to which businesses sent their young workers and apprentices every week. Alongside this they have accepted students for academic qualifications, like A-levels and degrees, acting as a counterbalance to the exclusiveness of sixth-forms and universities. Recognizing that all knowledge and skills are liable to become obsolescent, they have increasingly made available opportunities for updating and retraining. They have also offered chances of catching-up for those who for some reason have fallen behind or who have only recently come to this country. And, last but not least, they have offered opportunities in learning unconnected with qualifications in everything from aerobics to Zen.

The balance of their provision was largely a matter of agreement between the college and local authority. The bulk of the funding came as a block grant from the LEAs: 77 per cent in 1990–1 (Smithers and Robinson, 1993). Of the rest, about 15 per cent came from contracts and grants which would have pulled the colleges in particular directions – for example, for earmarked spending on work-related schemes (Employment Department, European Social Fund) or English language and basic skills (Home Office). Only about 5 per cent of the income came directly from tuition fees and charges paid by students and employers.

On incorporation under a Conservative government, the colleges were effectively turned into businesses run by a chief executive answerable to a board of governors. What they did was now to be determined by the marketplace. Public money which had been channelled through the local authorities was passed to the FEFC which created a market of its own in 'funding units'. In addition, the colleges were to compete for income from TECs (which were roughly the employers' equivalent of local authorities), from the local authorities themselves for adult and community education, from contracts and grants for specific purposes, and through the generation of fee income of various kinds. The 1992 Further and Higher Education Act also added specialist functions to further education when it included within the sector the art and design, and horticulture and agriculture colleges. But having set the legislative framework, the Conservative government was then content to see further education take on a shape determined largely by customer choices, expressed through what they were willing to pay for.

From incorporation on 1 April 1993 to the publication of *The Learning Age* in February 1998 the shape of the sector has changed appreciably. There are now fewer colleges and campuses. Some neighbouring colleges that found themselves together in the new sector agreed to amalgamate (for example, Tameside College of Technology and Hyde Clarendon Sixth-Form College; Pershore College of Horticulture and Worcestershire College of Agriculture), one or two colleges have withdrawn following poor inspections (for example, St Philip's RC Sixth-Form College's provision was transferred to South Birmingham College) and several have merged into the higher education sector (for example, High Peak into the University of Derby). There has been at least one new arrival (Richmond Adult and Community College), but overall there are some thirty fewer colleges than at incorporation and the process is continuing (FEFC, 1998b). The number of campuses within colleges is also reducing, partly as way of liberating funds to pay for the physical renewal of the remaining buildings (see Chapter 9).

Since incorporation there has also been a rush to franchise courses. The FEFC's Annual Report for 1996–7 shows a four-fold percentage increase in collaborative provision from 1994–5 to 1996–7, when 'an estimated 19 per cent of student numbers in the sector and 10 per cent of funds supported off-site enrolments run in partnership with third-party organizations'. As we have already seen (particularly in Chapter 13), there are concerns that this may have be driven more by economic than by educational reasons. Subsequently, there has been some decrease in franchising following a funding change to make it less profitable. Money may also have been at the heart of the progressive switch from collective learning to individualized study in resource centres (Chapter 7), but it can also be claimed that it has been for educational reasons. Dimbleby, for example, argues in Chapter 6 that individualized learning made possible by advances in information technology is more compatible with the nature of human intelligence.

It is difficult to separate out the effects of incorporation from the financial constraints under which the colleges have been operating. There has not been enough money to go round. The colleges have been required to make steep year-on-year savings, referred to euphemistically as 'efficiency gains'. From 1993–4 to 1997–8 the amount received per full-time equivalent student was reduced by 21 per cent (FEFC, 1998a). All colleges have been affected, but some more than others and, according to FEFC's *Annual Report 1997/1998*, ninety-four colleges (21 per cent) that year fell into the 'most vulnerable' category for financial health, compared with only twenty-five in 1994. The squeeze on colleges has impacted on the conditions of service of their staff who in many cases, as Dan Taubman reports (Chapter 7), feel badly let down by incorporation. Neither is the Labour government satisfied in terms of student learning. In a speech to the 1999 annual conference of the FEFC, the Minister for Lifelong Learning, George Mudie (DfEE, 1999c), complained that 'at least

7 per cent of colleges have achievement rates below 50 per cent; a further 5 per cent have part-time retention rates below 60 per cent; the average absenteeism rate is 23 per cent and there are wide variations in the performance of colleges serving similar areas'.

Having come through and been forged by incorporation, the colleges now face a fresh set of challenges for the new millennium. They are going to have to find their way around a new educational landscape in a new language. They are going to have to reckon with a government which wishes to be more directive than its predecessor and which is not always satisfied with what it sees. As with schools, it has taken to 'naming, acclaiming and shaming' (DfEE, 1999e) and Isle of Wight College is yet another to be identified as having serious weaknesses in governance and management.

A central question for the colleges at the turn of the millennium has to be: what are the main features of the new topography? An important issue for the government is: what changes should it seek to bring about in further education to try to ensure that its policies are realized? How the respective answers come together will have a considerable bearing on what further education will look like in the new millennium.

The New Landscape

Labour policy-making since taking office has been characterized by a wide range of initiatives and reforms, each of which has been given a distinctive label. Among those which are most likely to impact on further education are Lifelong Learning, New Deal, Wider Access, Fresh Start, University for Industry, Individual Learning Accounts and Lifelong Learning Partnerships. Others in similar vein include New Start, Fair Play, Skills Challenge and Employment Zones. Although intended to be catchy, because these tags are manufactured and seemingly unconnected, they can get in the way of understanding rather than facilitating it. In plotting their strategy for the new millennium the management of the colleges will therefore not only have to weigh up the relative importance of the policies and initiatives, but do so in a language which might almost have been designed to disorientate them. Even the bullet-pointed approach of *Learning and Working Together for the Future* (DfEE, 1998f) – which is meant to draw all the initiatives together – in practice conceals as much as it reveals.

Lifelong Learning

Perhaps the major change which the colleges will have to assimilate is the Labour government's attempt to recast all that goes on beyond compulsory schooling as Lifelong Learning. In doing so it is seeking to bring about a profound shift in perception. There have been earlier efforts, the Recurrent Education movement of the 1960s and early 1970s, for example, urged us to reject the notion that education is 'a terminal apprenticeship for a working life' (Houghton and Richardson, 1974). But this is the first concerted action by government. A National Advisory Group on Continuing Education and Lifelong Learning was established under Bob Fryer, principal of the Northern College in Barnsley, soon after the election victory and in its first report it called for 'a new learning culture, a culture of lifelong learning for all' (Fryer, 1997). This was carried forward by government in a Green Paper, *The Learning Age* (DfEE, 1998a), the main proposals of which are listed in Figure 16.1.

Figure 16.1 *The new agenda*

- Expansion of further and higher education to provide for an extra 500,000 people by 2002.
- Making it easier for firms and individuals to learn by creating the University for Industry and launching it in 1999.
- Set up individual learning accounts to encourage people to save to learn and begin by allocating £150 million to support investment in learning accounts by one million people.
- Invest in young people so that more continue to study beyond the age of sixteen.
- Double help for literacy and numeracy skills among adults to involve over 500,000 adults a year by 2002.
- Widen participation and access to learning both in further, higher, adult and community education (including residential provision) and through the UfI.
- Raise standards across teaching and learning after the age of sixteen through our new Training Standards Council, by ensuring implementation of the Dearing committee's standards proposals and by inspection in further and adult education.
- Set and publish clear targets for the skills and qualifications we want to achieve as a nation.
- Work with business, employers and their trade unions to support and develop skills in the workplace.
- Build a qualifications system which is easily understood, gives equal value to both academic and vocational learning, meets employers' and individuals' needs and promotes the highest standards.

Framed in this way, lifelong learning embraces the whole of higher education, further education, adult education, training delivered by the TECs and employer-funded training. It is clearly designed to affect the way we think and speak about education, shifting the focus from the first years of life to the whole lifetime. As such, it is necessarily a broad conception, but it could be too broad to implement in a meaningful way. It clearly extends well beyond further education, but has important implications for it.

National Learning Targets

While 'lifelong learning' may embody the aspirations, the government believes that targets give them definition. In setting specific goals the government has taken over and modified an approach embraced by its predecessor which, in order to underline its seriousness of purpose, adopted from the Confederation of British Industry eight targets for post-school education. In 1993, it established the National Advisory Council for Education and Training Targets (NACETT) to monitor and report publicly on progress towards achieving them. Following a consultation exercise conducted through NACETT, the present government decided to extend and reformulate the targets. The new National Learning Targets, set for 2002, are shown in Figure 16.2. All except the first two impinge of the work of the colleges.

Figure 16.2 *National Learning Targets*

- 80 per cent of 11-year-olds reaching the expected standard for their age in literacy
- 75 per cent of 11-year-olds reaching the expected standard for their age in numeracy
- 50 per cent of 16-year-olds getting five GCSEs at grades A*–C or equivalent
- 95 per cent of 16-year-olds getting at least one GCSE or equivalent
- 85 per cent of 19-year-olds with a Level 2 qualification
- 60 per cent of 21-year-olds with a Level 3 qualification
- 28 per cent of economically active adults with a Level 4 qualification
- 50 per cent of economically active adults with a Level 3 qualification
- 45 per cent of organizations with 50 or more employees to be recognized as Investors in People
- 10,000 organizations with 10–49 employees to be recognized as Investors in People

Although apparently precise, the targets are now framed in terms of levels. This assumes that there is a quality of 'levelness' and that it is feasible to equate qualifications which were designed for quite different purposes – ranging from identifying those who can be educated to a high standard at university to badges of achievement for the workplace. If, as Smithers argues (Chapter 5), there are strong reasons for doubting whether numbers can be assigned meaningfully in these circumstances, then the exactitude is illusory. At best the targets remain aspirational rather than a basis for planning. Nevertheless, NACETT (1999) is still going strong counting apparent progress towards them.

Widening Access

In redefining the priorities for post-school education to include social cohesion as well as economic competitiveness, the government has been encouraging a redistribution of resources away from those most likely to succeed to those who so far have not achieved. Widening participation, rather than merely increasing it, was brought to the fore by the Widening Participation Committee of the FEFC which was set up in 1994 under the chairmanship of Helena (now Baroness) Kennedy. In its report, *Learning Works* (Kennedy, 1997), it makes a strong case for drawing back into education those who have not made full use of earlier opportunities. In its response, *Further Education for the New Millennium* (DfEE, 1998b) – published at the same time as the Green Paper, *The Learning Age* (DfEE, 1998a) – the government 'endorses the vision of the report'. As we shall be seeing, this endorsement has been translated into a weighting of 10 per cent of funding for 'Kennedy students'.

This shift is not entirely uncontroversial since in terms of a sporting analogy it means moving financial support away from potential champions and international representatives towards encouraging everyone to take some healthy exercise. Neither is it technically easy to determine who should receive the extra funding. But it does gain some credibility from authoritative reports like *A Fresh Start: Improving Literacy and Numeracy* (Moser, 1999), which found that some seven million people have problems with 'functional literacy' or 'functional numeracy'. As Moser comments, this is 'a sad reflection on past decades of schooling and policy priorities over the years'.

New Deal

The New Deal schemes (DfEE, 1997b) have identified new client groups for further education supported by new money. The Labour party promised in its 1997 election manifesto that it would impose a one-off windfall tax on the privatized utilities and use the money to get people into employment. It made good that promise when, in the first budget of the new parliament in July 1997, Gordon Brown as Chancellor of the Exchequer announced that £3.5 billion would be spent on the New Deal. This targeted four groups: the young unemployed, the adult long-term unemployed, lone parents and people with disabilities. Administered by the Employment Service, it offered four options: a job with a private sector employer, work with a voluntary organization, work with an environmental taskforce, or full-time education or training. Colleges have been benefiting particularly from those choosing – and funded for – the fourth alternative (Education and Employment Committee, 1997).

University for Industry

One of the main ways by which the government is seeking to catalyse lifelong learning is through the University for Industry (UfI). This is somewhat oddly named since it is neither intended to be a university nor exclusively for industry, but it took its inspiration from the Open University. As it has emerged, it has two strategic objectives: 'to stimulate demand for lifelong learning among businesses and individuals' and 'to promote improved access and availability of training and education through the use of information and communications technologies' (DfEE, 1999e). In the first instance, it will be proceeding down four lines: it will be seeking to provide an information and advice service operating through broadcasting and local organizations; it will be working with companies to encourage their employees to do more learning; it will be working through existing educational institutions, businesses and other organizations to establish franchised learning centres; and it will be commissioning open-, distance- and digital-learning materials (Sainsbury, 1999).

The UfI is therefore conceived of mainly as a brokering organization and its likely impact on the FE sector is at this stage hard to judge. At one extreme it could bring in a lot more students with the colleges being the main providers of 'learning centres'; at the other, it could initiate their gradual dissolution, with the locus of learning eventually becoming multimedia packages at home. We are more inclined to the former view, because of what we would call 'the Weight Watchers phenomenon': while it is perfectly feasible to diet alone and in the comfort of one's home, many people prefer to pay quite large sums of money to join a club to be with and be motivated by other dieters. Similarly, while books, programmed learning, and information and communications technology have progressively made individualized learning more feasible, it is our view that learners will continue to want to come together to learn collectively and that for the foreseeable future schools, colleges and universities are safe. (The Open University, in fact, builds in a lot of collective learning, but to do so it relies on the existence of other universities.) Nevertheless, the UfI is likely to become an increasingly prominent feature of the education scene and it is something with which the FE colleges will have to reckon.

Individual Learning Accounts

Individual learning accounts are potentially the development that will have most impact on the shape of further education in the 21st century. Although lifelong learning may be thought by politicians to be a good thing, much will depend on an individual's willingness to pay for it. As we have seen, people have not been used to paying directly for the costs of their education in this country and the pattern of further education that has emerged has been largely in response to the funding mechanisms of first the local authorities and then the FEFC. Individual learning accounts are an attempt to create the means by which individuals can save to pay directly for their learning. This importantly gives choice between opportunities and influence over what is provided.

The details are yet to be settled, but in the pilot schemes involving some thirty-four of the TECs (DfEE, 1998d) up to a million accounts are to be opened in which a maximum of £150 could be added against a minimum deposit of £25. It is intended that the account should be opened with banks or other financial institutions, but these august bodies have been slow to come forward. It is also likely that eventually individuals will find themselves having to put in much more than £25 to be able to purchase anything substantial. Nevertheless, if the accounts do take off they have the potential to revolutionize post-school education, impacting strongly on further education, by putting its shape much more into the hands of the students.

Like Lifelong Learning itself, the New Deal and Fresh Start initiatives, although presented in an unfamiliar language, reinforce the traditional strengths of further education in continuing education, practical education and helping people to catch-up. Even the University for Industry has its roots in the National Open College Network which began in 1975 and which has similarly operated by brokering (FEDA, 1999). However, whether this means that the colleges will go on largely as before or have to considerably reorder their priorities will depend on the potential sources of income. That is what makes the individual learning accounts, as a new departure, all the more interesting.

Government Priorities for Further Education

While *The Learning Age* and the Comprehensive Spending Review have a considerable bearing on what goes on in further education, it is in general terms. The government's precise intentions were conveyed in an extensive letter of formal guidance to the Chief Executive of the FEFC in December 1998 (DfEE, 1998g). This spelt out three key objectives: to raise standards, to widen participation and to meet the skills challenge. In support, it drew attention to a new Standards Fund, reminded the sector of the qualification reforms and notified it of a statutory consultation on the modified instruments and articles of government.

The plans which the Secretary of State outlined provided for a major expansion in student numbers. Of an extra 700,000 students by 2001–2, some 50,000 were expected to be sixteen- to nineteen-year-olds (full-time) and 650,000 to be adults (mainly part-time). The formal guidance indicated that additional places were intended to help widen participation and a quarter of the new recruits should come from the 15 per cent most-disadvantaged wards in the Index of Local Conditions (DETR, 1998). Some 100,000 young people in jobs without training and some 100,000 not in jobs nor receiving education or training were to be targeted. The Secretary of State also indicated that he expected a growing proportion of the year-on-year increase in adult students to be drawn from those groups whose background had disadvantaged them (identified by a refined postcode method).

The Secretary of State also listed a number of key elements in the policy to help colleges meet the skills agenda:

- improved financial support for students;
- working closely with the University for Industry;
- providing a bridge back to learning through adult and community education;
- re-engaging fourteen- to sixteen-year-old pupils at risk of dropping out;

- supporting the development of individual learning accounts;
- addressing the major basic skills deficiencies of many adults;
- meeting national skills needs;
- contributing to the National Childcare Strategy.

Funding

In order to make these things happen the government, as is its wont, has adopted 'a something for something' approach. An extra £256 million has been made available for 1999–2000 and a further £470 million for 2000–1, but it is all tied to particular developments. The first year's settlement, for example, is mainly linked to the increased participation of sixteen- to nineteen-year-olds and adults, including a 10 per cent premium for 'Kennedy students'. The rest is assigned to the new standards fund (£35 million), a capital and information technology infrastructure allocation of £40 million, and £1 million extra for FEFC administration. Increases in 2001–2 can similarly be accounted for. While the standards fund can be used for (among other things) intervening in colleges causing concern, there is little to enable the colleges to dig themselves out of their current financial hole.

In recent years further education has suffered from chronic under-funding and, while the settlements may appear generous, in reality they do little to ease the colleges' financial plight. Rather than making good some of the money that has been taken away in recent years, a further 'efficiency gain' of 1 per cent is imposed. The sum allocated also assumes that employers will contribute an extra £35 million in the first year, rising to £60 million in the second. This may be overly optimistic since, in the past, employers have shown themselves extremely reluctant to contribute to training costs which they think should be borne by the state. The total settlement also includes a small transfer from the ethnic minority achievement grant previously paid by the Home Office. Significantly also, only the funding for the first two years of a three-year cycle has been announced. This may be because another review upon which the government is engaged may affect the future of the FEFC itself.

Strategic Planning

Although the government has shown every sign of wanting to control from the centre the strategy for further education, as for schooling, other aspects of its policies seem intended to delegate decision-taking to the regional or local level.

Regionalization

As part of its election pledge to devolve power, which has seen the establish-ment of a parliament for Scotland and an assembly for Wales, the Labour government also promised to give more say to the regions of England. It made good this promise in a White Paper, *Building Partnerships for Prosperity* (DETR, 1997), which detailed the plans for nine Regional Development

Agencies (RDAs), one each for the North East, the North West, Yorkshire and Humberside, the East Midlands, the West Midlands, Eastern Region, the South East, the South West and London. It envisaged that the

> RDAs will work closely with further and higher education, TECs, local authorities and National Training Organizations to pool information and development strategies which take account of national, regional and local objectives. RDAs will help the Government raise standards in education and training and tackle deprivation and social exclusion. It will be essential that RDAs help the Government make a reality of the concept of lifelong learning by promoting initiatives which help individuals and employers to undertake more learning.

The RDAs will be potentially very powerful bodies taking forward much of the strategic work that has previously been developed or coordinated by the Government Offices. They will have at their disposal some £800 million from programmes such as the Single Regeneration Budget and through tapping into European Union structural funds. Since, however, they have only recently come into being – on 1 April 1999 – we cannot be sure what their actual impact will be.

The government's view was stated by Blackstone (1998).

> I do not think that the RDAs have a role in planning the FE sector. What the RDAs do have an important role in doing is providing evidence of skill shortages, providing evidence of training needs in the regional economy for which they are responsible. That evidence should be fed into the FE sector via the Funding Council and particularly via the regional committees of the Funding Council.

The Select Committee (Education and Employment Committee, 1998a) agreed, 'RDAs will have a strategic role. We do not believe that they should take the lead in planning FE, not least because they have little direct influence or control over FE colleges.' The RDAs can however be expected to liaise with the nine regional committees of the FEFC that the Secretary of State was required to set up under the 1992 Further and Higher Education Act. These consider the adequacy and sufficiency of FE provision in a region. So far the regional committees have generally concurred with FEFC decisions and have not yet emerged as an independent voice.

Lifelong Learning Partnerships

The regions are, of course, large and somewhat remote from individual colleges. The FEFC also only has responsibility for the FE sector, but there is considerable overlap with school sixth-forms, training through the TECs and employers, and adult education remaining with the LEAs. It is possible to envisage, therefore, that there could be a strong element of local planning through bringing the parties together. The Select Committee (Education and Employment Committee, 1998a) was told that the Local Government Organization, the TEC National Council and the FEFC had been working together on an initiative to consider planning issues for further education at a local level.

That idea has been taken up and developed by the government. In November 1998, the Secretary of State announced that Lifelong Learning Partnerships would be established across the country during 1999. This was followed by the issue of a remit letter (DfEE, 1999a). The partnerships will comprise as a core FE colleges, schools, the local authority, Careers Service and TECs, but they may also include representation from higher education, the Employment Service, employers, trade unions, the churches, voluntary and community bodies, the Youth Service and agencies in the social inclusion field. They will be responsible for pulling together the different strands of lifelong learning activity and developing local targets linked to the National Learning Targets. This will be expressed as a local learning plan, the majority of which were expected to be in place by September 1999.

Given their wide and diverse representation, it is not clear to what extent they will influence provision at individual institutions, but an issue they will surely address is the basis of funding for post-16 education and training (DfEE, 1998c). It is widely held that FE colleges are less generously supported than schools for this phase of education, even though they ostensibly appear to be doing very similar things. But when the Select Committee (Education and Employment Committee, 1998a) attempted to investigate the extent of the differences, it did not find them as great as is sometimes perceived. Nevertheless the funding methodology for schools operates on different principles from the colleges and there is the question of whether they should be harmonized. The government has already asked the partnerships 'to promote consistency and coordination on issues such as home to school/college transport' (DfEE, 1998h).

Beyond the FEFC

The government began a review of post-16 provision in March 1999, the results of which were published in June as a White Paper, *Learning to Succeed* (DfEE, 1999f), accompanied by a consultation document on sixth-form funding (DfEE, 1999g). The White Paper proposes that from April 2001 the responsibilities of the FEFC would be subsumed by a new Learning and Skills Council. Since it was the FEFC which defined the colleges as a sector in their own right alongside the schools' and the universities' sectors, this could have profound consequences for the future of the institutions.

The new review comes in the light of a quinquennial review of the FEFC (DfEE, 1999b) which decided that the functions which it currently performs would continue to be needed by government and that in the medium term the FEFC was the best way of carrying them out. In all, six options were considered in detail:

- continuing with the FEFC;
- returning the colleges to local authority control;
- working through Regional Funding Councils;
- direct funding by the Secretary of State;
- privatization and strategic contracting out;
- transfer, merger and other forms of rationalization.

The high-level review group rejected a return to LEAs, largely on the grounds that they have enough on their plate with schools and that local democracy has not always yielded high standards there. The Regional Funding Councils option was rejected on the grounds that it would unnecessarily increase complexity. Allocating funding through an intermediary body rather than directly through the Department was thought to carry the important advantage that decisions would be at arm's length from political considerations. The review did not think the time was right for contracting out. It could see a number of attractions to the merging of FEFC and HEFC, but took the view that it would create a mega-quango which might become too powerful for the government's comfort. Furthermore, the diverse functions that it would encompass have hitherto been discharged in different ways, and a joint approach to common activities and support services was seen as a preferable alternative to outright merger.

The review group therefore concluded that 'in the medium term the FEFC should continue as an independent non-departmental body. However, in the longer term the government should consider the merits of creating an integrated system of funding in order to rationalize present arrangements.' It further recommended that the FEFC's powers of intervention at the governing body level should be extended so that it could influence them directly rather than via recommendations to ministers, and also that the FEFC 'should be invited to allocate a proportion of its non-core funding for regional purposes so that on the advice of its regional committees it could respond quickly to perceived local needs'.

The review group did not, however, consider the option of separating post-16 education into two phases, 16 to 18 and 19 plus. The latter could be achieved either through a merger of the relevant parts of FEFC with the HEFC or by continuing to keep adult education separate. A funding council for the two years beyond compulsory schooling would have a number of advantages for those arguing for a level playing field and a common inspection system (it is currently split between OFSTED, the FEFC and the new Training Standards Council). However, many of the arguments that the review group adduced against merging the HEFC and FEFC would still apply even if the FEFC were included in reduced form. The price of a funding council for sixteen- to nineteen-year-olds might be to introduce yet another non-departmental public body into an already crowded field.

In the event, the government settled on a measure of separation. The White Paper (DfEE, 1999f) proposes 'a single national Learning and Skills Council responsible for the planning, funding and managing of all post-16 education and training other than higher education' (as summarized in DfEE, 1999g). As such, it will take over the roles of not only the FEFC, but also the TECs and NACETT. It will however have two committees: a Young People's Learning Committee, with direct responsibility for sixteen- to nineteen-year-olds, and an Adult Learning Committee for post-19s. The importance of this distinction is underlined by creating a new adult learning inspectorate and extending the remit of OFSTED to cover provision for sixteen- to nineteen-year-olds in colleges.

The government also wishes to move towards equivalent funding for equivalent courses for sixteen- to nineteen-year-olds while maintaining support for school sixth-forms. Even with this qualification, any steps towards integration are likely to strengthen the hand of the colleges *vis-à-vis* sixth-forms, especially small ones, since hitherto the colleges have been less well funded in this respect. In its consultation document on sixth-form funding (DfEE, 1999g), the government offers the options of LEAs continuing to distribute funds within the current local government finance system or the LSC funding LEAs in respect of the school sixth-form provision in their area.

The new LSC is intended to provide coherence and reduce bureaucracy, but it will operate through a network of up to fifty local LSCs which, in turn, will work with Local Learning Partnerships. The Regional Development Agencies are also intended to have a key role in planning arrangements for learning and skills, and there will need to be close liaison between the various bodies. The White Paper sees this as 'a family of organizations – not a hierarchy'. But the potential for duplication and confusion carries the risk for the colleges that the clear identity they were establishing under their own funding council will be dissipated.

Future Prospects

What then is to become of the colleges as further education is redefined as life-long learning? The future may be uncertain, 'challenging' as the White Paper puts it, but throughout their existence the colleges have been nothing if not resilient. They have coped with the vagaries of local authorities, numerous reclassifications which have seen some of their number budded off as higher education institutions, and they have more or less survived in the marketplace. No doubt most will take the new framework for post-16 learning in their stride. It is likely therefore that in the immediate future the colleges will not be so different from how they are now. A developmental progression could be expected, with modifications to the funding arrangements, improved governance along the lines suggested by Shattock in Chapter 8, and an evolving qualifications structure as foreshadowed in *Qualifying for Success* (DfEE, 1997e). But the establishment of the LSC, with its two main committees, would be as much of a punctuation mark as was the coming of the FEFC. The FEFC brought about the birth of the FE sector; the LSC would see its transformation.

Since it is the existence of the FEFC which has bound together a heterogeneous collection of institutions, its replacement by a council with a much wider remit is likely to lead to a reconfiguration of the sector. With the distinction increasingly being drawn between adult learning and learning for sixteen- to nineteen-year-olds, it seems likely that the colleges will go their separate ways, with some resuming their close affinity with schools, while others adapt their various strengths to the concept of lifelong learning. Still others might continue to pursue their aspirations to become more like universities.

It is also unlikely that all current colleges will survive as independent institutions. In his guidance to the FEFC in November 1997, the Secretary of State (DfEE, 1997d) indicated that he would like to see 'a more proactive approach to mergers so that the sector will be better placed to live within what will always be limited resources'. To catalyse the process, a rationalization fund of £10 million was contained within the settlement. While, however, mergers can make sense (as we have seen in the adjustments the sector has made already), merging is no panacea. It can take the eye off the ball during critical times. Strategic collaboration between colleges may be a better alternative. The colleges around Northampton, for example, have agreed to secure a range of provision and share out the benefits and risks, including of those of expensive construction and engineering courses (MacDonald and MacDonald, 1999). As with other kinds of partnership, strategic collaboration can be continued as long as it meets a need but dissolved quickly when it has outlived its usefulness (see Gravatt and Silver, Chapter 10).

The plans for Individual Learning Accounts can also be expected to have a major impact on the future of the colleges. If they do take off, encouraging the habit of saving to pay for learning, they would put educational purchasing power into the hands of individuals. Up to now what has been provided is largely what has been thought good for us. Indeed, on occasions politicians appear to have been pursuing their own agendas. It is possible to infer, for example, that recent governments have been trying to ward off the threat to social cohesion that excessive unemployment poses by locking people into education and training. (Musgrove, 1964, interestingly, was able to show through historical analysis that the school-leaving age seems to been raised mainly in response to youth unemployment; the recent rapid expansion of further and higher education could be viewed in the same light.) But if people are purchasing their own education and training, they will have the ultimate say.

This could contain some nasty surprises for those who would govern. It could be that people would not be so enamoured with qualifications as the political wisdom suggests they should be. They could regard inclusion as a kind of imprisonment. It is already difficult to keep a significant minority of young people (the 'disaffected') in school to the end of compulsory schooling. Imagine would what happen if everyone were free to go and had to pay. This is the market in which further education already operates, but which would be considerably sharpened by Individual Learning Accounts. It could also be that what people would want to study would not be thought entirely appropriate. Astrology springs to mind as something which has continued to thrive with people paying for courses outside the respectable education system. It could be very unsettling for politicians if the shape of lifelong learning were to be decided in a truly democratic fashion.

Whatever the medium term holds, it is clear that the colleges' immediate future depends on attracting more students to generate income. He who pays the piper... . Pursuing money in order to survive has contributed to the explosion of franchising and the drift away from engineering and construction. In any changes to the funding arrangements, it is important that consideration be given to ways of protecting the state's interest in particular areas of training, perhaps through specifying fields, as the Higher Education Funding Council does to some extent.

A third force which could dramatically alter the shape of further education is information and communications technology (ICT). There are some who would argue that schools and other educational institutions are obsolescent (Hargreaves, 1997). Since ICT will enable people to tailor-make courses and study at times and in places convenient to them, it is envisioned there will no longer be a need to bring people together in special buildings. Similar thinking underlies the University for Industry. But this is to overlook the motivational importance of studying alongside other people – seeing how well they can do and learning from them. Individualized learning has been technically possible since the invention of the printing press, but it has never really caught on. This is because learning, like dieting in the Weight Watchers example (see p. 198), is fundamentally a social activity. Thus while ICT will bring greater flexibility to learning in colleges, it is highly probable that the colleges themselves or something derived from them will still be needed.

What then will FE look like in the new millennium? Our best guess, certainly for the first few years, is not so very different from now. It has battled to get through so much to be where it is, that it is likely to be able to pick its way through the policy context of whichever government is in office. But, in the medium term, it could be radically altered through the redefinition of further education to lifelong learning, financial arrangements that put more power in the hands of learners to decide what education and training *they* want, new modes of learning made possible by advances in technology, or to some unforeseen cataclysm. The colleges can be very proud of their first 100 years, even though their impressive achievements have too often been unsung. If the present government backs up with the necessary funding its wish to see them in the forefront of lifelong learning, the next 100 years could be even better.

References

Blackstone, T. (1998) *Oral Evidence*, 11 March, in Education and Employment Committee, 1998b.

Dearing, R. (1996) *Review of Qualifications for 16–19 Year Olds*, London: School Curriculum and Assessment Authority.

Dearing, R (1997) Report of the National Committee of Inquiry into Higher Education, *Higher Education in the Learning Society*, London: NCIHE.

Department for Culture, Media and Sport (1997) *The People's Lottery*, White Paper, Cmnd 3709, London: The Stationery Office.

DETR (1997) *Building Partnerships for Prosperity*, London: DETR.

DETR (1998) *Index of Local Deprivation, Regeneration Research Summary No. 15*, London: DETR.

DfEE (1997a) *Excellence in Schools*, White Paper, Cmnd 3681, London: The Stationery Office.

DfEE (1997b) 'Blunkett's call to the nation to join his crusade for jobs', *DfEE News*, 178/97, 3 July.

DfEE (1997c) '£3.5 million to "turn on" children through work-related learning', *DfEE News*, 311/97, 6 October.

DfEE (1997d) *Letter of Guidance to FEFC*, November, London: DfEE.

DfEE (1997e) *Qualifying for Success: A Consultation Paper on the Future of Post-16 Qualifications*, London: DfEE.

DfEE (1998a) *The Learning Age: A Renaissance for a New Britain*, Green Paper, Cmnd 3790, London: The Stationery Office.

DfEE (1998b) Response to the Kennedy Report, *Further Education for the New Millennium*, London: DfEE.

DfEE (1998c) 'Lane Group Report on further education student support', *DfEE News*, 310/98, 19 June.

DfEE (1998d) '£2 million to develop individual learning accounts' framework – Howells', *DfEE News*, 330/98, 25 June.

DfEE (1998e) '£19 million boost for education', *DfEE News*, 360/98, 14 July.

DfEE (1998f) *Learning and Working Together for the Future: A Strategic Framework to 2002*, London: DfEE.

DfEE (1998g) Letter of Guidance to FEFC, *Further Education Funding for 1999–2001*, 2 December.

DfEE (1998h) *New Arrangements to Support Students in Further Education and Post-16s in Schools*, December, London: DfEE.

DfEE (1999a) *Secretary of State's Letter to Chief Education Officers, College Principals, TEC Chief Executives, Careers Service Chief Executives and Attached Partnership Remit*, January, London: DfEE.

DfEE (1999b) *Quinquennial Review of the Further Education Funding Council: Prior Options Review Report*, London: DfEE.

DfEE (1999c) 'Good colleges to become beacons, failing colleges face "fresh start" – Mudie', *DfEE News*, 79/99, 17 January.

DfEE (1999d) 'Blunkett welcomes plans for millions of new learners', *DfEE News*, 122/99, 18 March.

DfEE (1999e) 'Blackstone welcomes further education beacons of excellence', *DfEE News*, 212/99, 12 May.

DfEE (1999f) *Learning to Succeed: A New Framework for Post-16 Learning*, White Paper, Cmnd 4392, London: The Stationery Office.

DfEE (1999g) *Learning to Succeed: School Sixth-Form Funding – A Consultation Paper*, London: DfEE.

Education and Employment Committee (1997) Second Report, *The New Deal*, vol. 1, *Report and Proceedings*, 263-I, London: The Stationery Office.

Education and Employment Committee (1998a) Sixth Report, *Further Education*, vol. 1, *Report and Proceedings*, 264-I, London: The Stationery Office.

Education and Employment Committee (1998b) Sixth Report, *Further Education*, vol. 2, *Minutes of Evidence and Appendices*, 264-II, London: The Stationery Office.

FEDA (1999) *Embracing Credit at Open College of North West*, www.feda.ac.uk

FEFC (1997) *Annual Report 1996–97*, Coventry: FEFC.

FEFC (1998a) 'Towards an inclusive learning society in the new millennium – the contribution of further education', in Education and Employment Committee, 1998b, Appendix 4.

FEFC (1998b) *FE: The New Agenda – Annual Report 1997–98*, Coventry: FEFC.

Fryer, R. (1997) *Learning for the Twenty-First Century*, London: DfEE.

Hargreaves, D. (1997) 'New technology will challenge status quo', *Times Educational Supplement*, 30 May.

Houghton, V. and Richardson, K. (eds) (1974) *Recurrent Education: A Plea for Lifelong Learning*, London: Ward Lock Educational with The Association for Recurrent Education.

Kennedy, H. (1997) *Learning Works: Widening Participation in Further Education*, Coventry: FEFC.

MacDonald, S. and MacDonald, S. (1999) *Further Education: Strategy for the Future*, Kettering: Tresham Institute of Further and Higher Education.

Moser, C. (1999) Report of the Working Group, *A Fresh Start: Improving Literacy and Numeracy*, London: DfEE.

Musgrove, F. (1964) *Youth and the Social Order*, London: Routledge & Kegan Paul.

NACETT (1999) *Progress Towards the New National Learning Targets*, Sheffield: NACETT.

NAO (1999) *Investigation of Alleged Irregularities at Halton College*, HC 357, 1998/99, London: NAO.

Sainsbury, D. (1999) MacLaren Memorial Lecture, *Modernising Learning: The Role of the University for Industry*, Aston University, Birmingham.

Smithers, A. and Robinson, P. (1993) *Further Education in the Market Place*, London: CIHE.

Tomlinson, J. (1996) *Inclusive Learning: Report of the Learning Difficulties and/or Disabilities Committee*, London: The Stationery Office.

Contributors

Patrick Coldstream was for ten years founding Director of the Council for Industry and Higher Education, after an earlier career in journalism, the City and the voluntary sector. The Council encourages long-term thinking between academic and business leaders, and is their joint voice to government. Currently Visiting Professor at London University's Institute of Education, he chairs the Employability Skills Overview Group bringing together employer, academic, quality, funding and government bodies. He also chaired the churches' recent Inquiry into Unemployment and the Future of Work.

Clive Cooke is Vice Principal (Curriculum and Customer Services) at the Bournemouth and Poole College of Further Education. He has worked in a number of further education colleges and also has considerable management experience in the private sector. He is currently responsible for the areas of curriculum management and development, teaching and learning processes, student services, quality assurance and the raising of standards, and marketing. He is a member of a number of national and regional committees, including those concerned with the development of a 'Signature Qualification' for the FE sector and the mapping of the FE curriculum to enable credit accumulation and transfer.

Richard Dimbleby is Principal/Chief Executive at the Bournemouth and Poole College of Further Education. Before that he worked in colleges in Hertfordshire, Surrey and Somerset and he spent an exchange year at the University of North Carolina School of the Arts. He is a member of the QCA Committee for General and General Vocational Qualifications, the FEFC Quality Assessment Committee and the FEFC South West Regional Committee. He is also a member of the AQA Education and Training Committee, a Chair of Examiners for A-level Communication Studies and contributes to AoC and FEDA Curriculum and Qualifications groups. He is co-author of *Teaching Communication, Between Ourselves: An Introduction to Interpersonal Communication*, and *Practical Media: A Guide to Production Techniques*.

Jim Donaldson is Chief Inspector and Director of Audit of the FEFC. He previously held the post of chief inspector of schools at the Scottish Office with special responsibility for post-16 education. He has also served with the Scottish inspectorate as chief inspector for vocational education and training, and as chief inspector for higher education. Between 1992 and 1996 he was seconded to the Scottish Higher Education Funding Council where, as Director of Teaching and Learning, he set up arrangements for assessing the quality of higher education programmes. Before his career in the Scottish inspectorate, Jim Donaldson was a lecturer in economics in further and higher education at Telford College, Edinburgh (1979 to 1982), Queen Margaret College, Edinburgh (1974 to 1979) and Napier University (1968 to 1974). He was educated in Dumfriesshire and holds degrees from the Universities of Strathclyde and Edinburgh. His professional interests include widening access to further and higher education, performance indicators and quality systems.

George Edwards was educated at the University of Edinburgh where he graduated as BSc in 1965 and again (after being awarded a Post Office Scholarship) with a Diploma in Business Administration in 1971. He worked in the Post Office from 1965 to 1987 in a variety of roles, including Head of Long-Term Planning Unit, Head of Letter Mail Transport, on secondment to the United Nations in 1976 and Head of Capital Appraisal and Control Unit. In 1988 he joined the newly formed Polytechnic and Colleges Funding Council, where he was a property adviser specializing in the recovery of the estate, and project assessment. He created the Hunter programme for the recovery of dilapidated estate and initially developed that procedure in the PCFC sector and, after moving to the FEFC in 1993, in the colleges of further education. He is at present the regional property adviser of the North West, West Midlands and South West regions of the FEFC.

Julian Gravatt is Registrar at Lewisham College, a job he has held since 1993 and which means he has been responsible for student administration and student data throughout the time of FEFC control. He has a history degree from Oxford University but trained as an accountant with the National Audit Office and Price Waterhouse. He started work at Lewisham College in 1992 as its financial accountant, just in time for incorporation. He is a prolific writer on further education issues, particularly those relating to its funding and systems.

Tom Jupp is Principal of the City and Islington College of Further Education. He taught overseas before setting up a national scheme for work-based learning in the 1970s called the Industrial Language Training Service. He is co-author of *Language and Discrimination: A Study of Communication in Multi-Ethnic Workplaces*. Since 1982, he has worked in central London, first as an inspector for further and adult education for the Inner London Education Authority, and later as chief inspector of schools in the newly formed London Borough of Camden

Roger McClure is a Pro-Rector of the London Institute where his responsibilities include strategic planning, finance, registry, management information, and information technology. As a management consultant he has wide experience of public sector institutions. In the mid-1980s he contributed to the Jarratt study of the efficiency of universities and was subsequently seconded to the University Grants Committee as its first financial adviser. In 1988, he became the first Director of Finance for the Polytechnics and Colleges Funding Council and played a leading role in establishing that sector, especially its funding and financial systems. In 1992, he took on a similar role for the further education sector as the first Director of Finance for the FEFC.

Deirdre Macleod is a policy analyst with the FEFC. Previously, she worked for the Scottish Higher Education Funding Council. She has degrees in geography and politics from the Universities of Cambridge and Edinburgh.

David Melville is Chief Executive of the FEFC. He was a lecturer and senior lecturer in physics at Southampton University and then Professor of Physics and Astronomy at Lancashire Polytechnic. He was subsequently Vice-Chancellor of Middlesex University. He has been the chairman or a member of a number of committees of the research councils and vice-chairman of the Committee of Vice-Chancellors and Principals. He has been a visiting professor at universities in Italy and Portugal, and has published and broadcast widely on his research interests in physics and biophysics.

John Pratt is Professor and Director of the Centre for Institutional Studies at the University of East London. He has an extensive record of research into the history and policy of post-school education and has written a dozen books arising from this, including most recently *The Polytechnic Experiment 1965–1992*. He has been a consultant to the Ford Foundation, the World Bank and OECD, and is editor of *Higher Education Review*.

Pamela Robinson is Deputy Director of the Centre for Education and Employment Research at Liverpool University. Following wide experience in teaching, examining and the training of teachers, she was appointed to a research fellowship at the University of Manchester in 1984. Here she began a collaboration with Alan Smithers of which this volume is but the latest example. Their policy-related research on such issues as teacher supply, subject choice at A-level, science and technology education, further education, and trends in higher education has become internationally recognized. After a spell as a lecturer in education at Brunel University she returned to full-time research with her appointment to the University of Liverpool in 1998.

Guardino Rospigliosi is Principal of Plymouth College of Further Education and a Director of Plymouth Training for Commerce and Industry Ltd. After national service in the Welsh Guards he read classics at Oxford University. Although privately educated in the USA, Zimbabwe and the UK, his teaching career has been spent in the state sector in England. Teaching posts in grammar, secondary modern and comprehensive schools were followed by the headship of the Elliott School in Putney from 1974 to 1982, and then from 1982 to 1988 by the principalship of Richmond upon Thames College, London's first and largest tertiary college. His professional interests include equal opportunities, vocational education, learning difficulties and organizational culture.

Michael Shattock CBE, is Visiting Professor at the Institute of Education, University of London, having been Registrar at the University of Warwick from 1983 to 1999. He conducted a public inquiry into the affairs of Derby Tertiary College, Wilmorton, on behalf of the FEFC. He is chairman of the governing body of Hereward College and of the West Midlands Regional Advisory Committee of FEFC. His most recent books have been *The UGC and the Management of British Universities* and *The Creation of a University System*. He is editor of the journal *Minerva: A Review of Science, Learning and Policy*.

Ruth Silver is Principal of Lewisham College in London. She studied psychology and literature at Glasgow and Southampton Universities, trained at the Tavistock Institute for Human Relations in adolescence and transition, and is a qualified and very experienced teacher. Her employment has spanned service as a teacher and inspector, service at the Department of Education and Science and the Manpower Services Commission developing national education policy on the Certificate of Pre-Vocational Education and Youth Training Scheme, followed by a period spent in senior management in further education. Ruth holds a number of national posts linked to learning in further education, has written and broadcast extensively on educational matters, and is the mother a fifteen-year-old daughter. She is committed to inclusiveness, particularly in the inner city.

Alan Smithers is the Sydney Jones Professor of Education and Director of the Centre for Education and Employment Research at the University of Liverpool. He has previously been Professor of Education at the University of Manchester and Professor of Policy Research at Brunel University, London. He has been a member of the National Curriculum Council, the Beaumont Committee on Vocational Qualifications and Special Adviser to the House of Commons Education and Employment Committee. His recent research has taken him into many areas of education including (as well as further education) qualifications structures, education for sixteen- to nineteen-year-olds, technology in schools, vocational education, graduate employment, flows into science and engineering, trends in higher education, and industry and education links. He has published a number of influential books and reports, and over 100 papers in biology, psychology and education.

Geoff Stanton is a Senior Research Fellow at the University of Greenwich School of Post Compulsory Education and Training. He also works as a freelance consultant and is a part-time inspector for the FEFC. He has taught in schools and colleges, and has been an FE teacher trainer. He was one of the FEU's first two development officers when the unit was founded in 1977, after which he went on to be Head of Department at Lewisham College and then Vice Principal of Richmond Tertiary College. He was Chief Executive of the FEU from 1987 to 1995. He has served on policy committees of NCVQ and the National Curriculum Council, and on the Council of the Institute of Education. He is currently a member of the Education and Training Committees of the OCR Examinations Board and of City & Guilds. He has been elected to fellowships of the RSA and the College of Teachers. He has written widely on further education matters, with a focus on post-16 qualifications policy and curriculum management.

Dan Taubman is the National Officer for Colleges and Adult Education with NATFHE, the university and college lecturers' union. He graduated from the London School of Economics in 1970 with a degree in government and in 1992 gained an MA in human resource management from Middlesex University. He has extensive experience in adult education and lifelong learning. Dan Taubman started as a community education worker and then as manager in the ILEA's adult education services. His responsibilities at NATFHE include policy formulation and advice across the fields of further and adult education. His particular areas of expertise are in curriculum and qualification reform, the government of further education and the funding of further education. In 1998 he published with the Post-16 Centre, Institute of Education, a study of the effects of the FEFC's funding methodology on the curriculum and working of colleges, *Funding Learning*.

Annette Zera is Principal of Tower Hamlets College of Further Education. She has worked in education in London's East End for over twenty years, as a teacher of English as a second language and later as a principal of an adult education institute. Most recently she has been a member of two DfEE committees: the Lane group, looking at issues of student financial support, and the Moser Committee, which reviewed adult basic education.

Index